THE AGE OF
MULTIMEDIA AND
TURBONEWS

THE AGE OF
MULTIMEDIA AND
TURBONEWS

Jim Willis

Westport, Connecticut
London

Library of Congress Cataloging-in-Publication Data

Willis, William James.
  The age of multimedia and turbonews / Jim Willis.
    p. cm.
  Includes bibliographical references and index.
  ISBN 0–275–94377–1.—ISBN 0–275–94378–X (pbk.)
  1. Multimedia systems.   2. Mass media.   I. Title.
  QA76.575.W55   1994
  302.23'0285'66—dc20   93–43445

British Library Cataloguing in Publication Data is available.

Library of Congress Catalog Card Number: 93–43445
ISBN: 0–275–94377–1
      0–275–94378–X (pbk.)

First published in 1994

Praeger Publishers, 88 Post Road West, Westport, CT 06881
An imprint of Greenwood Publishing Group, Inc.

Printed in the United States of America

The paper used in this book complies with the
Permanent Paper Standard issued by the National
Information Standards Organization (Z39.48–1984).

10 9 8 7 6 5 4 3 2 1

Copyright Acknowledgments

The author and the publisher are grateful to the following for granting the use of
material:

Communication in History: Technology, Culture, Society edited by David Crowley and
Paul Heyer. Copyright © 1991 by Longman Publishing Group.

New Electronic Pathways by Jerome Aumente. Sage Publications, 1987.

White Paper Report, *Videotex: A Growing Public Awareness*. The Newspaper Association
of America, 1991.

For John Kao

Contents

Preface

There is no media topic as important today as new media technologies and the impact they may have on all of our lives. We stand at the threshold of a revolution in the news and entertainment media, and the media as we know them today may cease to exist in just a few short years. Whereas it has always been a simple matter to distinguish between newspapers, broadcast television, cable television, computers, motion pictures, and the telephone companies, those distinctions are quickly eroding as a new, universal media looms on the horizon. This new form has come to be called *multimedia* because it embraces elements of all formerly distinct media. Often it carries the adjective *interactive* because it asks the consumer to become more involved in selecting its content. In the near future we may be telephoning a friend via our television or telecomputer, and we may be talking back to our television, telling it what we want to see and when we want to see it. Many of us are already doing our shopping via the television and its home shopping networks, and we are already using the phone to dial up movies on demand. In England and France viewers are reading their newspapers over the television screen—an experiment that is being tested in the United States, along with fax newspapers. These services are only the tip of the iceberg of what lies ahead for us with multimedia.

As mind bending as the interactive multimedia concept is, it is also interesting to look at the sheer amount of information that is possible with these media and their information providers. Not only is a tremendous amount of data possible electronically, but the speed with which it is being delivered is unparalleled in history. You might call this new form of news and information *turbonews*, and it carries with it some implications for all of us. For instance, in an age where the media is often assailed for the inaccuracy of its information, what will the increased delivery speed of this information mean for the reporter who is already having trouble getting to the bottom of a story under the old deadline system? Further, will the increased desire for an all-at-once news experience only exacerbate the problems already associated with short, quick stories that highlight the video and dramatics over the deeper content of the story?

In short, there are a great many opportunities as well as serious challenges posed by multimedia and turbonews. The new information age is already upon us, and interactive multimedia will only increase the amount of information available. But, will the fees and costs associated with public access to this information be such that some segments of society will be denied access because of their low incomes and education? Will there exist a knowledge gap of greater proportions than exists today?

Trying to harness a topic such as new media technology is an impossible task if one is trying to write the last word on the subject. This is the most fluid topic in existence today. Every day brings new stories, new developments, and new revelations as to the effects of the changing media technology. A favorite topic of *USA Today's* focus stories in its "Lifestyle" and "Money" sections is the changing media technology. Several times a month, stories appear concerning everything from HDTV to fiber optics to new alliances between telephone and cable companies, to wireless, handheld communication devices. The same is true in the pages of newspapers such as the *New York Times, Los Angeles Times*, and *Washington Post*. Business magazines like *Forbes, Business Week*, and *Fortune* also chronicle changes in media technology on a regular basis, as do the weekly news magazines *Time, Newsweek*, and *U.S. News and World Report*. In short, media technology is a bulky and bumpy subject to get our arms around because it refuses to stay in one shape. It just keeps evolving and changing, and it does so at fairly rapid speed.

This book is an attempt to show where media technology is today and what some of the developments might be down the road. Owners of media companies will change, and executives will be lured to greener pastures at other media companies. Corporate snapshots are presented here only to show the intensity of merger activity. This book is also an attempt to predict some of the changes in store for journalism, the news media, and our lifestyles as a result of these evolving media and the effect they are having on news and entertainment. Those individuals, companies, and consortia developing new media products and services are looking to the needs and desires of consumers in designing these new media. They realize, as some of the failed electronic newspaper experiments of the 1970s and 1980s showed, that when the consumer is left out of the planning stages, disaster will follow. You may have developed a technologically amazing product or service, but find no one wants it. In the end, these marketing questions may be some of the biggest problems confronting research and developers: What does the American consumer really want in the way of interactive news and entertainment media? How much time will the public really spend with it? How much are they willing to pay for it?

This book is appropriate for students of the mass media in colleges and universities, as well as those media managers who are trying to determine what these new technologies mean for them and their media companies. Again, however, this is a snapshot of where the technology is today. The story is continued in your daily newspaper—probably today's edition.

Acknowledgments

The topic of new media technologies is as current and dynamic as any media subject today. For that reason, it offers a fertile field for authors, writers in the daily press and television as well as some of the most respected magazines. Among the key sources of information used for this study are the *New York Times, USA Today*, the *Los Angeles Times*, the *Washington Post*, the *Boston Globe* and *Sunday Globe*, and the *Christian Science Monitor*. Additionally, articles in magazines such as *Business Week, Forbes, Fortune, Newsweek, Time, U.S. News & World Report, The Futurist, The Nation, MediaWeek*, and *AdWeek* have also provided good insight. Authors in the field who have written widely on this topic include Jerome Aumente, Phillip O. Keirstead and Sonia-Kay Keirstead, Stewart Brand, E. W. Brody, Wallys Conhaim, Michael M. Mirabito, Barbara L. Morgenstern, and Marshall McLuhan.

I would also like to acknowledge the assistance of the Newspaper Association of America, for allowing me to excerpt from its White Paper Report on Videotex, and of the MIT Media Lab, which provided me with research papers from its faculty and staff who are currently researching the latest developments in media technology.

Last, but certainly not least, I want to express my gratitude to Peter T. Rison, a recent graduate of Boston College. Mr. Rison, a gifted researcher in the field of communications technology, is responsible for contributing much of the information found in chapter 2.

1

·····

The Media Blur

Each year I take a class of newswriting students to the O'Neill Library on the campus of Boston College to have a reference librarian guide them through the maze of background material available to them for preparation of their stories. Many of the students expect the traditional library tour, generally not too exciting, wherein the librarian shows them stacks of Reader's Guides, Who's Who volumes, statistical abstracts, and printed census data that come in print volumes. Many assume that I will advise them later that, if they were serious about poring through this kind of fine-print research, they had better be prepared to start wearing glasses by age 30 if not sooner.

But their expectations of the nature of research materials are nearly always burst when the librarian ushers us into a section on the main floor replete with computer terminals and signs offering electronic databases such as Nexis, InfoTrac, Dialog, PIAS, QWIL, BCAT, and many others. It is as if they had entered a world of the electronic alphabet, and they soon realize that research just might be more interesting than it ever has been before. Logging onto Nexis, for instance, they are provided with an electronic display of the contents of hundreds of hard-copy newspapers and magazines. Over on InfoTrac, they not only can get electronic citations of print sources, but also electronic abstracts in case the article is not what the title suggests. BCAT offers electronic citations of books, and, QWIL offers leading scholarly journals.

In addition to the enormous amount of information offered on these and other electronic databases, these databases offer each student personal service geared to their own research needs. The pathway is through "keywords" of their own choosing. Want to read some in-depth material for background to a story on the high cost of college tuition? Just punch in a couple keywords such as "tuition" and "increase." Preparing a story about the risk that investors are willing to assume in buying stocks during a recession? Try keywords such as "investing," "risk," and "recession." Up pops an index of several stories from the nation's leading newspapers and magazines, together with abstracts in many cases, and you—as a budding reporter—are off and running. And you're doing it in a fraction of the time it would cost by doing traditional library research.

Students quickly realize that they are entering the world of the great *media blur*, where print, electronic, and telephonic communications converge. In a large sense, that section of O'Neill Library is a microcosm of what American living rooms and home studies may be like in the near future. In some respects, many homes already take advantage of the kind of high-speed information services—the kind of turbonews—offered in that and other major college libraries.

The decade of the 1990s is witnessing the emergence of a new kind of universal news medium. It is not so much a new medium, however, as it is a convergence of several formerly *distinct* kinds of media into one multipurposed, multifaceted, easily accessible, and painlessly digestible medium. It is also a medium that has the power to make profound changes in the way messages and personalities are delivered to us, in the way in which those messages and personalities are perceived and inter- preted by us, and on our learning habits. It is as though the ghost of such media seers as Marshall McLuhan and Harold Innis were still with us, whispering into our ears that the future is just as they predicted: that our rabid desire for the "all at once" experience of consuming infor- mation would lead us to the exact threshold of future news—of turbo- news—that we are at now.

Indeed, those of us who have been focusing on the innovations of *USA Today* and the promise of HDTV over the past several years may have been confusing the foothills for the mountain range or reading the symp- toms of a culture as the cause. It is apparent today that these revelations of the past decade have only been the tip of the iceberg, with the much larger expanse of new media technology lurking just below the surface of our consciousness.

What is the new medium? It is whatever one gets when one combines telephones, computers, television, cinema, newspapers, magazines, and even books into one—certainly no more than a few—electronic databases that also feature as many colors, lights, graphics, whistles, and buzzers as are necessary to get audiences interested in stopping whatever they are doing and pay attention to the message that both the editor and the advertisers want them to see and hear.

FEATURES OF THE NEW MEDIA

Whatever the exact shape this future media takes, there are likely to be several features that different versions of it will have in common. Among them are the following:

1. A strong customer orientation in which the shape and content of the media mirrors the public's information and entertainment needs and desires. Media will no longer be defined by what they *do* so much as what customer needs they meet. This market orientation is already here, obviously, as most major media have been following the lead of readership and viewership studies for some time. *USA Today* is the most obvious—so far—consumer-based news and entertainment product other than television. But there are many more waiting in the wings. This customer orientation will be the focus of chapter 6.

2. *User modeling* is the concept most often used to describe just how personalized these new media products will be. This personalization will focus on smaller and more distinct groups of individuals—and eventually individuals themselves—as marketers become more adept at classifying individuals on the basis of their personal behavior patterns. These personalized media will respond to an audience that will continue to become more fragmented in their individual interests, tastes, vocations, and avocations.

3. An electronic base using CD-ROM technology will replace hard copy as the physical format of the new media for information and entertainment. In other words, as the price of personal computers (PCs)—and telecomputers—decreases, and phone lines—which now can carry video as well as audio digital signals across the country and around the world—become more connected to those PCs, the stage will be set for an electronic medium that will combine some of the best features of print, broadcasting, cable, and electronic databases. Home printers will allow consumers to obtain hard copy of news, feature, and sports pages, so the advantages of the printed word will not be lost among those who still value it.

4. Immediacy and continual updates will almost certainly be vital features of this turbonews media. Just as the Associated Press, Reuters, and United Press International have traded for several decades in "deadlines every minute," so will the new media. The nature of this type of immediate, "real-time" coverage were seen in Operation Desert Storm in which the American public saw news being made and rumors commanding as much airtime as truth, with reporters having no time on live TV to sort out the two. America also received a hint of the kind of traumatic effect such real-time coverage can have on the senses and the psyche, especially when such earth-shaking events are the object of the media's scrutiny.

The reality is that Americans can no longer find a guaranteed escape in the media they so often turn to for relief from the strains of everyday life. Indeed, the strains caused by turbonews may be more than many consumers are willing to accept. Chapters 9 and 10 will discuss the impact of this future media.

5. An explosion of information from a greater variety of media sources than ever before will also be a product—and a rather welcome one at that—of turbonews. This feature may appease such media critics as Ben Bagdikian, who sees only a media monopoly or oligopoly controlled by a few dozen company CEOs at media conglomerates such as General Electric, Time Warner, and Gannett.

6. Although the new media will be able to deliver more news and information than ever before, Americans will probably turn to them more for entertainment. Those risking millions of dollars believe enough of us will want to stay inside and talk back to our television sets through new interactive mechanisms than go outside and entertain ourselves. Chapters 2, 4, and 5 will look at some of these proposed new media forms.

7. Although the telephone lines will likely be the medium of transmission for these new services (and certainly these phone companies are few in number), the information they will transport—and are now transporting—will come from a multiplicity of media sources instead of the reporters and entertainers who work for just one or two media organizations. In the traditional medium of newspapers, for instance, there has always been some media plurality even in a one-newspaper town. The reason is that, even apart from broadcast competition, the newspaper features stories done from outside the newspaper by news services such as the Associated Press and Reuters. But with the age of turbonews, information will emanate from hundreds, even thousands, of newspapers, magazines, journals, and other information providers that are catalogued on electronic databases such as Nexis, DataTimes, Dialog, and VuText, which are subscribed to by more and more media companies for presentation in their media product.

The disadvantage of this feature is the reality that there will be too much information for the audience to access in a reasonable amount of time. In an age when Americans are beset by so many leisure-time choices, the choices involved in being one's own news editor may be too daunting for many individuals. That is why media seers are trying to decide just how much the new media should edit the day's news and how many choices they should leave up to the consumers who may or may not feel up to making such selections. Perhaps user-modeling, in its sophisticated form that relies on behavior patterns and expressed interests of the news consumer, will bridge this gap by offering information that seems genuinely to be of interest to the individual customer. Another concern regarding advanced user-modeling, however, is that a company will be able to accumulate a great deal of private information about individuals' tastes, behaviors, habits, lifestyles, likes, and dislikes. The ramifications of this will be discussed in later chapters.

8. The new age of turbonews and future media will likely be more expensive for the audience to tap into than the current 35 cents it costs to buy a newspaper or the free newscasts one receives on commercial broadcast stations, or even the basic and pay cable viewing that much of the country pays for in the 1990s. The new media, which will rely on telephonic and satellite transmission, will charge a subscription fee to hook up and obtain monthly service—such as cable does now—and/or some kind of search fee, based on the amount of time the medium is used by the consumer. As an example of such subscription fees, pay-per-view (PPV) television charges customers for the events they wish to watch. The 1992 Summer Olympics, which were carried in their entirety by NBC on a pay-per-view basis, charged viewers more than a hundred dollars to see. At the time, there were relatively few takers, and NBC was forced to lower its rates during the games. Still, there were tens of thousands of viewers who were willing to pay the steep sum to watch events that they really cared about. Pay-per-view movies, which cost much less to see, have been growing in popularity around the country.

There is a general feeling among many media marketers that special-interest groups of viewers and readers will pay what would normally seem a prohibitive sum of money if they are able to watch what they want to, when they want to. Locating that threshold of top dollar versus consumer turnoff is the marketing challenge that has been taken on by several media marketing experts.

9. The longer these new media are in operation, the more research and upgrading will be done, and the more the subscription fees charged to the consumers will decrease, as will the price of equipment needed to access it all. There is always a learning curve when new technology is invented and becomes operational. That curve applies to the user of the technology and those producing it. As these manufacturers become more skilled in creating the new products, they will find ways to develop them more cheaply. This will enable the companies to offer them for sale to consumers more cheaply. This has happened in every high-tech industry from the hand calculators, to digital watches, to personal computers. In 1982 the PC was out of reach of most customers, by 1992 one-third of all U.S. homes owned at least one.

10. The new media may lead consumers to a more cursory examination of the news, even though more information will be available to them than ever before. This is happening already on television. Before the age of cable and the remote control unit, viewers focused longer and steadier on news and information programs. Most would watch a 30-minute or hour-long episode of a station's or network's evening newscast from start

to finish. Changing channels would mean getting up from the sofa and crossing the room to the television, and there were only a couple other alternatives once they did decide to switch. Today,"changing channels" has become "zipping," "zapping," and "grazing," adding new meanings to the dictionary for these words. The latest concept, "channel surfing," is an apt description. It's all done from the couch and, with cable, the alternatives may number from 30–50. In some cities, such as New York and Los Angeles, experiments are underway with as many as 150 different channels.

Now ratings services such as Nielsen and Arbitron measure viewership in chunks of a few minutes as opposed to longer segments. If sound bites of political candidates are longer than 5 to 10 seconds, the viewer may not stay around for the end of the quote. If commercials run longer than 15 seconds, they may not be seen in their entirety. Most distressing to many, if interview segments of talk shows run longer than 2 to 3 minutes, the audience will become bored and move on to another show.

Obviously, surfing has some fearsome implications on the media, as well as on society as a whole. At minimum, it means many viewers will just stay tuned to get the headlines (indeed CNN already offers a syndicated news program to stations called "Headline News") and, at worst, it makes the public much easier to manipulate by politicians and government officials who get elected by—and then govern by—the 10-second sound bite. More will be said about these implications in later chapters.

11. Increasingly, it appears that *fiber optic lines* will be the transmission vehicle for much of this turbonews. Fiber optic lines use modulated light beams to carry information—whether written or spoken or visual—and are glass lines with the same diameter as a human hair. The bonus of fiber optic technology is that light waves can also be used to store information and play back that information from an optical disc, which is a storage system with tremendous capabilities. Fiber optic lines have a number of advantages over direct satellite broadcasting (using satellites to deliver personalized news and information to viewers). For example, fiber optics are relatively immune to atmospheric conditions and other interference that sometimes plague satellite or traditional broadcast or cable delivery systems.

These hair-thin glass lines, now being lain across the country by AT&T and the *regional Bell operating companies (RBOCs)*, have permitted the creation of a system called the Integrated Services Digital Network (ISDN). Under this system, voice and data travel side by side over the same wire. Subscribers to interactive systems will be able to talk on the phone, have their utilities metered, watch a video picture on their television, and receive their electronic mail, all at once without interference. The connecting loop will probably be fiber optics instead of conventional copper wire because fiber has the expanded band width needed to carry the transmission and can carry them at lower costs.

Among the RBOCs laying fiber optic is New Jersey Bell, which plans to bring fiber optic cable to the curb outside every home and office in New Jersey by the year 2010. It is an ambitious plan that will phase in new technologies as the glass fiber replaces nearly 57 million miles of copper wire. The project, dubbed Opportunity New Jersey, is the result of a deal struck last year between the state and New Jersey Bell, the Bell Atlantic subsidiary that provides telephone service to 96 percent of the state.

Even cable television companies have announced plans to begin laying fiber optic lines. In fact, there are likely to be several joint business ventures between cable and telephone companies cropping up in the near future, and chapter 3 discusses some that have already been formed. In many ways, the cable and telephone industries are rapidly converging. In the near future, consumers will be able to get video services from their regional Bell company and make calls by television. This will also mean they can see the person on the other end of the phone call by looking at their television screen, or they can dial a phone number to view a favorite movie. This latter service is already operational and is marketed under the concept of video on demand.

In late 1991, Congress helped speed up the laying of a "fiber optic highway" across the country with the passage of a $3 billion High-Performance Computing Act, which was then signed by President George Bush. Funds from this act were to be used for creating and implementing computer hardware that would help carry data to and from the country's top centers of research. The transmission vehicle is fiber optics.

12. Of great importance is the fact that these new media will be *interactive*. The public will not only receive the news, information, and entertainment over their televisions or PCs; they will actually be able to interact with and manipulate the 10 information or story plot lines, if the programming is fictional entertainment. Interactive media is not a new concept. Media companies experimented with it during the late 1970s and 1980s in places such as Columbus, Ohio, where Time Warner developed an interactive television system called Qube. Under this system, viewers used portable keypads to indicate their choices as the programming was underway. In one example, for instance, during city council meetings, viewers could indicate their on-the-spot reaction to issues under discussion.

Still, for other interactive media experiences such as Knight-Ridder's Viewtron in Florida, the service was either too expensive or complicated or didn't meet the viewers' needs that well, or was hampered by the low percentage of homes with personal computers, or all of the above. As a result, most of these interactive experiments failed.

IMPORTANCE OF CD-ROM

Helping the new wave of interactive media reach new heights is the technology known as CD-ROM or compact disc, read-only memory. These products, which resemble old LP records but which are smaller and are recorded with lasers, can hold a great deal of information on a single disc and can allow users to interact with and manipulate this data for their own needs and desires. Compact disc technology was introduced in 1983 by Philips and Sony and quickly gained popularity in the form of the now-familiar audio CDs, which are competing with audio tapes. The specifications for CD-ROM, called the Yellow Book, were introduced in 1986. There is no physical difference between audio CDs and CD-ROM discs. Both are small aluminum-coated plastic discs that are etched with digitally encoded information. Like the audio CD player, the CD-ROM drive directs a laser beam at the disc and then "reads" the pattern of reflected light created by the encoding as digital data. The most obvious disadvantage to CD-ROM is that it is read-only and cannot be written to. The most obvious advantage is the room it offers to spread out, and a number of multimedia software developers have simply used CD-ROM to expand existing disk-based products. Another advantage—and a big one, as computer buffs know—is that it is virus proof. As an indicator of the growing popularity of CD-ROM, InfoCorp Computer Intelligence, a Santa Clara, California, market research firm, reports that some 900,000 CD-ROM drives were sold in 1992, as compared to 650,000 in 1991. Also, the number of CD-ROM titles has expanded even more rapidly. The *CD-ROM Directory*, published by UniDisc Inc. of Soquel, California, listed 3,000 commercial CD-ROM titles in 1992, almost double the number available in 1991.

In the 1980s, the largest segment of the CD-ROM publishing market was in text-based information databases. In the early 1990s, that use still dominated the industry and was likely to continue to do so for some time. CD-ROM is such a handy and economical way of sharing huge amounts of information. A single CD-ROM disc can hold approximately 650 megabytes (MB) of data and is much cheaper to produce and mail than an 800K floppy disc, which would hold an equivalent amount of information. Therefore, they became the vehicle of choice for such database storage services as Nexis and Lexis, as well as many others.

Yet the capabilities of CD-ROM extend far beyond the realms of news and information retrieval services of the type that are in use in major research libraries throughout the country. Books are now being published on CD-ROM (interactive novels are especially growing in popularity), computer games are showing up on this medium in great numbers, and electronic publishers are finding it is an ideal way to combine learning with entertainment for young people. Both visual and audio elements have been incorporated into CD-ROM technology, as is evidenced by Apple Computer's introduction of its innovative QuickTime architecture.

More will be said about CD-ROM technology in later chapters. Suffice it to say for now that this technology, along with technology such as fiber optic lines and direct broadcast satellite reception—which allow information to be updated continually—are making a major difference in the way we will receive our news, information, and entertainment in the future in the sheer amount of information we receive, in the personalization of that information, and in our ability to interact with that information.

SUMMARY

It is important that we realize these new vehicles of information—as well as the form of that information—have the potential of creating almost as many problems as they pose, especially for information consumers who are used to getting their news and entertainment in more traditional ways. The scenario of a knowledge-gap, to be discussed later, is not an unlikely occurrence.

In short, in the 1990s we are at the crossroads of information creation and processing. It is a crossroads similar to the one the world faced when it moved from an aural to a literary mode thousands of years ago. Some will be prepared for it, others won't be, and still others will be caught in the middle, realizing the need to change their communication patterns but unsure about how to do it. These technological changes, and the impact they may have on American society, form the focus of the remaining chapters of this book.

2

· · · · ·

The Media's New Means

Chapter 1 introduced some of the technology that lies behind the multimedia concept. Technology such as fiber optics and direct broadcast satellite (DBS) transmission are two of the transmission means that are being tested now in many experiments around the country. Conventional coaxial cable is also being used by some companies as an interactive vehicle for multimedia. On the receiving end is technology such as high-definition television (HDTV) and the high-resolution personal computer monitors. Behind much of the development of interactive television, telecomputers, and HDTV lies the concept of digital compression, needed to transmit much more data across cable, conventional copper telephone lines, and—ultimately—fiber optic lines. This chapter will look at some of these new means of two-way communication, their status by the mid-1990s, and the promise they hold for the future of communication technology.

DIGITAL COMPRESSION TECHNOLOGY

Interactive communication technology requires a tremendous amount of data to be transmitted, especially when video signals as well as audio and text are being transmitted. For this reason, it is necessary to compress as much of the data signals as possible so enough data can travel through the lines of communication that are used, whether that medium is fiber optic lines, copper telephone wires, or coaxial cable. Digital technology enables such signal compression to take place at the needed rate and pace for multimedia requirements. But before discussing digital compression, we should first look at the older transmission system of analog technology, which is being replaced at a rather swift pace.

Analog Technology

Analog technology refers to nondigital, terrestrial signal transmission through conventional ground wires. The telephone as we know it uses analog transmission technology. Telephone instruments, facsimile machines, and telephone answering machines are all referred to as customer-premises equipment (CPE). Telephone instruments are connected to one another through wires called intrapremises wiring that are brought into the customers' homes at a central point.[1] When the user lifts the receiver, that action completes an electrical circuit which triggers the dial tone and sends a signal. The electrical power comes from the telephone central office and not the electric company, so telephones continue to work during blackout periods.

When making a telephone call, the signal travels from the intrapremises wiring, through the central point outside the building to the local loop that connects it with the central office. The central office provides the dial tone, receives the dialed number, and makes the next connection for the signal to reach its final destination.

The public switch network is a system of transmission circuits that instantly connects voice to voice, computer terminals to electronic databanks, facsimile machines to faxes or video to video. The overall analog connection occurs as a result of the four major parts of the telephone communication system: the telephone instrument, transmission, switching, and signaling.

In using analog technology for transmission of video signals, some significant problems arise. First, analog video is intimately tied to a particular distribution standard with all of the attendant disadvantages associated with it. Specifically, video such as might be stored on a videodisc or tape is, by definition, tied to a national standard for current television technology that is quickly becoming outmoded by the introduction of HDTV and other similar systems. Every image of analog video contains 525 lines of vertical resolution (used in current television technology) of which 483 are visible, and it can never look better than a broadcast signal, no matter what the resolution of the display monitor is.[2] That is why an HDTV receiver, with double the amount of lines as traditional TV, will not make an analog signal look nearly as clear as a signal sent by digital technology. By contrast, a digital representation is standard-free. It can contain the basic information from which a sequence of frames may be reconstructed at any rate, with any resolution, on any machine that can receive the bits.[3]

Second, and probably more important to viewers, television images resulting from analog technology are noticeably inferior to signals sent by digital compression technology. MIT researcher Andrew Lippman has noted:

An individual still image from that (30-frame-per-second) sequence is noisy and blurred; it is not generally suited to prolonged or critical viewing. Television was never intended to be viewed frame-by-frame or even especially closely. It was a solution to the problem of providing moving pictures to the home in a time when electronic design constraints were quite different from what they are today. . . . In interactive use, video is used alternately as a medium for motion and separate stills. Quite often stop points are provided where the ongoing action may be interrupted to either take a new path through it, make measurements on elements within the frame, or change some graphics associated with the picture. . . . A digital representation can merge the virtues of photographs with movies.[4]

Third, Lippman adds, analog representation does away with all data not relevant to the native display format, but a digital representation can retain it. It is this tightly coupled data that forms the basis for the notion of merging video with data prior to screen display.[5]

Digital Technology

Digital technology differs from the older analog signal technology because it consists of discrete pulses of binary 1's and 0's. Digital encoding uses bits and bytes composed of the binary language of 1's and 0's of computer language. It emits this encoding through pulses. For this reason, the data—whether audio or video—is read easily by multimedia computers. Digital signal processors help conserve data size for video compression and fiber optics. A switch to digital communications will provide more effective ways of coping with the large amounts of video data information and increased traffic through phone lines. Current creations and applications of algorithm-based compression for digital video signals are referred to as compressed digital video (DCV) technology.[6]

Both analog and digital telephone systems utilize a transmission component that uses multiplexing systems to transmit the information. Digital systems are transmitted through other communications technologies such as copper phone lines, coaxial cable, radio, cellular, fiber optics, and satellites. Multiplexing is the ability of the system to send several signals simultaneously. Two major multiplexing schemes exist in telephone technology today. They are frequency division multiplexing (FDM), used for analog signals, and time division multiplexing (TDM), used for digital signals. TDM is also easily adaptable for computer systems, which makes it a favorable candidate for use with emerging multimedia systems.[7]

Pulse code modulation (PCM) is the most basic waveform method to convert traditional analog speech into a digital stream. The telephone frequency range for voice is between 300 to 3,400 Hz. The dynamic range of this frequency range allows for 256 levels of telephonic voice. As a result, 64,000 bits per second are required to encode analog human speech into digital form. PMC is classified as a form of both modulation and signal processing. PMC analog-to-digital techniques convert the analog speech to the digital stream. From there a multiplexer stacks them onto higher bit streams that allow for greater frequency capacity.[8]

Switching enables users to connect with other users and their telephone systems. Digital technology uses switching based on TDM. Topology is a mathematical equation of geometrical configurations. TDM switching uses bus topology in which the information is shared and linked by a single line, as opposed to a square or star configuration.[9] In fact, time division switching in digital technology is called TDM Bus Switching. In order for the switch to occur, the telephone lines are connected to a bus, and the time on the bus is divided into slots. A path between two lines is created by correlating common slots along the bus. Each line places the data from the signal into a buffer, and a multiplexer then analyzes them and sends it along the telephone lines.

Since digital technology is transmitted through other communications technologies, several pieces of digital carrier equipment are available to provide digital connectivity. Traditional analog communications use channel banks or terminals to transform the analog data direction into a digital stream. Digital multiplexers allow different bit rates to be attached to each other along the specified carrier wave by multiplexing blocks of data streams. Digital cross-connects provide a common point where information from terminals, multiplexers, and transmission facilities meet. Here, the cabling is cross-connected. Both telephone companies and end users have access to these devices, which can aid in network rearrangement and connections for multimedia devices in the future.

An emerging standard for digital video transmission in the United States for video conferencing and video telephones is the 56 kilobits per second (Kbps) digital service. This network actually operates at 112 Kbps with two multiplexed 56 Kbps lines working together. Internationally, the 64 Kbps standard is becoming popular. This network runs at 128 Kbps with two multiplexed 64 Kbps lines.[10] The two are not compatible.

Digital technology is an underlying link with other emerging communication technologies whose goals are increased frequency capacity. Digital technology will have to expand and be compatible with these other technologies. Together they will be able to compress the data enough to provide the transmission and reception of video image data. This is a key element to the success of multimedia systems and equipment.

Video Compression

The goal of video compression is to condense the amount of information needed to display the video image so that the information will pass through telephone lines. Video images use about 92 million bits per second, but existing copper phone lines can handle only 19,000 bits per second. Developments in video compression offer options for all future users of multimedia systems. Video compression techniques are correlated with digital technology for a number of reasons. For example, once a video signal is digitized, it becomes pure data and thus can be transmitted at any pulse rate. If the user wants to pay for the property of immediacy, he or she may buy a high-bandwidth channel; if such a channel is unavailable, slower methods are available. Therefore, digital video allows for use of whichever distribution means are at hand; they need not even be television channels at all.

A welcome development occurred in 1990 when researchers at Bellcore found a method to squeeze video signals through telephone wires. The technique of video compression is known as asymmetric digital subscriber line (ADSl).[11] This was good news for AT&T because of the introduction of its VideoPhone 2500 in 1992 and its multimedia aspirations on the horizon. Even with this development, however, the amount of data that fiber optic lines can carry is much greater.

Audio Compression

Digital audio broadcasting (DAB) is the new technological development in radio transmission that promises to deliver sound quality higher than CD transmission. In fact, DAB was being touted in the early 1990s as the single most important event in decades for radio. The goal of DAB developers was to design and establish a universal DAB system that would cause a minimum amount of economic upheaval to broadcasters, provide the most sensible technological solution, and at the same time, generate the greatest enthusiasm by the listeners. DAB would enable radio stations to broadcast with CD quality and virtually no interference or static. Basically, the idea is the same as with digital video: compress the signal into digital form which can then be sent either over landwires or up- and down-linked off communication satellites. The main issues in the early 1990s was which DAB system to implement, which radio band spectrum to use, and how to deal with potential competition from satellite-based systems. In 1990, the radio industry was favoring terrestrial transmission and fearing the satellite delivery of perhaps hundreds of DAB channels direct to listeners.[12]

By 1990, the board of directors of the National Association of Broadcasters (NAB) had taken the following approach to DAB implementation:

1. It officially opposed the concept of national satellite distribution of radio programs directly to consumers.
2. It appointed a task force to study and monitor the impact of DAB on listeners and on the industry.
3. It urged the federal government to support the World Administrative Radio Conference in 1992 as well as the establishment of world technical standards for terrestrial (transmission via ground-based towers) DAB in other forums.

Since then the DAB task force has, through numerous meetings, attempted to learn all it can about DAB in order to shape and influence DAB so that its eventual introduction would result in a new and vastly improved radio broadcast system for all broadcasters.

In January 1992, NAB approved a plan for the radio industry that was developed by the task force to manage and influence the implementation of DAB technology. This plan calls for broadcasters to implement DAB to improve the current system of broadcasting and has since been endorsed in one form or another by Canadian and Mexican broadcasters and many American broadcasters.

Not all broadcasters, however, agree with NAB's plan. That debate tends to revolve around the following issues:

1. What happens to the AM signal if DAB is carried over FM only.
2. The likely number of DAB signals in a given market.
3. Whether DAB should be located in the N spectrum, which means shoehorning it into an already crowded FM band, or in some new location such as an L band or S band.
4. The potential economic impact of DAB as it relates to equipment costs, receiver costs, and station values.

Several DAB systems have been under development. They include the Eureka 147 system, one from USA Digital, and two from AT&T. The Eureka and USA Digital systems have created a great deal of interest in the radio world, although the American-developed USA Digital seems to have gained prominence in the United States over the European-developed Eureka system. Eureka 147 had the backing of many in the industry when it was first announced, but then it created controversy because it would require opening up a new spectrum on the dial to a third radio service that would compete against the current AM and FM spectra. Nevertheless, Canada has adopted the Eureka 147 standard and in 1993 planned to start offering DAB transmission soon.

The distinction between the AT&T systems and USA Digital's (developed by CBS, Gannett, and Group W Broadcasting), is just where in the current radio bands the digital signal will be located. USA Digital's system is in-band, on-channel (IBOC), which means it is placed on a station's current analog signal or actually just beneath it at lower power. In radio jargon, USA Digital's DAB uses a station's own spectrum "real estate." As a result, any regulatory obstacles would more than likely be small. One AT&T system, co-developed by Amati Corp., is also IBOC, but only on the FM band. This raised an obvious question of what might happen to AM licensees. Would there be some way to accommodate them as well or would they be unable to use DAB signals? The other AT&T system is in-band, adjacent channel (IBAC), meaning it puts the DAB signal in the spaces between existing FM stations. Again, however, the question is who will get to utilize those adjacencies. Would they be for current FM licensees only, for AM or FM, or for some entirely new third party who applies for a broadcast license?

All of these proposed DAB ventures are terrestrial-based, as opposed to satellite-based, and all but Eureka use the existing N-band of the radio spectrum. The Eureka 147 system uses the L-band (1500 MHz), a section of spectrum higher up the band than AM and FM. In the United States, the military has jurisdiction over the L-band and wants to keep commercial traffic off of it.

An attractive feature of USA Digital's IBOC is that current licensees would have the right to add DAB signals as a simulcast enhancement to their analog service. It would also provide 15 kHz stereo for AM and CD-quality for FM.

For individual radio stations, costs of DBA conversion are likely to run in the $50,000 to $85,000 range, according to industry analysts.

Digital audio compression has also extended to recorded audio tapes, and digital audio tapes (DAT) are on the horizon, which would provide competition for the CD industry. This is especially so since DAT has the added advantage of recordability. This benefit may not last long, however, as companies are experimenting with ways of making recordable CDs; these improved CD systems were in the developmental stages in 1993, and hopes ran high that they would soon be marketed to the general public.

DIGITAL CELLULAR TECHNOLOGY

Another conceived way of transmitting and receiving the audio and video images of multimedia systems is by way of cellular transmission. In fact, many of the developers of multimedia products assert that their products will be portable, cordless, and cellular in the future. In cellular transmission, now widely used in mobile telephones, signals are sent over radio frequencies using frequency modulation carrier analog radio technology like that of a car radio. The Federal Communication Commission (FCC) has allocated the frequencies between 30 MHz and 500 MHz for all types of users. In addition, the FCC has allocated 825 to 845 MHz of the radio spectrum for use by cellular communicators. The operation of cellular communication utilizes the fundamental technology used in radio. The cellular system divides an area into a number of smaller units or cells in which each cell uses its own antenna. The antennae are relatively small, and the cells are located to provide an overlap of signals. When a call is made, its signal is picked up by the closest cell, and it is monitored by the Mobile Telephone Switching Office (MTSO) that transfers the signal to a closer cell as the signal from a moving car becomes weaker. This transfer is called a hand-off, and it occurs in less than a second. The MTSO also links the signal to a conventional land line telephone network for long-distance calls outside of the cells to anywhere in the world.

The same frequency can transmit many signals at the same time. As more signals are transmitted to the cells, they subdivide into a series of smaller cells to increase the number of available channels. The cellular radio transmits and receives the voice signals through the same fundamental process as regular radio under frequency modulation waves. The radio transmitter uses an oscillator to create a carrier wave and a modulator to combine the sound wave and the carrier wave through the frequency component of the wave. The antenna, which acts as a transducer, converts the electrical energy from the waves to physical energy so it can travel over the airwaves. The detector in the receiver then separates the sound wave from the carrier wave. This process is performed in cellular radio, except that the cellular radio is both a transmitter and a receiver, whose signals are aided by the cell antennas and the Mobile Cellular Unit (MCU).

One problem that has plagued cellular transmission, however, has been geological terrain and tall buildings, which occasionally interrupt signals from cell to cell. Also, cellular phone users sometimes report problems at the fringe areas of cells, some of which may not overlap.

Many experts predict that cellular radio technology will play a major role in the development of video telephones and multimedia systems discussed throughout this book. Adapting multimedia devices to the cellular system, however, poses a problem. Cellular technology currently is analog technology. The bandwidth space through which the data can be transmitted is very limited, and cellular traffic is very congested. With the introduction of video image data along the bandwidth, the problem of bandwidth spaces increases dramatically. If progress is to be made in overcoming this barrier, one or all of three things would have to happen.

1. Least likely is the hope that the FCC will allocate additional and broader bandwidth for cellular communications.
2. There is the possibility that the FCC will allocate special bandwidth for computer communications.
3. If cellular transmission could convert to digital cellular technology, then both audio and video images could be compressed to occupy less space.

Currently, cellular companies are working on developing digital transmission standards. Among the standards under review are the following:

1. *Narrow-band advanced mobile phone service (NAMPS)*. It is a modified narrow band analog system that actually coaxes additional capacity from the existing AMPS system through frequency reuse and the use of microcells. But, because it is not digital technology, it is seen as only a short-term solution that would nevertheless increase carrier capacity by a factor of three.[13]
2. *The frequency-division multiple access, time division multiple access (TDMA) system*. The Telecommunications Industry Association (TIA) chose TDMA as the access technology for the next digital standard even though it failed to meet the capacity standard set under its User Performance Requirements (UPR), which outline the requirements for future digital technology for manufacturers. Like the NAMPS system, it increases AMPS capacity three times, and it has the benefit of being digitized.[14]
3. *The code division multiple access system (DCMA)*. It claims to improve capacity by 10 to 20 times that of AMPS. It also provides for better quality for handoffs, privacy, and audio. An upgraded version of DCMA is expected to appear in 1994 that will contain digital control channels. This technology may allow personal communication networks such as computer communication and possibly multimedia devices that use DCMA to coexist with other cellular communication in an already allocated bandwidth. The FCC, however, must still approve of the broadcast at any frequency.[15]
4. *The cellular digital packet data (CDPD)*. The data is actually packaged and piggybacked on voice, and it decreases the cost of a cellular call by about 20 percent. Using idle cellular channels, CDPD sends packets of 9,200 bits per second over a standard 30 Hkz channel. This technique does not affect voice quality, and it is compatible with both present and future analog and digital cellular standards. Therefore, even as the technology expands and evolves, wireless modems will not become obsolete. Existing cellular carriers can utilize CDPD by adding parts to their base stations and cell sites.[16]

In order to accommodate any of the new standards that are emerging, the cellular network must be modified. The network through which analog, cellular, and digital cellular communications will be connected has been coined the personal communication network (PNC). The PNC will have to be composed of three layers: one that provides unrestricted, universal access, another that handles switching and transport, and a third that provides intelligent services to manage the different types of data and technologies. These three layers must work with each other and be able to link the wired and wireless networks they transport. The layers as a whole will have to utilize the infrastructure already in place, and they will have to adapt to the changing and improving technologies and standards.[17]

Some of the wireless, cellular communication products now in prototype versions or operational include the following:

- *Personal communicators.* Companies such as IBM and Motorola have developed these hand-held devices that allow on-the-go users to receive E-mail, make cellular calls, and serve as a cordless phone at home.
- *Speed checkers.* A company called Symbol Technologies has developed this handheld product, which store clerks can use as a portable price scanner or use to take credit card payments and record the sale wirelessly.
- *Handheld computers.* Apple, for instance, has developed the Newton, which is a personal digital assistant that eventually will handle wireless faxes and E-mail.
- *The iridium phone.* Developed by Motorola, the iridium satellite system would allow calling anywhere on earth.

By the mid-1990s, only a few companies were willing to invest large sums into developing wireless products, but their numbers are growing. Included in the group of risk-takers are Federal Express Corp., which has constructed its own private radio network, and United Parcel Service of America, Inc., which has done the same by piecing together cellular-phone systems. Some communications experts, however, predict that by the year 2000 as many as 20 million American employees will be using new wireless data terminals.

FIBER OPTIC TECHNOLOGY

No matter which pieces of the communication technology puzzle actually become a reality, it is a certainty that fiber optic technology will be one of the important surviving ones. It is inevitable that copper telephone wires will be replaced by fiber optics, which technology analyst Jerome Aumente has called "the communications equivalent of replacing a small stream with Niagara Falls."[18] The amount of data that the hair-thin, glass fiber optic lines can handle is amazing. With fiber optics, laser impulses are transmitted through hundreds of thousands of these thin strands, and each can be a channel for voice, data, text, and video services.

It is hard to pick up a news magazine or business magazine—or even a metropolitan daily newspaper—without reading a story about the new data highway that will be paved with fiber optics. Private industry is beginning to lay out huge sums of money to help build this highway, but it may take a large commitment on the part of the federal government to lay it nationwide. John D. Abel, executive vice president of operations at NAB has said of fiber optics:

Fiber is going to come. There are a lot of reasons why it should come, and it's NAB's view that it is good for America. It is a very powerful thing to have such unlimited broad-band capability. It is like building the new interstate transportation system for America—only this is a communication system.[19]

Fiber optic development was brought into existence by researchers' perfection of the laser, which has proved to be an ideal light source for a communications system that is lightwave based. Such a communication system uses modulated beams of light to transmit information through hair-thin, glass lines. The use of light has also proven to be highly beneficial in the storage of information and in the playback of that data from special storage media called optical discs. Fiber optic lines, as mentioned before, carry a great amount of data and the transmission going through them is immune from weather and atmospheric conditions. Such is not the case with other forms of transmission media, such as satellites.

In fiber optic systems, a light beam becomes an optical signal, serving as the vehicle to carry data to the desired points. The light travels through the fiber and, when it reaches its destination, it is picked up by a light-sensitive receiver and is reproduced into an electrical signal, which is the original form it took before it was transferred into light at the start of the transmission process.

In terms of the carrying capacity of fiber optic lines and the speed with which data can be sent, the figures are startling. Transmissions have exceeded a billion bits per second (a gigabit), and one 0.75-inch fiber cable can do the work of up to 20 conventional 3.5-inch coaxial cables. Information is more secure on fiber optic lines, and it can be sent longer distances without the use of repeaters, which are necessary with other forms of transmission vehicles, such as cable.

The chief problem with fiber optics is the expense of creating what is often referred to as a new information highway made up of light lines. Such a highway, which should eventually connect everyone in the United States, is analogous to the nation's interstate highway system that takes traffic to virtually anywhere in the country. Cost for such a fiber optic data system has recently been estimated at $200 billion to $400 billion, and the time needed to complete the project at 20 years.[20] This time frame may lessen if the demand for such services as interactive television shifts into high gear. As noted before, private communication companies are starting to fund some of the cost of laying fiber optic lines because they see it as necessary to advance their interactive systems.

OPTICAL DISC TECHNOLOGY

Optical disc systems are often classified into two major categories: (1) those with prerecorded information, such as musical compact discs, and (2) those that allow a user to store his or her own information.

Both types of optical discs utilize the same kind of light-based communications that fiber optic transmission uses. The first category of optical discs include CDs and CD-ROM. The second category of optical discs include such systems as Write Once, Read Many (WORM) discs that are interfaced with personal computers.[21]

Basically, optical disc technology stores digital audio—and even video—information in the form of microscopic pits on a round plastic disc. A laser-produced light writes or stores this data on an original master disc, and this disc becomes a kind of parent disc, playing a major part in the production of the commercially sold copies. Then, when the CD is placed on a player, a laser is used to retrieve and play back this information.

Tremendous amounts of data can be stored and retrieved from optical discs, and their durability surpasses many other forms of data storage, since the laser focuses on the data that lies beneath the disc's plastic, protective surface. Optical discs are also not subject to erasure (unless one is made purposely with that feature in mind) and, therefore, have a secure form of permanence.

All types of optical discs are receiving attention in the world of multimedia. One of these types is the CD-ROM, which looks like a regular audio CD. The read-only-memory portion of the name indicates that the disc cannot be used to store any additional information but instead is used only to read or playback information already stored on it. A CD-ROM is also computer compatible and is interfaced with a computer through a special CD-ROM drive and software. Once the disc is inserted into the drive, software that is bundled with the system allows the user to search through and retrieve the information stored on the disc.[22] CD-ROM optical disc technology is applicable to electronic publishing and electronic data storage and playback systems and services such as Nexis and Lexis. The tremendous amount of storage capacity makes them especially useful for storing large amounts of information. For instance, one CD-ROM title alone, *Grolier's Academic American Encyclopedia* contains 30,000 articles and can be stored on a single optical disc.[23] Other standard library research publications such as the *Reader's Guide to Periodical Literature* is also being stored on CD-ROM discs by libraries nationwide. Such enormous volumes of information can be used easily by simple keyword searches in which the user types in a keyword on a PC and the disc is automatically scanned electronically for all articles in which that keyword might appear in the headline or title. Then bibliographies are generated as well as abstracts of the articles in many such systems.

Another type of optical disc that is emerging in the field of interactive video is the Compact-Disc-Interactive (CD-I) and Digital Video-Interactive (DV-I). Both are parts of one system and are found in one configuration. Michael M. Mirabito and Barbara L. Morgenstern explain this technology as follows:

The CD-I is a sophisticated audio-visual tool that supports a variety of recording and playback formats. . . . A user interacts with the database of information through the computer and its operating system. Two potential applications include computer games and training systems. . . . The DV-I system is centered around a highly efficient data compression technique. In addition to storing thousands of individual images, a DV-I disc can support a full- motion, full-screen video display. . . . A single DV-I disc has a playing time of a little over an hour, and it could make strong inroads into our educational and training markets dominated and targeted by videodisc and CD-I systems, respectively. Actual applications could range from storing picture libraries on a disc to creating high-quality simulators and computer games supplemented by full-screen video displays and animated graphics.[24]

A third kind of optical disc with wide-ranging applications is the videodisc, which has applications for general consumers and schools. Consumer applications, in which movies are stored and played back on videodiscs, have largely been supplanted by videotaped movies played back on VCRs. Nevertheless, the CDs, which surpass the playback quality of audio tapes, videodiscs likewise produce greater video playback quality and resolution than videotapes. In school usage, videodiscs can be interfaced with a personal computer by way of a videodisc player to create an elaborate interactive environment for students. The educational uses of videodiscs seem to be the most popular and may hold the most promise for this form of optical disc technology.

COMMUNICATION SATELLITE TECHNOLOGY

On July 10, 1962, Telstar I was launched, which marked a significant event in worldwide communications. Telstar was an experimental "bird" that was the first to receive, amplify, and simultaneously retransmit telephone and television signals. It was, in fact, a forerunner of the modern communication satellite. Telstar's first transmission, a phone call to Vice President Lyndon B. Johnson ranked with such historic accomplishments as the first transmission of a telegraph message by Samuel F. B. Morse in 1844.[25] Today, communication satellites by the scores are traveling through space, orbiting the earth and making possible a new era in communications.

Recent innovations in satellite communications include tiny dishes that news organizations can assemble like petals of a flower to broadcast live from remote war zones and disaster areas. By the mid-1980s, average Americans were able to purchase similar small home satellite dishes for a few hundred dollars to receive television programming beamed directly off designated communication satellites. Each satellite can retransmit a great deal of video and telephone data. Some 30,000 telephone calls and three television channels can be carried by a single satellite at the same time.[26]

Television networks and local stations have been using live, satellite transmission for years to conduct real-time reporting from across town or around the world. Portable satellite dishes, as well as larger dishes mounted on expensive satellite news vans (SNVs), are now in use across the United States by television news crews.

One of the most recent entries into the field of telecommunication is direct broadcasting by satellite (DBS). With this technology programs are uplinked to a satellite that is parked in stationary orbit more than 20,000 miles above the earth's surface. The satellite then downlinks the programming directly to viewer's homes that are equipped with a receiving satellite dish. It is called "direct" because the signal does not have to pass through a retransmitter at a television station or a cable operator.

Several communication companies have moved into the DBS field. K-Prime (a blue-chip cable consortium of nine multiple system operators) began beaming 10 television channels by satellite directly into homes in 1991. Later that year, SkyPix announced intentions to transmit 80 more channels. By mid-decade, NBC, News Corp., Cablevision Systems, and Hughes Communications hope to switch on an additional 100 or so channels.[27]

As the 1990s began, companies were scrambling to get into the DBS competition. It was at that same time, however, that the future of DBS began to look a little blurry because of competition from fiber optics. This development has drastically altered the economics of the satellite business, and there seems to be more serious talk and research in the 1990s concerning fiber optic transmission than concerning direct broadcast satellite transmission. Additionally, like fiber optics, a great deal of financial investment is needed to develop a nationally supported DBS system. Another problem for DBS is the enormous growth in popularity of home VCRs and movie rentals via the neighborhood video store. If movies can be seen that way in the living room, it dramatically lessens the need for satellite transmission of movies. The DBS industry has also been harmed by the Satellite Television Corporation's suspension of plans to build a DBS system, joining other communication companies, such as CBS that left the field earlier.[28]

Nevertheless, for the near-term future, satellite-distributed television programming is the chief means by which cable television networks such as HBO, Lifetime, and A&E transmit their programming. In a typical situation, a cable network uplinks its programming to a communications satellite, which then downlinks it to a number of cable companies operating around the country. The programs are then transmitted locally to home subscribers via coaxial cable. The broadcast networks also use satellite transmission extensively.

After more than a decade of false starts, DBS television appeared ready for widespread use in the United States as the mid-1990s approached. The first two genuine DBS TV services were expected to be on line by March 1994, pending a successful December 1993 launch of a Hughes HS601 satellite via an Ariane rocket. A second similar satellite was to be launched in mid-1994 to complete these services' offerings. When fully operational, the two companies—Hughes Communication's DirecTV and Hubbard Broadcasting's United States Satellite Broadcasting (USSB)—are planning to deliver more than 150 television channels of programming to the continental United States from two satellites parked in space.

If successful, these two DBS operations hope to rewrite the story of direct broadcast satellite transmission in the United States and give it a happy ending. Among the improvements in these two new ventures over previous ones—most of which failed—are high-power satellites, improved low-noise amplifier (LNA) technology in receivers, different frequencies, wider orbital spacing of satellites, and digital video and data compression technology. The transmission these satellites send can also be accessed with 18-inch dishes on the ground, lowering the cost to consumers to about $700 for the hardware, plus subscription or PPV fees which would be comparable to that of cable TV service. Receivers are to be made by Thomson Consumer Electronics and sold under its RCA brand name at consumer electronics stores and satellite equipment vendors.

COAXIAL CABLE

While not a new technology (cable television has been in widespread operation since the 1970s), coaxial cable should be a part of this chapter's discussion because it still figures prominently in the entertainment and information industries. In fact, cable companies are in an enviable position. Like the telephone companies, which connect virtually every home in America with telephone lines that can be used for other data transmission as well, cable was within reach of more than 85 percent of American households in 1993. In addition, cable companies such as TCI and Warner Cable are providing much of the research and development dollars for more sophisticated audio/visual/textual transmission systems and are doing so in collaboration with other industries, such as the telephone industry and electronics manufacturing industry. Further, as noted earlier, it has been discovered by scientists at Bell Laboratories that coaxial cable can serve as a transmission medium for some compressed digital signals, although it cannot handle nearly the amount of data that fiber optic lines can. Cable networks also work in tandem with the satellite systems discussed in the previous section, as they bounce their signals off communication satellites for distribution to far-flung local cable operations, which, in turn, send them out over cable to subscriber's homes.

Basically, cable television is a method of distributing television programs that uses coaxial cables, which are fed into subscriber's homes. By 1990, cable television was bringing in some $15 billion every year in revenue, with all but about $2 billion of that accounted for by subscriber fees. The rest was in the form of advertising sales. The number of homes subscribing to cable mushroomed to over 50 million in that same year. In addition, of the households accessible to cable, about 65 percent of them subscribed. Projections for mid-decade were that cable would result in over $22 billion in revenue, and some 60 million households would subscribe to basic cable, with cable penetration at just over 60 percent.[29]

As most viewers know, cable TV is made up of basic and pay cable, although every household pays something to subscribe to either kind. Basic cable programming includes networks such as TBS, CNN, A&E, Lifetime, and ESPN. Pay cable programming includes networks such as HBO, Showtime, and the Disney Channel. One of the aspects of cable that makes it fit so nicely into the coming interactive television era is its ability to offer narrow-interest programming networks. *USA Today* reported that the following new cable networks were being prepared in 1993.[30]

* *Caribbean Satellite Network.* Cultural and sports programming from the islands.
* *ESPN 2.* Even more sports.
* *The Game Channel.* Owned by The Family Channel, this is one of two entries offering originals and repeats of game shows, together with some new interactive game show programming.
* *The Game Show Channel.* A second in this category from Sony.
* *The Golf Channel.* The name says it all.
* *History TV Network.* It is from A&E and is targeted to anyone who is interested in what has happened in the near or distant past.
* *IT Network.* Interactive classified ads.
* *Jones Computer Network.* Teaches viewers to operate computers.
* *The Sega Channel.* Interactive service offering the popular Sega Genesis games.

- *Television Food Network.*

- *Romance Classics.* From the AMC movie network featuring classic love stories on film.

- *World African Network.* A pay channel featuring programming targeted to black Americans.

In the early 1990s, some 50 multiple system owners (MSOs) dominated the cable industry, with some such as TCI, Warner Cable, ATC, Viacom, Cox Cable, Storer, United Cable, Newhouse, and Comcast supplying over one-third of all U.S. cable subscribers in 1990.[31] The large MSOs own many local cable delivery systems across the country, and it is these operators who run cable programming into the subscribing households. As the 1990s began, the number of cable systems around the country had grown to more than 9,000.

A subject of much controversy has been whether the cable industry should be regulated by the federal government and, if so, how closely. The Cable Act of 1984 swept away much of the regulation that had been imposed on cable by the FCC and put strict limits on municipal authorities over local cable operators. This trend was reversed in 1992, however, with the passage of the 1992 Cable Act, which—among other things— allowed local governments to cap the fees charged to subscribers for basic cable TV service. More will be said about this milestone legislation in chapter 8.

HDTV AND EXTENSIBLE TELEVISION

Up to this point, most of this chapter has focused on technology used to transmit and retransmit communication signals. A great deal of interest, however, is also centered on the receiving end of the process, especially with the growing popularity of the interactive—or two-way— television concept. To date, much of this research and development—as well as political and economic debates—have focused on high-definition television sets. HDTV has already been developed by several firms in Japan, Europe, and the United States and is operational now in Japan, where sets cost several thousand dollars each. An HDTV screen, as its name implies, delivers much clearer resolution because the screen is composed of twice as many horizontal lines (1,150 in one popular version) than the traditional 525-line television screen. Problems in international standards for this new form of television are impeding the implementation of HDTV in the United States, even though it is widely believed that this type of image resolution is vital for true interactive television. This section will look at the state of HDTV in America and at a form of television one step beyond HDTV, which many think is already making the HDTV concept obsolete even before it is operational in the United States.

HDTV

HDTV is a completely new concept in television. The television screen takes on dimensions and features of a movie screen, partly because there is a new "aspect ratio" of five units wide to three units long as opposed to the current standard screen that has a size ratio of four to three. That means the HDTV screens more clearly resemble the rectangular movie screens as opposed to the more boxy television screens now in use. In addition—and more importantly—there is a much clearer picture resolution. The standard screen in the United States is composed of 525 lines of vertical resolution, whereas HDTV screens are composed of from 1,050 (the standard developed by CBS), 1,125 (the Japanese standard) to 1,250 (the European standard) vertical lines of resolution. The more lines, the clearer the picture resolution, making either of the HDTV standards twice as clear as the picture that appears on current American television screens.

Another key feature of HDTV design is the stereophonic sound that gives viewers crystal clear sound reception, probably even clearer than current stereo television sets. The words and special effects are more audible and easier to comprehend, and sound is transmitted digitally in time sequences with the video. One of the developers of the CBS system, Renville McMann, explains, "The system is based on a TMC (time multiplex component) video processing system, in which luminance (brightness) and chrominance (color) are not mixed together as in the NTSC systems. Rather, it is sent in a time sequential form."[32]

Although HDTV is a fairly new concept for American industry, the Japanese have been working on it since 1970. Europeans have been working on improving HDTV since the early 1980s. The United States was one of the first countries to initiate the idea, but other countries picked up on it and developed it faster. This has left the United States trailing Japan and Europe in a critical industry.

HDTV improves picture quality by attacking the problem at the source: the broadcast signal. This produces a problem, however. One of the main reasons industry is slow in accepting HDTV is because the signal transmitted needs to be compatibly converted to the already existing receiving system. HDTV also requires extremely wide bandwidths to transmit.

In September 1988, the FCC decided to require that HDTV broadcasts be compatible with conventional and standard NTSC sets, in the same way NTSC color broadcasts are compatible with black-and-white sets. There are many proposals as to how to make HDTV and NTSC compatible, but none had been accepted by the early 1990s, nor has any worldwide screen standard been approved. The U.S. and Canadian governments did evaluate four competing HDTV systems in early 1993 and hoped to decide on one of them as the North American standard later in the year.

The problem of acceptance of national and/or worldwide HDTV standards is not the only hurdle HDTV is facing in the United States. Funding the conversion project is another major problem. An intense struggle came about during the Bush administration over the future of funding for certain projects such as Sematech, Pentagon projects, and HDTV. The White House has been concerned about where the development money would come from and if it would result in a profitable HDTV system in the United States. Another means of funding would be outside of the government and would come from broadcasters and broadcasting consortiums.

In addition to funding, there is the problem of international competition. Japan has already developed and is selling its HDTV system, known as the NHK 1125 or Muse System. In Europe, Eureka 95 is being field tested as another HDTV system. American manufacturers are worried that Japanese will start selling HDTV video equipment in the United States shortly. This threat is pushing cable operators and broadcasters to figure out how they can also deliver HDTV pictures before the Japanese move to take over the U.S. market. Michael Sherlock, head of operations and technical services for NBC, put it this way:

How can we address the competition now, while we grow into whatever is needed as we go over the long term? The broadcasters' best defense is a good offense: designate a system that is immediately implementable. . . . It is a situation in which the Japanese and Europeans are in the eighth inning of a tightly contested ball game, and America is about ready to hop in the station wagon and look for the ballpark.[33]

The U.S. government has been slow in taking the lead in HDTV policy. House Telecommunications Subcommittee Chairman Ed Markey told a Washington seminar in 1989 that he wanted to see the United States develop a national policy that would ensure that the United States competes in the HDTV marketplace.[34] Markey then had action memos submitted, which contained a number of suggestions on how Congress could help HDTV by getting U.S. industry involved. His project was estimated to generate approximately $250 billion in revenues from the sale of HDTV equipment.[35] But it was not until 1993 that the FCC got around to deciding that the consortia remaining in the race for HDTV development should pool their efforts to develop a single usable standard for the United States.

The issue of how much revenue is at stake in the race for HDTV is still in doubt. Some estimates put the bonanza resulting from HDTV revenues at lower figures than those expressed earlier in this section. For instance, a Congressional Budget Office report put it at about $30 billion over the next two decades, while many in the television industry put it at $120 billion over the same period of time.[36]

Whatever the future revenues, Japan and Europe progressed faster in research and development of HDTV in the 1980s than did the United States. It was Japan's clear, ambitious industrial policy that helped the Japanese build TV sets in 1970 for one-third the cost of building them in the United States. Also in 1970, Japan started thinking ahead to the next generation of TV sets, which are now the HDTV sets. Since that time, according to a U.S. Department of Commerce report, NHK has spent more than $500 million on HDTV research and development. And with the help of the Japanese Ministry of International Trade and Industry (MITI), which set up an HDTV promotion center and loan program, Japanese manufacturers have put another $400 million into HDTV.[37]

Nevertheless, even though the NHK 1125 system is the first one in widespread operation, it does not follow that it is the most technologically advanced system. Nor does it follow that it has become highly successful in Japan. Indeed, the *New York Times* proclaimed Japan's HDTV industry "a flop so far" in mid-1993.[38] The reason? The Japanese government had anticipated annual revenue from HDTV sales to reach two trillion yen—about $17 billion—by the year 2000 in Japan alone. However, the high prices of the sets (from $9,000 to more than $12,000), Japan's sluggish economy in the 1980s and early 1990s, and a paucity of HDTV programming in Japan held sales to only 10,000 or so sets by mid-1993. Nevertheless, Japan was continuing to pump money into the industry and began a new push in 1993 to snare video buffs by readying laser-disc and video players and software for the high-priced sets. Not only do they expect these efforts to bear fruit in Japan, but they are also gearing up to attack the huge American market for HDTV equipment, which the *New York Times* estimates will be close to $70 billion from 1995 to 2005, which are expected to be the inaugural years of American HDTV.[39] Given that there is only one large American manufacturer of television sets left—Zenith—and that the Japanese control most of this manufacturing niche in the United States, a dominant Japanese presence in the construction of most American HDTV sets is a strong possibility.

In Europe, where trade protection and state industrial policies have staved off Japanese control of conventional, television manufacturing, the European Economic Community launched an HDTV research and development program, Eureka 95, similar to the Japanese-funded program in 1985. By 1990, it spent about $100 million—60 percent from private sources and 40 percent from government—on HDTV.[40]

Meanwhile, in the United States, industry and government were still debating the value of the HDTV industry in the early 1990s, and the amount of research and development funding has amounted to only a few million dollars. By 1993, however, the U.S. government seemed convinced that an American HDTV standard should be adopted as soon as possible.

In addition, research and development of HDTV systems has picked up at research locations such as MIT Media Lab, where work has been underway for years to help give the United States a competitive edge in the HDTV battle. It was at the Media Lab that Professor William F. Schreiber theorized that the HDTV market could revive America's critically ill consumer electronics industry. And it was Schreiber who realized, when the world was looking around for an HDTV transmission standard, that the U.S. government seemed to be advancing a standard that would hand control of the HDTV industry over to the Japanese. It was Schreiber who put forth the arguments that European countries used to stop the Japanese takeover plan, and it was Schreiber, working with the Media Lab, who designed an HDTV system that could spell real trouble for the international competition and bring future television manufacturing business back to America.[41] Another MIT researcher, Jae Lim, headed a research group that, in partnership with Chicago-based General Instrument Corp., developed an HDTV system that was one of the five evaluated by U.S. and Canadian governments from 1991 to 1993 for possible adoption as the North American standard. The MIT group's system— along with a second American system developed by AT&T and Zenith Electronics Corp.; a third developed by a U.S./European consortium of NBC, the David Sarnoff Research Centre, and the American subsidiaries of Thomson SA of France and Philips Electronics NV of the Netherlands; and a fourth U.S. consortium—are all based on digital transmission technology. The fifth competing system was Japan's NHK which, although it is the first in public operation, is based on an older analog transmission system, as is Europe's Eureka 95 system.

In analog television transmission, the physical properties of electrical impulses or of radio waves determine the image that appears on the screen. In a digital system, the television interprets encoded information that is transmitted directly from the source and uses that to create images.

Most North American experts predicted in 1993 that the FCC would select a standard for HDTV that would be a digital system and that other nations, including Japan, might be persuaded to follow and adopt the same digital standard.[42] Part of that prediction came true in February of that year when the United States decided against adopting Japan's HDTV standard as a contender for future U.S. broadcasts, apparently narrowing the field to the three remaining groups contesting for the prize. Then in June 1993, the FCC prodded the remaining consortia to form a grand alliance among themselves to merge the best of their technical schemes into a single industry proposal. Although the complicated and detailed tests did not produce a clear winner, all groups demonstrated better pictures than the current Japanese HDTV system. Markey called the work of the U.S.-based groups "one of the great late-inning comebacks of all time."[43] The quick American technical advances in the early 1990s even prompted the European Community to put its effort at developing its own analog HDTV system on hold.

Scientists feel that digital formatting will provide the HDTV receivers much clearer and sharper pictures, along with more flexibility and working efficiency. Additionally, digital systems—unlike analog systems—are capable of interacting with other similar electronic media, such as CD players and home computers. With interactive television such a much-discussed subject in the United States, it stands to reason that a digitally based HDTV standard, which accommodates such interaction, would be the one selected.

Writer William J. Cook, however, noted that even with the progress in an American HDTV standard, there are still industry concerns.

The computer industry wants the new standard to contain features that permit data to be exchanged seamlessly between digital devices, including computers and television sets, and be displayed in a certain way. Otherwise, it says, the full promise of coming information technologies won't be realized. Broadcasters fear that giving the computer industry everything it demands will sharply raise costs to stations and consumers and slow development.[44]

Another issue is how the video screen should be formulated. Television manufacturers and broadcasters want the same "interlaced" technique now used to compose television screens. In that technique, even-numbered, horizontal lines of dots that form the picture are scanned, then the process is repeated for the odd-numbered lines. But the computer industry wants the screen to be scanned progressively, each line in sequence, to produce flicker-free text and graphics imagery.[45]

A compromise is possible on this last issue due to the formation of the grand alliance of HDTV consortia. Both systems could exist side by side, with information transmitted in packets, bundles of digits each labeled with their contents and how they should be handled by very smart TV sets, which could display both formats. Thus, broadcasters could begin sending interlaced signals even as computer users could receive progressive scanning.

The alliance's new proposal was due to be tested sometime in 1994, and an FCC ruling on its feasibility was expected sometime after that. If everything goes according to plan, Americans could have HDTV available to them by 1996.

So, by 1993, it appeared that the FCC was giving the introduction of

HDTV in America a high priority. After a system was chosen, U.S. broadcasters would have five years to set up HDTV channels alongside existing, conventional channels, even though HDTV sets would cost in the range of $10,000 each, putting them outside the reach of most Americans. Still, by the year 2008, sets are expected to drop dramatically in price and become more widely affordable. At that time, broadcasters would be required to phase out conventional TV broadcasting to free the airwaves for other uses.[46]

The Case Against HDTV: Extensible TV

Not everyone sees a rosy future for HDTV, and some feel it is already not needed or outmoded. The first argument maintains that there is a demonstrated lack of consumer interest in the quality of their current television image. There has been no grassroots demand for a new system, and few consumers when faced with the question of what is wrong with today's television would answer that the picture is not clear enough.

The second argument—that HDTV technology may already be outdistanced by other technology—has been made by media researchers and developers as well as several observers of the television industry. The argument was made by the *New York Times*, for example, that the real advance in television pictures is the telecomputer, which couples digital and video technology along with fiber optics. Whereas HDTV offers only a fourfold increase in picture quality over existing television, "digital computer technology is fully interactive and responsible not only to keyboards, joysticks and mice, but to touch, movement, and the human voice.[47] Since that 1989 *Times* article, however, three U.S.-based research and development groups, as noted in the previous section, produced digitally based HDTV technology that—it would seem—might allow the same kinds of interaction that digital telecomputers would. In addition, the main hurdle to the introduction of telecomputing is the lobbying underway in Congress in support of HDTV. Some critics of HDTV feel that, by diverting resources and congressional attention away from the drive to replace broadcasting with digital fiber networks, HDTV poses a threat to the future of American communications technology.[48] Again, however, fiber optic technology will be needed by a digitally based HDTV system as well as a digital telecomputer system, so one wonders how strong this argument actually is today. Still, the so-called intelligent TV made possible by the evolution of TV receivers into personal computers optimized for display is intriguing. Such television would need no new regulated standard—such as HDTV does—since a complete set of resolution options could exist for digitally revising the signal, both visually and with text, to generate higher-quality imaging as well as individualized telecasts. In the final analysis, the program could actually be created in the TV set as the result of negotiation between the viewer and the information in the channel.[49]

Another scenario that looks beyond HDTV is also being researched. It is an option, described by MIT Professor Andrew Lippman, for the evolution of television that simply "bypasses the jump to the double the number of lines on-screen and entails a new architecture for image distribution."[50] Many at MIT champion this open-architecture plan for television, and they are gaining allies among some manufacturers of computers and others committed to digital imaging. Lippman explains:

Images no longer need to be defined by the number of lines or the frame rate. Instead, you specify the precision or resolution of the image in terms of clarity and frame rate. The underlying bandwidth (or storage requirement) of an image is proportional to the volume it occupies in a three-dimensional space where the axes are its resolution vertically, horizontally, and temporally. For example, imagine a cube that is as wide as the image is clear, as tall as it is sharp, and as deep as the frame rate. The theme of extensible TV is that the bandwidth is proportional to the volume of the cube but the actual system can allow many different shapes. You would use this notion to build a TV system in which each component in the image chain processes its image data to the best of its ability, independently.[51]

This orientation is "extensible" and can evolve as the technology of cameras, processors, channels (or other storage media), and displays evolve. Lippman points out that a small, under-the-kitchen-counter television set does not need a 1,000-line screen to produce a clear image, but a 25-inch screen might need that kind of line image resolution to look as good as the smaller set. Still a larger, possibly wall-size, television panel may require more lines than any of the HDTV systems currently feature in order to get as clear a resolution as the smaller sets. Basically, this kind of extensible television is simply taking computer industry technology and applying it to television screens. In personal computers, the number of lines on a display is determined by its size. Therefore, bigger monitors have more lines, and lines per inch rather than lines per page is the operative parameter.

Lippman concludes that this approach is called extensible "because it makes no attempt to define the 'right' line count for TV systems that will come into existence in the indefinite future. Instead, the system is allowed to grow, as laser printers (dots-per-inch parameters) and computer screens do."[52]

VIRTUAL REALITY

In seeking a greater sense of presence—an entry into worlds one cannot literally encounter—researchers have come up with a media form that has come to be known as *virtual reality* (VR). Sometimes the concept is also connected to the idea of artificial intelligence, and one idea is inseparable from the other. One must have a device that is capable of creating artificial intelligence before he or she can enter a state of virtual reality. If it lives up to its promise—and that is a big if—VR will be a multisensory merger of the telephone, graphic workstation, and the television set. VR media have been touted as the "ultimate form of interaction between humans and machines,"[53] and "the first medium that does not narrow the human spirit."[54] Some even refer to VR devices as dream machines in that they could have the ability to take us into dream worlds.

Where does this medium stand now? According to the University of North Carolina's Frank Biocca, VR technology is in the prototype stages as improvised introductory system abound that "remind us of the very early television set; a low-resolution array of black and white lines barely sketching a snow-spotted image."[55] He continues:

Inside the low-resolution head-mounted displays, we can barely see the outlines of a new way to produce and experience mediated information. When fully implemented and diffused, the medium could be the catalyst for a revolutionary change in the way we communicate. At least, this is the vision.[56]

In one form of VR technology—dubbed *highly immersive systems*—users' senses are enveloped with virtual stimuli. Equipment used to do this consists of a head-mounted display (which looks like a pair of night-vision goggles), speech recognition system, spatial audio system, position tracker, data glove, tactile feedback system exoskeleton, treadmill, and motion platform. While this is the full-blown system, few systems combine all of these elements and instead settle for three or four. One abbreviated VR system that seems to produce the desired effects consists only of the head-mounted display, speech and audio systems, and data glove. Some VR systems have been described as the next wave of video games, where the player is actually placed inside the game and must maneuver his or her way toward his or her goals as the animated characters do.

Virtual reality has also been applied to what happens when a digitized image can be altered without a trace such as when a photograph or videotape is altered digitally and made to appear real. Chapter 8 discusses the ethical problems of this technology. But more often, VR is seen as a kind of latter-day trip-taking drug like LSD (only much safer) that can take users into worlds they only dreamed of before. In donning the VR equipment, users can enter all sorts of escapist fantasies, taking trips to a distant planet or deep into the past, shoot it out with John Wayne, and even experience "virtual sex." There is even a culture growing up around VR, just as LSD and Timothy Leary produced their own cult. The VR cult is called *cyberpunk*, and it is now a handy term for combining the related cults of techno-bohemians—primarily computer hackers—and "phreaks" or practitioners of the art and science of cracking the telephone network. Cyberpunk has been described as follows:

It's things like music, art and video done with a hacker sensibility. It's using technology just to see if you can do it. It's where the wizardry of the hacker meets the alienation of the punk.[57]

In 1993, there was a proposed bi-monthly magazine for cyberpunkers called *Wired*, supported in part by MIT Media Lab director Nicholas Negroponte. Not surprisingly, it touted itself as the *Rolling Stone* of technology.[58] The direction that virtual reality takes in the future, however, depends on time and the imagination of its creators and developers.

SUMMARY

Digital compression of audio and video, fiber optics, direct broadcast satellites, upgraded coaxial cable, HDTV, extensible television, and virtual reality are all cutting-edge technologies that are moving the world into the age of multimedia at a breakneck speed. Although some of these technologies are competing with one another for dominant means of transmission or reception, in a sense most of them are extremely complementary and locked in symbolic relationships, as is the case with cable and satellite transmission, as well as digital compression and HDTV. Large companies like TCI, Time Warner, AT&T, General Instruments, US West, Southwestern Bell, and many others are racing at swift speeds to research and develop new links in the evolutionary chain of mass communications, which are taking on a distinctly personal touch as the program and information offerings are tailored to individual tastes.

Whatever the future usage patterns of multimedia in the United States, interactive media will not be impeded by a lack of research and development but rather by market considerations discussed elsewhere in this book. Even at present, there is probably more technology in the world of communications than will ever be needed or used by the average American.

NOTES

1. A. Michael Noll, *Introduction to Telephones & Telephone Systems*, 2nd ed. (Boston: Artech House, 1991), 3.
2. Andrew Lippman, "Feature Sets for Interactive Images," *Communications of the ACM*, April 1991, 93.
3. Ibid.
4. Ibid.

5. Ibid., 94.

6. Report on Compression Labs, Inc., Securities and Exchange Commission Report, May 20, 1991, 2.

7. Daniel Manoil, *Telecommunications Technology Handbook* (Boston: Artech House, 1991), 103–104.

8. Ibid., 11–12.

9. Noll, *Telephones & Telephone Systems*, 167.

10. Report on Compression Labs, Inc.

11. Philip Elmer-Dewitt, "Take a Trip into the Future on the Electronic Superhighway," *Time*, April 12, 1993, 54.

12. Jim Willis and Diane B. Willis, *New Directions in Media Management* (Boston: Allyn & Bacon, 1992), 175.

13. Tom Crawford, "Why CDMA Should be the Digital Choice for Cellular Carriers," *Telecommunications*, March 1993, 51.

14. Ibid., 49.

15. Ibid.

16. Patrick Flanagan, "Wireless Modems: CDPD Standard Gaining Acceptance," *Telecommunications*, February 1993, 8.

17. Anil T. Kripalani, "A Seamless and Smart Network Is the Key to Great PCS," *Telephony*, March 8, 1993, 24–25.

18. Jerome Aumente, "Battling the Telcos," *Washington Journalism Review*, May 1990, 22.

19. Ibid.

20. Ibid.

21. Michael M. Mirabito and Barbara L. Morgenstern, *New Communications Technologies* (Boston: Focal Press, 1990), 201.

22. Ibid., 202–203.

23. Ibid., 203–204.

24. Ibid., 207.

25. Peter Coy, "Satellites Affect Face of Communications," *Albuquerque Journal*, July 12, 1987, D1.

26. Ibid.

27. Kevin Pearce, "Pies in the Sky?" *Channels Field Guide 1991*, 51.

28. Mirabito and Morgenstern, *Communications Technologies*, 183.

29. *The Veronis, Suhler & Associates Communications Industry Forecast, Industry Spending Preview 1991–1995*, 5th ed., June 1991, New York, 70.

30. Brian Donlon, "Cable Is Overflowing with New Options," *USA Today*, June 7, 1993, 3D.

31. Willis and Willis, *Media Management*, 98.

32. "CBS Breakthrough on HDTV Compatibility," *Broadcasting*, September 26, 1993, 77–78.

33. "All Eyes on HDTV at the NAB Convention," *Broadcasting*, April 18, 1988, 47–49.

34. "Congress High on High Definition," *Broadcasting*, March 6, 1989, 62.

35. Ibid.

36. Art Jahnke, "Not Just Another Pretty Picture," *Boston Magazine*, March, 1990, 90.

37. Ibid.

38. David P. Hamilton, "Japanese Push to Switch on Sales of HDTV," The *New York Times*, April 1, 1993, B1.

39. Ibid.

40. Jahnke, "Pretty Picture," 91.

41. Ibid., 90.

42. Patricia Chisholm, "Getting the Picture," *MacLean's*, November 9, 1992, 115.

43. William J. Cook, "A Clear Picture for TV," *U.S. News & World Report*, June 7, 1993, 60.

44. Ibid.

45. Ibid.

46. Chisholm, "Getting the Picture," 117.

47. George Gilder, *"Forget HDTV, It's Already Outmoded,"* The *New York Times*, May 28, 1989, F2.

48. Ibid.

49. Andrew Lippman, "HDTV Sparks a Digital Revolution," *Byte*, December 1990, 303.

50. Ibid., 299, 301.

51. Ibid., 301.

52. Ibid., 303.

53. Frank Biocca, "Virtual Reality Technology: A Tutorial," *Journal of Communication*, Autumn 1992, 24.

54. Ibid., 25.

55. Ibid.

56. Ibid.

57. Nathan Cobb, "Cyberpunk: Terminal Chic," *The Boston Globe*, November 24, 1992, 32.

58. Ibid.

3

· · · · ·

Media Seers and Shapers

Who are the wizards behind the new media? Do they have their feet planted firmly on the ground or in midair? Do they have the resources—in terms of talent and money—to bring these star wars ideas into the realm of reality? These are some of the questions that this chapter will address. They are important ones because it is a long jump from an idea to a commercial reality, as some of the failed videotex experiments of the 1980s showed the newspaper industry.

A DO-OR-DIE MEDIA TECHNOLOGY THINK TANK

Undoubtedly the place that has received the most light—and heat—over the past decade as a hub for media technology research is the MIT Media Lab. The Media Lab is housed in the Jerome Weisner Building, a silver and glass futuristic structure that sits on the north bank of the Charles River in Cambridge, Massachusetts, and looks like something out of "Star Trek." Construction of this self-proclaimed "technological mecca" was completed in 1985. From the initial ribbon cutting, more than 20,000 engineers, scientists, artists, media managers, educators, corporate executives, and government officials have come to the Media Lab for a tour. Most have gone away impressed and awed by what they have seen, even though much of it was probably beyond their comprehension. There are many intriguing areas of research activity: One graduate student might be working on multicolored Legos as he analyzes one phase of media technology; another student is demonstrating an interactive television system that is geared to an individual viewer's own tastes and habits. It all looks interesting, but one wonders how much of it will actually find its way into the marketplace.

It is awesome, but does it work? That was the question that *Boston Globe* associate editor David Nyhan asked in a skeptical piece about the Media Lab. He had his doubts about how well the lab's projects would work in the marketplace. Nyhan referred to the lab as "a helluva toy shop" and "part Disney World, part Las Vegas."[1] He took the Media Lab to task for focusing too much on corporate sponsorship and also faulted it for paying too much attention to what forms the media might take versus quality of journalism that might come from this new media gadgetry. But journalism per se is something the Media Lab obviously feels is beyond its scope. It exists simply to create the technology that will bring us the information and entertainment. Still, within that focus seems to lie a belief that the technology will be somehow neutral and disassociated from the message and also neutral in the sense of having no major psychological effect on the consumer. One wonders if that is truly the case. Nyhan wondered how far technology could take us as he noted this about the Media Lab.

It sounds a little like an academic version of strip poker or a peep show: you pays a little more, and you sees a little more. . . . Judgment, commitment, and leadership—these are the human qualities that the media need, and they are the very qualities that the computer cannot give you. All I'm saying is that searching amongst the bits and bytes for clues to the next generation of media metamorphosing should not be the only way media managers look when they think about the future.[2]

Despite skeptics such as Nyhan, the Media Lab continues to flourish. As the 1990s began, for instance, corporate sponsors of these Buck Rogers-style projects at the lab included Knight-Ridder, Gannett, Times-Mirror, ABC, Warner Communications, Dow Jones, AT&T, NYNEX, BellSouth, and Ameritech. If companies like these are listening, then you know the researchers at MIT are saying something interesting.

The Media Lab's flamboyant director, Nicholas Negroponte, has described the Media Lab's mission as inventing and creatively exploiting new media for "human well-being and individual satisfaction without regard for present-day constraints."[3] It is comparable to using free association to spur managers in business on to greater heights of creative thinking. "Suppose money were no object," a creative thinking consultant might say to a group of business executives in charge of developing new products. "How would you design this new widget to overcome the inherent problems our traditional widget has encountered? In fact, let's not even think of it as a widget—let's think of it instead as something similar from another realm. How about a hockey goal?" Freed from present-day constraints, a lot of imagination is possible, and some of it winds up being transferred back into the realm for which it is intended. Some of the end products of such creative thinking are quite surprising in their commercial effectiveness. Pringles Potato Chips is one such product of creative thinking, and the Media Lab expects to deliver some high-tech surprises through such creative thinking and demonstrations. Negroponte notes that the Media Lab employs "supercomputer and extraordinary input/output apparatus to experiment today with notions that will be common technologies tomorrow in areas as diverse as music and learning, entertainment, film, and quality of life in the coming electronic millennium."[4]

The means that MIT uses to achieve its lofty goals are many and varied, and most of them are very expensive. Still, with corporate sponsors such as those noted earlier, money and resources are not necessarily a problem for the Media Lab. One of the reasons the lab continues to attract such sponsorship is because of its focus on demonstrating the technology and devising a way to apply it to real-life use. "Demo or die," has thus become the Media Lab's dominating motto, reflecting an emphasis on creating products and services that will actually work rather than on developing theories about what might or might not work. Experimenting, prototyping, and reducing to practice are three chief methods of learning by doing, theorizing by making, and inventing by trying. To accommodate eager young minds bent on reinventing the media, the lab is open 24 hours a day, so that each member of the faculty, staff, and student body can access an almost endless array of computer equipment.

In using the word *media*, the researchers at the Media Lab are not referring to traditional display-oriented, passive mass media. Rather, they mean a more personal kind of media, such as interactive TV and PCs that can handle a vast array of functions. These personal, interactive computers would understand content, abstract concepts, and use common sense to filter and present information in accordance with their understanding of the user, his or her schedule, and mood. This is the essence of the concept of *user modeling*.

One of the products under development at the Media Lab in the early 1990s, for instance, was an electronic newspaper called Newspace, which would join the worlds of mass media and personal computing. Newspace would offer a broadsheet-sized electronic news presentation to the reader, complete with state-of-the-art graphics and human interaction. Much of the product would be built around individual users' habits, interests, tastes, hobbies, and lifestyles. It would have a "front page," simultaneous presentations, and various juxtapositions. The news content would be supplemented with information from local and remote databases, including electronic mail, or personal mail for the individual user, that the writer has sent electronically. This compilation of data is presented in the style of a newspaper, complementing rather than supplanting it. Further personalization would be accomplished by creating and maintaining dynamic user models. These models include information such as the user's day-to-day time schedule and areas of interest. As if that were not enough, Newspace would also monitor user actions to bolster precision and accuracy of the model over time. It would use a wide spectrum of information from several sources, including various news wire services, television news, local newspapers, and electronic mail. In addition to textual material, Newspace would also feature a range of maps, graphics, charts, and audio and video presentations. The user-modeling system, Doppelganger, collects information about a population of users, makes inferences from this information, and provides the results for clients. The data gathering is as unintrusive as possible, fueled by the monitoring of the articles and features the user "clicks in" over time. The system monitors this usage pattern, and it, in turn, helps personalize the content even more in the future, possibly without even having the user click that which he or she wants to see or read.[5]

MIT has also been at work developing a new kind of broadcast news that would distribute data and computer programs that—like the personalized newspaper—would lead to a more personalized television newscast instead of prepackaged material sent out to the masses. These broadcasts are not targeted at a human viewer so much as at a local "computational agent acting on his behalf." Thus, responding to instructions from both the broadcaster and the reader, this agent scans the incoming information, selects appropriate pieces of it, and presents it in a manner similar to that of the traditional media. At the core of this new system is a news retrieval system in which the personal computer replaces the news editor as gatekeeper. A wide range of local and remote databases operates passively and interactively and is accessed by "reporters." These reporters are actually software interfaces that are programmed to gather news. In a sense, they are "broadcasting," or watching all TV channels; reading all newspapers, magazines, and journals; and listening to all radio stations and picking out that which the individual users might wish to see. One result of this system would be the merger of all four traditional news media: radio, television, newspapers, and magazines.

In its information sheet for applicants to the study of Media Arts and Sciences, MIT explains they will be involved in the study, invention, and creative use of new information technologies in the service of human expression and communication. The field is deeply rooted in the modern communication, computer, and human sciences, and its academic laboratory is intimately linked with research programs within MIT's Media Lab. MIT researchers note that computers are the most prominent common denominator of this multidisciplinary merger of previously separate domains. Underlying the explosive advances of the various technologies involved, MIT feels it is discovering and cultivating a new set of shared intellectual and practical concerns that are the foundations of an emerging academic discipline.

Within its academic areas of study, MIT students analyze, probe, and invent new forms of entertainment and information technology; computer graphics and design; interactive cinema; connections between computers, music, and cognition; virtual reality; holography and 3-D imaging; and advanced human interface, speech research, computer animation, and how all this relates to epistemology and learning. Projects that the faculty and staff of the MIT Media Lab have developed in recent years include those with such enigmatic titles as Open Architecture Television, Optical Simulators, Portable News, Holographic Video, Data Gloves, Voice Windows, Society of Mind, Storyteller Systems, Elastic Movies, Desktop Movies, and LEGO/Logo.

A sampling of Media Lab publication titles illustrates the areas of research among the students and faculty. Among recent titles are *A Prototype for the Electronic Book; Network Plus; Image Enhancement; Newspace: Mass Media and Personal Computing; Edge-Lit Rainbow Holograms; Photographic Holography; The Integrated Multi-Modal Interface; Conversing with Computers; Using LEGO Robots to Explore Dynamics; LEGO, Logo and Life; Open Architecture Television; Computers and Design; Building an Alternative to the Traditional Computer Terminal; Aesthetics and Culture in New Media; Interactive vs. Observational Media; Interactive Shopping; Fifth Generation Television; Electronic Publishing; Music, Mind and Meaning; Communications with Alien Intelligence; Studying the Effects of New Communications Technologies;* and *Expressive Typography.*

In sum, the MIT Media Lab has been on—indeed has often defined—the cutting edge of technological innovation and discussion over the past several years, and its level of funding and expertise indicates it will continue to exert a prominent influence over new communication technologies for many years to come. The test as to how useful its innovations are may lie in the ability of others to adapt and apply MIT technology to the media marketplace.

It may not be long before other major research universities build their own media labs, but MIT definitely has the jump on them. The University of Michigan has started in the field, and a half-dozen other universities were drawing up plans for media centers in 1990. Some analysts believe that, by the late 1990s, most major universities will have some type of media research program.

BRINGING TECHNOLOGY TO THE MARKETPLACE

The advance of communications technology to new heights is good and bad for executives of media companies. On the one hand, for example, the CEO of a major newspaper group might welcome an alternative form of the traditional newspaper that might be better utilized by the consumer of the future. This is good news because newspaper readership has suffered over the past two decades in America as readers have largely turned to television for their news. So, if the newspaper industry can find a way to use television to get its product across, why not send forth a cheer? The bad news is that other electronics industries—such as the nation's telephone companies—are better equipped with resources, expertise, and existing equipment to launch such efforts than the paper-oriented newspaper industry. It is only natural to assume that such electronics industries will try to develop their own electronic information products, which is exactly what is starting to happen today. So the good news to the newspaper executives is opportunity, but the bad news is increased competition from companies that may know how to produce electronic information products better and quicker. In sum, there are many reasons for this ambivalent—often reluctant—welcoming of new technologies into an industry, and it is this kind of good news/bad new paradox that characterizes the thinking of media executives today. It is a paradox that is also characteristic of other industries, as researcher Stephen Wilks has noted:

While a dominant strain in industrial society is sustained celebration of scientific progress and technological accomplishments, there has always been an undercurrent of unease and criticism. Awareness of the ill-effects of scientific and technological change nowadays prompts a quizzical footnote to every announcement of technological advance. . . . Achievements in communication have produced an information society with, some fear, the potential for total social control as envisaged by Orwell. . . . Above all the way in which technology is employed has a distributional impact. It produces elites within societies and between societies.[6]

It is useful to recognize that research and development in any industrial sector takes place in three main institutional locations: universities, private industry, and government laboratories. It is also important to realize that each of these institutions may have their own unique motives, agendas, and goals in developing certain types of new technology. Some universities are more interested in pure research; some are more interested in applied research. With its slogan of "demo or die," the MIT Media Lab would seem to fall into this latter category. Yet an examination of the projects and publications done by its students and faculty indicates there is still a big gap between what MIT researchers and what media company executives might view as applied research. As will be seen in chapter 6, media executives are only interested in new technologies that will (1) be economically feasible to purchase and implement, (2) cut operating expenses, and/or (3) result in more readers or viewers. These are three difficult standards to meet for any new technology. Just because a certain type of technology is out of the experimental stage and into operation does not mean it will meet any or all of these three tests. MIT, for example, prides itself on staying out in front—often way out in front—of current technological discussion. For instance, as chapter 2 noted, a major discussion in the television industry now centers on the feasibility of HDTV. The industry is debating it, government is debating it, and it is operational in Japan. But some researchers at the MIT Media Lab have already declared it an obsolete issue and are thinking past it. In short, some research is running on a much faster track than the television industry.

As far as the government is concerned, there has been historical interest primarily in the military adaptability of new technologies. Often there has been the opinion that science is too important to be left to the scientists, and scientific research has been co-opted by the government and military through large grants that come with strings attached as to what is to be researched and what kind of application it is to have. If one was to study the beginnings of broadcasting in America, one would find that the government encouraged the development of radio, seeing its primary application as as means of communication with and between naval ships and to improve other types of military communication, especially in times of war. The government basically dissolved all radio patents during World War I to speed up the efforts at improving the quality of point-to-point radio communications for military purposes. It was during and immediately after World War I that most of the huge electronics companies, including RCA and General Electric, came into existence.

Recently, however, it has been the large corporations that have provided the impetus for developing new technologies. In addition to this kind of impetus, many large corporations have their own extensively developed research laboratories. Wilks notes that the continued growth and influence of large multinational corporations rests on their ability to harness and exploit technology. He writes:

[Technology] is so central it can no longer be treated as an adjunct, a separate division, a gain to be realized "if possible." Instead it must be placed at the centre of corporate activity and must become a strategic prerequisite in what Best has termed "the new competition." The concept of the new competition is built around the idea that the modern firm must engage in constant innovation and adaptation in order to survive . . . the systematic pursuit of technological innovation has been institutionalized within the corporation.[7]

In fact, from 1983–1988, the government was funding less research and development, while business was undertaking a greater proportion, approaching 75 percent in all countries.[8] The implication, Wilks points out, is that private industry was expanding its control over the content and direction of research and development.

COMMUNICATIONS COMPANIES STEP TO THE FORE

There is no shortage of companies venturing into the expanding communications technology today. In fact, the communications industry is still unsure of how many directions the new technologies will take and what kind of companies will need to become involved and lend their expertise. There is a sense that the communications functions of which they are aware are simply too much for a single industry to handle adequately, so many partnerships are being formed between companies that heretofore competed against each other as archrivals and shared few if any trade secrets. Some industry analysts fear that the market for the new communications products may be smaller than others predict, and they envision a scenario where, as too much technology competes for the same market, warfare among companies will loom. Analyst Nancy Hass has noted that "even with the fall of Soviet communism and the opening of China there is not market enough for the dozen or so technologies now in conflict (such as cable, traditional telephony, cellular, fiber optics, direct broadcast satellites) to all come out ahead. They are all racing to deliver a signal of equal clarity and reliability to many of the same customers."[9] She predicts that by the beginning of the twenty-first century there will probably be a few big pipelines that direct communications traffic globally. They will be hybrids; part land line, part wireless, part extraterrestrial. Others believe that there is more than enough work for many companies venturing into the development of new communications technologies. Alfred Sikes, chairman of the FCC, has alerted laboratories, manufacturers, and service providers to his belief that immense new opportunities are close at hand and that these companies soon will have reasons to put large amounts of money into the communications infrastructure.[10]

This section will analyze some of the companies and partnerships that surfaced in the early 1990s to take on the challenge of developing marketable communications technologies.

The Telephone Companies

The FCC has systematically dismantled the boundaries between communications fiefdoms, and the 1992 ruling by U.S. Judge Harold Greene allowing telephone companies—most notably the regional Bell operating companies or "Baby Bells"—to enter the information-providing business has also helped greatly in destroying many of the traditional boundaries between telephone systems and the news and entertainment media. Following the lifting of the ban preventing telephone companies from becoming information providers, as well as owners of the chief means of mass communication, the FCC gave the go-ahead to let telephone companies carry television programming. Overall, this action seemed likely to encourage the phone companies to move ahead with plans to deploy fiber optic networks. More specifically, the FCC's vote means that phone companies can transmit video for other companies, provide electronic menus showing video choices, and offer billing and collection services for video programmers. Phone companies are prevented from owning cable companies in their service areas, but they can own up to 5 percent of other cable companies or video programmers.

As a result of these rulings, the telephone companies are stepping up their research and development efforts and are considering expanded ways of serving their customers, including becoming information providers and part-owners in cable television systems. It is a high-stakes game with potential revenues soaring into the hundreds of billions of dollars. The business also has a multinational face, as phone companies at home compete with and worry about their counterparts overseas. Table 3.1 shows the world's 50 largest telecommunication companies and their 1991 sales and market value. By the early 1990s, for instance, the telephone equipment business had been consolidated into the hands of a half-dozen huge global companies, and the industry is expected to grow to $250 billion by the year 2000. Analysts such as Hass believe it will be dominated by "larger-than-life characters" such as Czech-born CEO Paul Stern of Britain's Northern Telecom and Perre Suard, CEO of France's Alcatel Alsthom.[11] About America's AT&T, Hass observes:

In this Grand Guidnol drama, AT&T, the only company in the world to engage in both manufacturing and network operations, is cast as Darth Vader —throwing off the harmony of the market by refusing to open the bidding process at its own operating subsidiary. Overall, AT&T's manufacturing units, never considered cutting edge or very efficient, are at best breaking even. "They are subsidizing themselves in a way that is destructive to everyone," says Alcatel's chief strategist, Josef Cornu.[12]

In other words, manufacturing companies from other countries would like a shot at supplying AT&T. That may not happen in the near future, however. AT&T's Randall Tobias argues that, while true that AT&T supplies a reasonably high percentage of its own equipment, even if it bought more from the outside, that would give them only 2 to 3 percent of the U.S. market. Besides, he believes, AT&T is in a better position to handle its customers than are foreign manufacturers.[13]

AT&T, under its chairman Robert Allen, was also gearing up in the early 1990s to be a major player in the multimedia era. The company's com-

Table 3.1
The World's 50 Largest Telecommunications Companies

Company•Country	Business	1991 sales — from telecom (mil.)	1991 sales — total (mil.)	Pretax income (mil.)	Total assets (mil.)	Employees	Stock price	Market value (mil.)
AT&T • *U.S.*	global services & equipment	$55,362	$63,089	$883	$53,355	317,100	$44	$57,120
NTT • *Japan*	global services	43,366	46,324	2,655	83,004	249,942	3,979	62,068
British Telecom • *U.K.*	global services	21,805	21,805	5,583	35,121	226,900	6	39,395
GTE • *U.S.*	regional svcs & telephones	19,621	19,621	2,191	42,437	161,567	35	31,001
Alcatel • *France*	systems & equipment	17,307	25,293	1,655	36,512	213,100	126	15,041
BCE • *Canada*	transmission services	15,164	16,807	2,030	38,632	124,000	39	12,160
STET • *Italy*	services & network systems	14,363	14,574	1,692	40,873	125,958	1	6,524
BellSouth • *U.S.*	regional services	11,719	14,446	2,260	30,942	96,084	53	25,673
Nynex • *U.S.*	regional services	11,462	13,229	793	27,503	83,900	82	16,610
Bell Atlantic • *U.S.*	regional services	10,197	12,498	1,996	27,882	76,900	47	20,552
Ameritech • *U.S.*	regional services	9,737	10,818	1,656	22,290	73,967	69	18,320
MCI Communications • *U.S.*	global & long-distance services	9,500	9,500	848	8,834	28,000	33	8,744
Telefonica de España • *Spain*	regional services	8,896	8,896	1,105	31,539	75,499	11	10,171
Siemens • *Germany*	systems & equipment	8,776	40,008	1,537	46,111	402,000	423	22,328
Pacific Telesis • *U.S.*	regional services	8,715	9,895	1,642	21,838	62,236	43	17,351
Southwestern Bell • *U.S.*	regional services	8,484	9,332	1,644	23,179	61,200	65	19,623
US West • *U.S.*	regional services	8,425	10,577	741	27,854	54,923	38	15,629
NEC • *Japan*	systems & equipment	8,178	27,323	372	29,548	117,994	6	9,350
Sprint • *U.S.*	global & long-distance services	7,954	8,780	559	10,464	43,000	23	5,100
Hitachi • *Japan*	PBX & fax equipment	7,287	56,223	2,714	64,131	324,292	6	18,951
Ericsson Telephone • *Sweden*	switching & cellular equip	6,843	7,120	327	7,716	71,247	23	4,643
Telefonos de Mexico • *Mexico*	regional services	6,509	6,509	3,444	14,965	49,912	2	25,240
IBM • *U.S.*	diversified equipment	5,300	64,792	121	92,473	344,396	87	49,836
Cable & Wireless • *U.K.*	global services	5,193	5,193	1,052	7,986	39,426	10	10,703
Motorola • *U.S.*	phones, pagers & radio equip	3,629	11,341	613	9,375	102,000	85	11,187

48

Company	Category							
Fujitsu • *Japan*	systems & equipment	3,486	24,920	373	28,899	52,039	3	5,527
Toshiba • *Japan*	systems & equipment	3,296	34,190	832	41,445	162,000	5	15,084
Matsushita Electric Ind • *Japan*	systems & equipment	2,194	53,938	2,631	65,303	242,246	10	19,978
Philips • *Netherlands*	systems & equipment	2,115	27,092	754	23,683	240,000	14	4,358
Sumitomo Electric Inds • *Japan*	fiber-optic systems	1,951	8,378	393	8,195	14,833	7	4,813
GEC • *U.K.*	switching & transmission	1,839	15,425	1,355	9,303	118,529	4	11,397
Racal Electronics* • *U.K.*	mobile & data comm equipment	1,701	2,959	251	2,571	35,384	1	1,775
KDD • *Japan*	global services	1,651	1,847	194	3,972	6,004	64	4,089
British Columbia Tel • *Canada*	regional services	1,644	1,644	301	3,168	15,015	18	1,941
Telecom NZ • *New Zealand*	global services	1,532	1,532	343	2,892	13,562	1	2,943
Nokia Group • *Finland*	mobile telephones	1,492	3,647	-72	4,749	29,167	13	824
SNET • *U.S.*	regional services	1,419	1,633	214	3,539	11,224	34	2,134
Oki Electric • *Japan*	transmission & terminal equip	1,395	4,932	23	6,021	20,278	3	2,034
Ascom Group • *Switzerland*	systems & equipment	1,369	1,896	40	2,149	18,215	1,311	596
Centel • *U.S.*	regional services	1,181	1,181	169	3,492	9,291	30	2,564
McCaw Cellular • *U.S.*	cellular telephones	1,135	1,366	-153	8,717	6,373	27	4,969
Telecom Malaysia • *Malaysia*	national services	1,112	1,112	399	3,486	28,797	6	10,874
Goldstar • *Korea*	switching equipment	1,092	5,487	53	4,931	32,436	13	930
Telus • *Canada*	global services	1,030	1,037	161	2,564	10,201	12	1,623
General Electric • *U.S.*	systems & equipment	1,000	60,236	6,436	168,259	284,000	76	64,786
Matra • *France*	transmission equipment	950	3,587	100	5,860	19,614	35	844
Alltel • *U.S.*	regional services	932	1,748	282	2,787	11,916	39	3,118
Corning • *U.S.*	fiber optics	750	3,295	327	3,853	33,300	36	7,041
General Instrument • *U.S.*	systems & equipment	727	929	-98	1,783	8,600	15	8,596
PacifiCorp • *U.S.*	regional services	724	4,007	710	13,229	15,722	22	5,911

*Includes Vodafone, which was spun off to shareholders in September 1991. Note: All figures are latest available and are converted into U.S. dollars using average exchange rates. Prices and market values are as of Aug. 7, 1992 and are for home stock exchanges. Sources: Worldscope; Arthur D. Little Inc.; FW.

Reprinted with permission of *Financial World* magazine, September 15, 1992.

bination of fiber optics, semiconductors, and software gives it a tremendous advantage as a multimedia company. Despite the fact that AT&T receives approximately 90 percent of its profits from the long-distance business alone, where it maintains a 67 percent share of a $60 billion market, the company is repackaging its network services for different customers with features defined by software. As *Forbes* magazine noted in 1993:

With so much calling capacity buried in the ground in fiber optics, communicating has become cheap, so cheap that distance means virtually nothing any more in determining the cost of a telephone call. . . . But if distance is not the issue, complexity is. Today's information consumer is connected to many networks around the world: electronic mail, wireless voice and data networks, teller machine networks, cable television networks, networks of digital libraries. Today more than ever there is a need to integrate these networks.[14]

Integration is in AT&T plans. It has the jump on other companies because of its extensive vertical integration and, thus, its ability to merge all the elements—fiber, chips, and software to run them. In software alone, AT&T is charging ahead, and in its research arm, Bell Labs, more than 10,000 of the professionals are software people. Among the many communications ventures AT&T has become involved in are the following:[15]

- A "neighborhood" phone that extends the range of a cordless phone to a mile.
- A converter box for the top of the television set to access and decompress up to a possible 540 channels. This is a joint venture between AT&T and TCI and General Instrument.
- A combination home computer/videogame/TV for interactive multimedia, through a joint venture with Time Warner, 3DO, and Matsushita.
- A portable computer that can communicate without wires, through an equity investment in a Silicon Valley research firm called EO.

General Telephone (GTE) has also been experimenting with expanding its services to include the transmission of video signals. The nation's second-largest telephone company after AT&T, with $18.4 billion in 1990 revenues, was experimenting in 1991–1992 in Cerritos, California, with fiber optic cables. The new wiring allows phone companies to offer home video and other types of television entertainment programs that cable television companies offer today. If the phone companies' ambitions prove true, future households may be able to consult with their family doctors over videophones or have their children tap into databases at the Library of Congress. As of 1992, the GTE residential experiment with television services and fiber optics was the most extensive test of any telecommunications company. That test, however, consisted of providing a wide range of interactive video services to just one family in Cerritos because of the expense of the wide range of services offered. For instance, this family had the ability to use their remote control to dial any of 20 of the latest movies at anytime, or to have a high-fidelity picture phone. Nevertheless, telephone company researchers and marketers were watching the experiment closely. Some telephone researchers have been able to do wonders with digital signaling techniques, increasing the carrying capacity of telephone copper wire more than twentyfold. But only the cable television industry's coaxial cables can carry enough information for a good television picture, which requires 700 times the carrying capacity of copper wire.

The major long-distance carriers (AT&T, MCI, and US Sprint) have come a long way in replacing crucial parts of their networks with fiber optics, and so have the Baby Bells. But these portions of the system are on the order of major arteries; there are numerous veins and blood vessels that need to be replaced, too. Substantially less than 1 percent of the wiring to homes by 1991 was fiber optic wiring.

Not to be outdone, NYNEX Corp. (one of the Baby Bells) hired a former television programmer in 1993 to serve as managing director of business planning and development. Alan B. Bennett predicted that by the year 2000, regional Bell companies like NYNEX will serve as one of the main providers of programming into the home. He called telephone companies such as NYNEX, "the next viable distribution platform."[16] According to Bennett, the most significant opportunity for NYNEX lies in providing video-on-demand services, allowing consumers to use their phones to order such programming as movies and news. Bennett and others at the seven regional Bell operating companies were hoping for a reversal of a 1992 law that prohibits them from offering entertainment programming to consumers. Many analysts have predicted that this restriction, like others before it, would give way in the face of the tremendous political influence the telephone companies have in Congress and with the FCC.

Yet another Baby Bell, Southwestern Bell, broke new ground in 1993 by paying $650 million for two cable TV systems in the Washington, D.C., suburbs. This was a deal that resulted in a new era for the television business. By purchasing the cable systems, Southwestern Bell became the first phone company in America to own a cable TV operation. Similar acquisitions were expected to follow. Robert Morris of Goldman Sachs, called the Southwestern Bell deal "the first shot over the bow. The lines between telephone companies and cable companies are all going to blur into communications companies."[17] Both of the cable systems bought by Southwestern Bell—Montgomery Cablevision Limited Partnership and Arlington Cable Partners—were owned by Hauser Communications and together had 228,000 customers. Southwestern Bell had already bought two overseas cable systems. Federal regulations prevent local telephone companies from owning cable systems in their operating areas, but they are free to buy systems elsewhere. Stephen McGaw, an official with Southwestern Bell, told *USA Today* that the phone company would run the cable systems as Hauser ran them but held out the option that the "cross-fertilization trend may lead to phone services offered through cable TV and video services offered through phone lines."[18]

Later we will take a detailed look at another joint venture between RBOC—US West—and a cable company, Time Warner. In this 1993 deal, US West agreed to pay $2.5 billion for 25 percent of Time Warner's entertainment division, which owns cable TV networks, movie studios, and cable TV's HBO. This is the first time a Baby Bell and a cable TV and programming giant have teamed together to put interactive information, entertainment, and telephone services at cable customers' fingertips. The services were expected to be available by 1998.

Whatever the outcome of this domestic and international competition among telephone companies, one thing is certain: phone companies will no longer be looking for profits solely from the manufacture of equipment or the operation of their telephone networks. Increasingly, phone companies will be more involved in the information services sector, providing information over lines they also own.

Cable Television Companies

Cable television is a distribution system for programming that is carried over coaxial cables into subscribers' homes. The cable industry has seen an unprecedented growth in popularity since the early days in 1952 when there were fewer than 14,000 subscribers to some 70 very primitive cable systems. That popularity grew as new and better forms of programming were offered and as more of the country realized the benefit of having more viewing choices on television than were provided by the big three commercial networks and PBS stations. In the 1970s, cable stations started proliferating and developed their own programming for transmission. With the growth of satellite communications and their ensuing capabilities for sending programming to remote local cable systems from a single source, cable grew tremendously.[19] The growth of the industry was also aided by the federal government's deregulation of cable in 1984, although reregulation legislation was approved eight years later in 1992, which brought the industry back under the watchful eye of the federal and local governments.

Today, the cable industry is dominated by about 50 multiple system owners (MSOs). Among the leaders of these basic cable operators, which are the distributors for the many cable networks, local stations, and "superstations," are Tele-Communications (TCI), ATC, Continental, Storer, Warner Cable, Cox Cable, Comcast, United Cable, Viacom, and Newhouse. These 10 companies alone accounted for about 20 million basic cable subscribers as the 1990s began, and those numbers are growing annually. The large MSOs, in turn, own many local cable delivery systems around the country. These local operators feed cable programming into the homes of area subscribers.

Cable companies are worried, as are newspapers, about the new-found freedoms that the telephone companies have received. If phone companies can deliver television programming, then that could affect the cable companies' franchises. The cable companies, however, are not wasting any time. They are now laying 75 percent as much fiber optic cable as the phone companies, and soon they will be ready to move into the telephone business, turning the tables on the phone companies who are considering going into the television business. TCI chairman John Malone noted in 1992 that "right now, the telephone companies are probably as scared of us as we are of them."[20] With TCI bringing in $3.8 billion in annual sales, the phone companies' fears are probably well grounded.

As an example of how aggressive the cable industry has become in competing with the phone companies, TCI announced in 1993 that it planned to build a fiber optic network that would include approximately 500 channels and would bring the concept of an information highway closer to the nation's living rooms. In all, TCI said it planned to spend $1.9 billion between 1993 and 1997 to build its fiber optic network in 37 states.[21] The plan was that, by 1994, the first TCI customers hooked to the network would notice sharper images and have the ability to select from dozens of pay-per-view movies and specials. Then, by 1996, some 9 million TCI customers (roughly 10 percent of homes in America) would be served by the network. These television sets would be able to receive as many as 500 channels carrying dozens of college sporting events each weekend, a series of home shopping channels, and pay-per-use video games. The network could also connect computers, letting them quickly and cheaply share information, which is the same concept that has the support of President Bill Clinton.

TCI is not the only communications company laying fiber optics, but it appears to be spending more and moving faster than other companies.[22] Pacific Bell, for instance, also unveiled plans in 1993 to build similar technology in California by 2015, and New Jersey Bell announced plans to spend $1.5 billion on fiber optics by 2010. TCI's network would consist of fiber optic cables that are made up of 24 hair-thin glass strands that can carry 100 times more information than copper telephone lines. These would run to underground computerized boxes serving from 500 to 2,000 homes. TCI planned to build the most fiber optics in seven cities: Pittsburgh, Miami, Denver, San Francisco, Salt Lake City, St. Louis, and

Hartford. The fiber optic cables would not connect to the actual homes. Instead, two coaxial cables—one going into the home for TV broadcasts and one coming out for two-way interactive TV and computer hookups—would connect home TVs to the neighborhood boxes.

COOPERATIVE COMMUNICATION VENTURES

As the battle to develop and harness the technology of the future moves into high gear, many communications company giants are finding that it is too big of a puzzle for them to solve alone. As a result, a number of joint ventures was created in the early 1990s between companies that traditionally have competed heavily and have closely guarded their research and development secrets. This section examines some of these new partnerships.

TCI/US West

One of the more ambitious television experiments of the early 1990s was the one conducted in a Denver suburb where cable giant TCI and its Baby Bell neighbor, US West, sent 1,000 movies, dozens of pay-per-view events, and about 60 channels of regular cable programming into some 400 homes. Residents participating in this experiment could access all of this—and more—through their own special remote control pads. The experiment brought these viewers one step closer to what has become a vision for the information industry: video on demand.

Technology used to create this phenomenon consisted of standard fiber optic lines and coaxial cables, which transmitted the programming to the test homes from a large switcher that stored the programs and movies. While this technology was not radically different from similar experiments at the same time, the difference was that two business competitors were jointly running the experiment. Writer Robert Wrubel describes this partnership as "a little like a mongoose and a cobra curling up together for a nap."[23]

The partnership was formed in the midst of regulatory battles that permitted telephone companies to do some things, and cable companies to do others. Since 1984, for instance, the Baby Bells have been trying to break the regulatory gridlock that keeps them from owning or operating video services. At the same time, cable companies have seen the wisdom in creating high-speed—or turbonews—communications networks that can offer much more programming than the cable companies currently provide.

The Denver experiment was called VCTV and formed the initial stage of the partnership between TCI and US West. The project began in 1991 when the two companies joined to create and operate cable systems in the United Kingdom, Hungary, Norway, and Sweden. Those partnerships grew into a cable/telephone experiment in England that became so successful that it threatened the giant British Telecom.

If the communications industries in the United States were looking for a way to inspire Washington officials to develop a favorable national information policy and begin appropriating funds for an interstate fiber optic network, they might do no better than to form partnerships such as TCI and US West have done. Computer consultant Patrick Springer describes the rationale for partnerships this way:

It is a natural alliance. You have the telephone industry with an abundance of cash flow, capital and few opportunities for diversification, and a cable industry which is heavily leveraged and has plenty of entrepreneurial drive and experience.[24]

The added advantages are complementary skills and technologies. Cable operators know how to operate and program a video system, while their telephone company counterparts are expert at switching and interconnecting electronic signals across communications networks.[25]

Partnerships between cable and telephone companies makes sense from another standpoint as well. The United States is just now beginning to attack the problem of an interstate fiber optics network. Although several major cities and research centers have been linked via fiber optics, the vast majority of cities and towns remain unlinked. Even when these cities and towns are connected to each other, however, running the fiber optic lines out the last quarter mile to each home seems a gigantic task. As *Time* noted in 1993, it has long been assumed that nothing much would really change in the strides toward interactive television until these last quarter-miles are wired for fiber optics, which has been estimated to take approximately 20 years to do. But a breakthrough may have been found that would allow interactive television systems to get around this last-mile bottleneck. Evidence indicates that coaxial cable can carry information quite well over relatively short distances of a quarter-mile or so, having almost as much bandwidth as fiber optics. Therefore, if the signal could be brought to within a few blocks of each subscribing home and have coaxial cable carry it to the actual homes, the cable companies could do away with their troublesome amplifiers, obtain more signal capacity that is easier to maintain, and get two-way interactivity almost cost-free.[26] The phone companies scored a breakthrough when they realized it is possible to squeeze a video signal through a telephone wire. While it cannot handle live pictures and the images are not as crystal clear as those sent over coaxial cable, the development holds out the promise that video signals can travel across conventional telephone wires.[27]

So the stage appears set for more joint ventures, although because of regulatory restrictions from the Cable Act of 1984, TCI and US West are not permitted to call the project a "joint venture." It must instead be called a "cooperative effort." Still, it is from experiments such as this that future technology will be developed.

IBM, Apple, and Japan

Some partnerships are international ones. In late 1992, for instance, IBM and Apple Computer, Inc., already joined in searching for a new multimedia standard for computer operating systems, were talking with various Japanese electronics companies to support their emerging multimedia system called Kaleida. Among the companies IBM and Apple were negotiating with were Matsushita Electric Industrial Co., and Sony Corp. It was unclear what role the Japanese company would be offered, but it was obvious that an international cooperative venture was deemed desirable to develop what could be an internationally accessible system.

Multimedia machines, which combine video, images, sound, and data, are expected to create a new generation of electronics, blending the functions of computers, televisions, video disks, and game machines.

According to the *New York Times*, U.S. companies such as IBM, Apple, and Microsoft are expected to shape the future of that market, but "their discussions in Japan illustrate that Japanese hardware manufacturers will have a key vote in determining which of the standards will be most successful."[28]

IBM and Sears

One of the more successful joint ventures has been the teaming of Sears Roebuck & Co. with IBM to produce the popular interactive personal service Prodigy. The Prodigy service enables families with personal computers to conduct transactions such as shopping, securities trading, banking, and travel bookings and to select a broad range of information, education, and entertainment. Users can also send mail electronically from their homes and offices. Each home accesses these features through its regular telephone line, which connects to a computer with a modem. Prodigy makes use of color and graphics to give it a distinctive look and feel. In all, there are more than 750 features that Prodigy can offer to its subscribers.

The service, which was begun in 1984, speaks simple English and eliminates the need for advanced computer skills. It is also personalized, as each member of the household (up to six persons) can set up a personal "path" that automatically calls up the 20 features of greatest interest in the same order each day, like a clipping service. Each member of the household creates his or her own unique password that protects such information as credit card numbers, bank account data, electronic mail and personal address book, travel profile, and personal stock portfolio. Prodigy's system architecture makes the individual member's home computer the "host" for most transactions, which is the reverse of traditional videotex, which requires that every keystroke be transmitted (and processed in) a large, distant host computer—a much more expensive process. The Prodigy service, on the other hand, requires only a local call to a neighborhood Prodigy site. Most of the processing is done right in the member's home computer, greatly reducing Prodigy's costs. This is one key reason the service can be offered for a low, flat fee. According to Prodigy press information, more than 8 million U.S. households had computers compatible with the service as of 1990. Ownership of these home computers was growing at a compound annual rate of 25–30 percent.[29]

Prodigy is the result of a partnership that combines the expertise of marketing, retailing, and creative computer insight and manufacturing. The *Wall Street Journal*, in a special story devoted to "companies for the future," named Prodigy Services Company as one of 66 enterprises "poised to lead business into the 1990s."[30] Members of the service paid a flat monthly fee of $9.95 for the whole family in 1990, but the number of subscribers fell far short of the millions that Prodigy had hoped to garner. Only about 160,000 households subscribed to Prodigy as of 1990.[31] Some of the complaints of the service focused on its slow response time and the fact that most of the pictures were part of advertisements. The *Chicago Tribune* noted, "Virtually every time you switch to a new screen, part of it is taken up by an advertisement for some product. More than 200 companies, from Pepperidge Farm to Budget Rent a Car to Sears, are shamelessly pushed."[32] This abundance of advertising, of course, is one chief way Prodigy keeps its monthly fees to the users so low.

The *New York Times* noted of the interactive service that:

Prodigy has a long way to go before it convinces videotex skeptics that it can turn profits where companies like American Telephone and Telegraph, Time Inc., Knight-Ridder, the Times-Mirror Co. and several big banks have lost millions. Prodigy's two partners (CBS, Inc., dropped out of the original partnership) have already sunk $600 million into the project and may need to invest $1 billion or more before reaching profitability, industry analysts say.[33]

David J. Waks, Prodigy's director of technology, told the *Times* that the company had to figure out how to limit the use of central computing resources because they are extremely expensive. He said the service also had to find out how to minimize national telecommunications costs because moving bytes of information across country is also very expensive. Thus, Prodigy's approach means that most of the traffic is between the user and a nearby minicomputer. The mainframe at Prodigy's White Plains, New York, headquarters is tapped only when the minicomputers do not have the necessary information. Still, the *Times* concluded that "although most videotex industry analysts remain to be convinced that Prodigy can be profitable, they give the service high marks for its innovative technical design."[34]

Other Consortia

Among other joint ventures and/or mergers in the communications business in the early 1990s were the following:

- *QVC, TCI, and Liberty Media.* In this venture, Hollywood entrepreneur Barry Diller bought into QVC, the television shopping network, which is part of the TCI-Liberty Media empire.
- *TCI and General Instrument.* In this venture, TCI—the country's largest cable system operator—announced it would use digital technology developed by General Instrument, making an initial move toward creating a 500-channel cable television system.
- *MCA, AT&T, Time Warner, and 3DO.* Large corporate investors risk $15 million that they put into California manufacturer 3DO, which plans to build an interactive, multiplayer box that attaches to televisions to play video games and educational CDs, as well as to control interactive cable TV.
- *Sega, Time Warner, and TCI.* Here Sega, the videogame manufacturer from Japan, linked up with the two largest American cable operators to create the Sega Channel, expected to be available by 1994.
- *Microsoft, Intel, and General Instrument.* In this consortium, General Instrument embraced two giants in the software and microchip industries to assist them in developing a cable converter box that has personal computing power.
- *Hewlett-Packard and TV Answer (now Eon Corp.).* A joint venture to build boxes to control interactive television using a radio-based system.
- *United Video, Zenith, General Instrument, Kaleida Labs, and Scientific-Atlanta.* A consortium that will develop converter boxes that will accept plug-in modules, providing access to new multimedia cable services.

As is evident from this list, several of the joint ventures are going after the so-called "black box" or set-top converting device needed for interactive television operations. Because the stakes are so high in this race (whoever controls the converter has a great influence on how the future of digital communication develops), companies that have heretofore kept close guard on their technology are more than willing to share it with companies from complementary industries, if it helps them win the race to build the converter box.

MULTIMEDIA PIONEERS

Until now, we have been talking mostly about industries and companies within them that are working hard to advance the new communications technologies and market them to the public. This section will look at some individual entrepreneurs, some of whom were heading these company efforts in the early 1990s and others who are charting their own courses in this great technological surge.

Bill Gates

In 1981, IBM tapped Bill Gates's Microsoft company to provide the operating system for the original IBM PC. This was a big break for a rather small company in the industry. By 1993, Microsoft was ranked first in overall development and sales within the software industry, and its software was compatible with most PC brands, including the leaders IBM and Macintosh.[35] *Fortune* magazine reported that Gates's 30-percent share of Microsoft was valued, on paper, at $7.3 billion, "which was enough to buy out an entire year's production of his 99 nearest competitors, burn it, and still be worth more than Rupert Murdoch or Ted Turner."[36] Microsoft's total $25 billion market value in 1992 was higher than that of Ford, GM, 3M, Boeing, RJR Nabisco, General Mills, Anheuser-Busch, or Eastman Kodak. Around the world, some 120 million PCs run on Microsoft's MS-DOS operating system, and that figure was expected to reach 140 million by the mid-1990s.

If these statistics are not staggering enough, Microsoft was outselling its three largest software competitors—Lotus, Novell, and WordPerfect—combined in 1992.[37] In 1993, Microsoft was pushing hard to establish its newest PC operating system, Windows NT, which was designed to provide better computer networking in the high end of the market.

Microsoft, under Gates, is not without its challenges. Microsoft will have to do battle with the emergence of interactive TV, which is designed to merge the television and PC into a single instrument. In confronting that challenge, Gates is faced with developing partnerships with consumer electronic companies, telecommunications, broadcasting, and cable TV operations or risk losing out on the huge portion of the communications market represented by the 85 percent of American households that still did not own PCs in 1993. Nevertheless, many industry analysts are betting Gates and Microsoft will not only survive, but prosper as the 1990s continue.

Gates is a visionary and is not afraid to gamble on what seems to be feasible projections. He feels the company's current success has arisen from the risks it took in the 1980s and how it has managed to stand beside those gambles. He wants the company to move now into the areas of multimedia, interactive TV, object-oriented programming, and other innovative project areas. In short, he wants to develop a new approach to how people around the world tap into information. Writer Alan Deutschman has noted, "Microsoft is unique in trying to compete in virtually every niche—and it never, never surrenders."[38] Gates has the tenacity—and his company has the money, momentum, and market recognition—to stay with gambles until they pay off.

In a way, Gates is like the CEO of a bygone era. He gets very involved in the research and development of new products and ideas, overseeing them and constantly challenging their creators. He has a near-photographic memory for details, reads voraciously, and is a virtual walking encyclopedia on computers and software. His long-term vision, which he feels will not be realized until the year 2000, is called "Information at Your Fingertips." "The idea here is very ambitious," he says. "Any piece of information you want should be available to you."[39] His vision does away with needing to recall whether a piece of data is stored in a database, spreadsheet, or elsewhere. The users will only have to tell their computers what they are looking for. The personal computer will actually become more of a personal communications tool than an intimidating computing instrument. And Bill Gates wants Microsoft to build that computer plus all the software anyone would need for it.

Nicholas Negroponte

Director of the MIT Media Lab, Nicholas Negroponte has been called the Henry Kissinger of the telecommunications industry. He has become a favored expert source for the news media on communications technology as well as a consultant—both official and unofficial—for top CEOs. His theme is fairly constant: the most important aspect of the new communications technology is the personalization of computer functions. In order to survive in the marketplace, he feels, computers must do more and more work for the consumer, and they must do it in language they understand. To do this, they will have to be user-modeled, so users will have to reveal a lot of personal information about themselves to their computer so it will be able to tailor programming and services for that particular consumer. Therein lies the trade-off for this kind of personalized service: the potential loss of privacy and turning over information to a computer database that others might access.

Negroponte is the leader of a large number of MIT researchers who are developing and demonstrating what this personalized multimedia universe might look like. He seems to pride himself on being at least one large step beyond other research and development leaders around the country. For instance, he is already thinking past HDTV, which has not yet become operational in the United States. In fact, he feels it is a waste of time and says if 50 people on the street are asked what is wrong with television today, very few if any of them will respond that the picture is too fuzzy. The problem, he says, is and always was the programming and the rigid formatting of programs, which require viewers to be home in front of their sets at certain times of the day or night to watch what they want to see. The VCR has alleviated some of that necessity, but not enough he feels. In short, the future belongs to those systems and services that will tailor programming and services to consumers and provide them when the consumer wants them. If the success of the Media Lab up to this point is a good indication, Negroponte may well be on the right track in his thinking.

Albert Gore

In 1993, Al Gore became vice president of the United States, and one of his goals for the next four years was to develop and create a kind of interstate highway system for multimedia communications. That system, often referred to as an *information highway* or *electronic data highway*, would be a network of fiber optics. A national policy seems needed to go along with the development of these high-speed and multivarying communications modes. Gore saw this highway as serving two functions: (1) to spur on the new age of telecommunications, and (2) to serve as a giant boost to the nation's economy. The original budget proposal included nearly $5 billion over the next four years to develop new software and equipment necessary for the construction of this information highway. Many industry observers believe it will take a government friendly to the idea of a new era of communications in order to usher in this new age. Without government funding, such a data superhighway would probably not become a reality. Gore seemed to understand this, and President Clinton seemed favorable to the idea.

Masao Yukawa

By the early 1990s, Masao Yukawa had accumulated some 30 years with the Japanese electronics giant, Mitsubishi, heading the company's industrial electronics business and its information services group. But, according to writer Maggie Topkis, his greatest contribution was the cofounding of Daini Denden (DDI), "an upstart long-distance phone company that was one of the first competitors to Nippon Telegraph & Telephone."[40] As of 1992, DDI was taking in some $160 million in annual sales, only five years after Yukawa began operations, and accounted for 20 percent of the lucrative Osaka-Tokyo phone traffic. In addition to his entrepreneurial skills, Yukawa is also an adviser to government regulators and politicians. That is important in Japan because the country has been slow in permitting Japanese carriers to compete internationally. As a result, by the year 2000, the Japanese may be more involved in international telecommunications.

Trip Hawkins

If Bill Gates has been working overtime to perfect a computer software system adaptable to several different computer brands, Trip Hawkins has been on a similar mission in trying to unite many different electronic communications functions into one "universal box." Hawkins, president of Electronic Arts, unveiled in 1993 the box he calls his Interactive Multiplayer. It is a VCR, slide projector, CD-interactive box, and laser disk video player, plus a jumbo Game Boy machine combined into one unit. In addition, he foresees other applications that could allow the television to perform some bizarre functions. Among these are updating viewers who sign on late with the plot of an episode by way of producing a comic book-like bubble on the screen with the text of the plot summary inside. It could even give the brand name of the apparel the stars of the program are wearing if asked. But the box's most popular feature may be its ability to enhance the resolution and speed of computer games. Specifically, the Interactive Multiplayer has the capability of processing images at 50 times the power of conventional video-game computers, and it offers spectacular graphics.[41]

With his new company, 3DO, he has joined hands with Japan's Matushita, which owns Panasonic, to create a model of the box, which was set to retail for about $700. A fan of partnerships that will move his vision forward, he has also teamed up with AT&T, Time Warner, and MCA, all of whom could get even richer in selling their software if Hawkins's system becomes the format of the 1990s. In short, the multiplayer is envisioned by many as a platform that will spur the development of newer, more sophisticated software products. But like every other visionary discussed in this chapter, Hawkins is not without his challenges and challengers. One big hurdle is the question of whether the consumer will want the multiplayer enough to pay for it. Another is whether or not there will be enough software products created for it to raise consumer interest and maintain it. As far as challengers go, there are plenty including Tandy and Philips Electronics N.V., Commodore International, Nintendo and Sega, Apple, IBM, Sony, and Microsoft. All of these companies are working toward developing their own formatted multiplayer system as well. The competition aside, Hawkins believes the floodgate of consumer acceptance will open when the industry embraces the multiplayer and all music, video games, and how-to videos are stored on discs.

Akio Tanii

Known as "Mr. VCR" in Japanese business circles, Akio Tanii may soon be known as "Mr. Matsushita" to the world. Tanii, president of Matsushita Electrical Industrial since 1986, earned the former nickname by taking over Matsushita's VCR Division in 1972, when VCRs were still bulky rarities, and transforming it into a profit-generating powerhouse. Now, with Matsushita suddenly a player to reckon with in the U.S. television business, Hollywood's eyes are on Tanii. The Japanese executive has placed priority on six growth businesses: information/communication, factory automation, semiconductors, new audiovisual equipment, automotive electronics, and housing and building products. Of the company's major wares, video equipment has registered the fastest sales growth. Tanii has also restructured Matsushita into a global company, localizing the management of its foreign subsidiaries. Although his aim is to make Matsushita, whose products are sold as Panasonic and Quasar in the United States, an insider in all its major markets, Tanii is something of a maverick outsider in Japan's conservative corporate culture. While he may lack the high profile of Sony's Akio Morita, he is determined to make Matsushita a stronger global player in the market for new electronic equipment, including HDTV. One way to do that is to follow Sony's lead in software-hardware synergy. Matsushita attaches equal importance to software and hardware. They are like two wheels attached to one axle. If one is smaller than the other, the wheel won't balance.

Cathleen Black

Although not a high-tech wizard, Cathleen Black has the power to influence some very large technological changes in the newspaper industry. She is the president of the Newspaper Association of America (NAA, formerly the American Newspaper Publishers Association), and the NAA thought enough of her talent and abilities to hire her at a reported salary of $600,000 in 1991. She is the former publisher of USA Today, and she knows the newspaper industry inside out. She is a leading fighter in the war against Baby Bells and fears what may happen if the Bell companies are given complete freedom to become information providers in their own phone service areas without limitations.

Black brings a high degree of enthusiasm, know-how, and persuasive ability to her job as head of the NAA. Many analysts credit her with the success of *USA Today*, and John Reidy of Drexel Burnham Lambert, Inc., states, "She was able to convince advertisers the paper was workable, that it would make a difference, and that she could deliver the demographics. She knows how to sell, understood the product, and was able to convey that to advertisers."[42] Her first two years with the NAA indicated she would prove equally successful in mapping out a future for the entire industry—a future that would include the assimilation of high technology and the possible merger of print into the electronic media. Through her efforts to stem the tide of telephone companies' incursion into turf formerly reserved for the traditional news media, and through her encouragement of executives in her own industry to put more effort into high-tech research and development, Black could make a strong impact in communications technology in the years to come.

Barry Diller

As chairman of QVC Network, Inc., Barry Diller has designs on changing the way America shops by creating a kind of electronic marketplace. His company is already in the interactive television field and is showing that this kind of shopping can be highly profitable. Diller leads a company that invests in its own infrastructure so it can offer a large number of different home-shopping formats over television. He envisions a narrowing of the traditional home shopping club format, much like the narrow-interest mail-order catalogs now blanketing the country. Some of these formats will offer electronics, some health and fitness products and services, some apparel, and some gardening products.

Diller and QVC are on the cutting edge of multimedia program opportunities. The home shopping niche that QVC is aiming at is an important one in the area of interactive television. There are a lot of competitors as a result, and the next few years should see a plethora of these home shopping services. Diller expects to be the impetus behind as many of them as possible. Indicative of the strides QVC has made in expanding its media interests is its 1993 bid to buy media conglomerate Paramount Communications for $10.5 billion. Paramount, a moviemaker, TV producer, and book publisher, announced in late 1993 that it would sell to Viacom, but Diller and QVC went to court in November of 1993 to get Paramount's anti-takeover defense overturned. The bid for Paramount was so large that it needed help from other communications companies to support it. Among companies investing $500 million each in QVC to help it acquire Paramount were BellSouth, Cox Enterprises, Advance Publications, Liberty Media, and Comcast Cable. In addition, BellSouth invested a whopping $1.5 million in QVC for the same purpose. As 1993 drew to a close, QVC was still fighting with Viacom and Paramount's ownership.

John Malone

As the CEO of TCI, John Malone leads the largest of the cable providers in America today. Like his competitors, he envisions a future of interactive television and a nation of families who will soon see their desire for user-modeled information and programming realized. He believes cable's next generation of residential equipment will be the most powerful computing device in the average home, according to *U.S. News & World Report*.[43] This equipment will open doors for new types of high-resolution television displays; new long-distance forms of education; videophones; high-speed computer networking; interactive armchair shopping; a huge spectrum of sports, news, and entertainment choices; and—one day—movies on demand. In short, he says, "It will give consumers more choice in their television service, and it will change the very definition of television. The new technology will give families control over their television rather than the other way around."[44] With experiments such as the Denver test, TCI and Malone expect to be leading the charge.

Robert Allen

No listing of important communication executives to watch in the 1990s would be complete without the name of the chairman of AT&T, Robert Allen. Probably more than anyone else at AT&T, he has helped it face the concept of multimedia and has prepared it for the battles of research, development, and marketing. Allen's vision is one of multimedia services where executives can decide from a vast array of choices how they might communicate with others. In describing some of these choices recently, he noted:

Office and mobile communications systems will respond to voice commands, whether to send a jotted memo, research a customer's questions or set up a business lunch. Many of us will become accustomed to seeing the people we're talking with, even on conference calls. During the call, we'll be able to read documents quickly, call upon experts or access remote systems to run analysis.[45]

Allen does not believe industry can bring about a multimedia age by itself. It must be helped by the federal government, which can clear the way in creating incentives and opportunities for industries who are working to bring the new age about.

Internally, Allen reorganized AT&T into five individual business units in an attempt to spur creative development and obtain greater account-ability among his managers. He has also reached out and taken in managers from outside the company to provide AT&T with fresh ideas and a different perspective. In place of a chief operating officer working under him, Allen has formed a kind of symbiotic committee made up of heads of his five key operating divisions, including communications products, long distance, the NCR division, switching and fiber optics, and finances. Every month this committee meets for four days to develop ways of capitalizing on the merging of telephone and computer communications.[46]

Gerald M. Levin

Just as Robert Allen is leading AT&T into the age of multimedia, so Gerald Levin is doing the same thing with corporate giant Time Warner. *Business Week* noted of Levin in 1993:

Levin has shelved [former chairman Steven J.] Ross's rhetoric about worldwide clout in favor of concentrating on technology's role. . . . Levin is convinced that Time Warner is uniquely positioned to become a dominant player in multimedia. . . . It has the words and pictures to fill the electronic pipeline (of fiber optics). It also has a cable network with 7.1 million subscribers.[47]

Like the CEOs of other companies mentioned in this chapter, however, Levin realizes he must seek alliances with companies from complementary industries (most notably computer and telecommunication companies) to bring Time Warner into a position of industry leadership. Several alliances do involve Time Warner, and most of them came about under Levin's leadership.

John Sculley

As the former chief executive officer of Apple Computer, John Sculley led this immensely popular PC firm into the age of multimedia. He is also a potent voice for the inclusion of personal computers in the race for interactive television. Sculley is a champion of the use of digital-compression television because it will offer companies such as Apple a chance to sell their PC software in new markets, such as the ones interactive television provides. With the FCC opting for a digitally based HDTV transmission standard, companies such as Apple are poised to become an important force in the age of multimedia. In late 1993, Sculley left Apple Computer to become chairman and chief executive of Spectrum Information Technologies. Spectrum, a small Manhasset, New York-based company engaged in transmitting data over wireless communications networks, has been working with Rockwell International, NCR, and IBM to jointly develop and market products using its technology.

Bruce Bond

Representing another foreign country is Bruce Bond, director of group products and services for British Telecom. Although he is American, he is the most senior black executive in the United Kingdom. His importance to the future of telecommunications is his efforts to awaken what has often thought to be a sleeping giant of a corporation. He does not mind bucking tradition, and he wants to make British Telecom more of a force on the international telecommunications scene. He has already added beef to British Telecom's thin marketing programs and cut the company down to scale by laying off approximately 80,000 workers. He appears very serious about his role, and many American competitors are worried he may take his job too seriously.

Joe Nacchio

The president of business communications services for AT&T, Joe Nacchio has performed a role similar to that of Bruce Bond at British Telecom. He has helped turn AT&T into a leaner company and made it realize that in order to succeed it will have to compete. That notion was something foreign to AT&T's monopoly thinking, but Nacchio seems to have helped the company realize they are no longer a monopoly. To be sure, the company has lost about a fourth of its long-distance market share since divestiture, but Nacchio has helped dam the loss by creating customized client phone packages such as Tariff 12, customized communications packages for large billers, and the kinds of win-them-back television and print promotions directed at defectors to MCI and Sprint. Nacchio designed the well-known campaign "We'll pay to switch you over."

George Fisher

An important facet of multimedia communications is mobile communications. Few people know this business as well as George Fisher, chairman of Motorola, Inc., which has become a leader in the electronics and semiconductor fields. Today, Motorola has also become a leader in mobile communications. Fisher envisions a kind of mobile or portable office made possible by the convergence of wireless communications and digital computing. We are already seeing some of the parts come together with the plethora of mobile phones and even mobile fax machines. Fisher is struck by the fact that about 40 percent of the American work force is on the move. This is the target audience for Motorola and other mobile communications companies. Although there were only about 200,000 wireless users in 1993, Fisher believes that by the year 2000 the market will see an explosion to more than 26 million users. By 2010, he sees a $3 trillion telecommunications market in equipment and services, with the wireless component accounting for some $600 billion of that.[48]

Fernando Morales

Mexican inventor Fernando Morales has incorporated his vision of interactive television with the creation of Eon Corp. (formerly TV Answer, Inc.), in Reston, Virginia, which, by the early 1990s, looked to be the key player in the development of interactive TV. In 1986, Morales obtained a U.S. patent for a wireless network that would let television viewers talk back to their sets. His invention was so impressive that he managed to raise some $80 million to develop and perfect it.[49] In the process of establishing Eon Corp., he recruited some key Washington insiders, including former FCC chairman Mark S. Fowler, to sit on his board of directors and use whatever inside knowledge and influence they could in getting the government to support the implementation of this new interactive system.

Eon Corp. feels so strongly about the results that it is asking companies such as Hewlett-Packard and Sony Corp. to contribute some of the $200 million needed to launch the interactive TV system.[50] Although he failed to receive a nationwide allocation of radio frequencies for his system from the FCC, Morales is moving ahead with his alternate plan of trying to recruit those who did win the licenses by lottery to become Eon Corp. franchises across America, using the system he has developed. Although the company faces many uncertainties in the market demand for interactive television and in the kind and intensity of competition in the interactive television field, it still has strong financial backing from Mexican investors and Morales's expertise in communication technology.

SUMMARY

This chapter described some of the intense competition existing in the telecommunications field today, but also some of the many opportunities facing entrepreneurs and consumers in the coming age of multimedia communications. It is not unlike previous pioneering ages in history, and, in fact, is similar to the competitive environment that immediately followed World War I, when an abundance of companies and individual entrepreneurs and engineers set their sights on developing radio into a mass medium and claiming as large a share of the market as possible.

Although the many number of competitors in the telecommunications field will make it difficult for some to survive with their dreams intact, the advantage for the information consumer is that a score of savvy people are working to bring about a new era of personalized, interactive communications that can be accessed from a number of sources. This new era will undoubtedly change the way society not only conducts business but also the way people interact with each other and their daily work and leisure habits. Some of these specific changes—and how they might impact society—are the subject of chapters to follow.

NOTES

1. David Nyhan, "MIT's Multimedia Marvels: Future Schlock?" *Washington Journalism Review*, April 1988, 16.

2. Ibid., 17.

3. The Media Laboratory, 5th Anniversary (Cambridge, MA: MIT, 1990), 5.

4. Ibid.

5. Walter Bender et al., "Newspace: Mass Media and Personal Computing," *USENIX*, June 1991, 1.

6. Stephen Wilks, "Science, Technology and the Large Corporation," *Government and Opposition*, Spring 1992, 190.

7. Ibid.

8. Ibid.

9. Nancy Hass, "Telecommunications: A Global Report," *FW*, September 15, 1992, 30.

10. Ibid., 31.

11. Ibid., 35.

12. Ibid.

13. Ibid.

14. Gary Slutsker, "The Tortoise and the Hare," *Forbes*, February 1, 1993, 66.

15. Ibid., 67.

16. Josh Hyatt, "Nynex Sees Video in Its Future," *Boston Globe*, April 14, 1993, 31.

17. Kevin Maney, "Southwestern Bell Wires into Cable TV," *USA Today*, March 19, 1993, B1.

18. Ibid.

19. *The Veronis, Suhler & Associates Communications Industry Forecast, Industry Spending Preview, 1991–1995*, 5th ed., June 1991, New York.

20. Robert Wrubel, "Strange Bedfellows," *FW*, September 15, 1992, 44.

21. Kevin Maney, "Cable Firm to Build $2 Billion Fiber Network," *USA Today*, April 12, 1993, B1.

22. Ibid.

23. Wrubel, "Strange Bedfellows," 44.

24. Ibid.

25. Ibid.

26. Philip Elmer-Dewitt, "Electronic Superhighway," *Time*, April 12, 1993, 54.

27. Ibid.

28. Rachel Kaplan, "Video on Demand," *American Demographics*, June 1992, 38ff.

29. Johnnie L. Roberts, Paul B. Carroll, and Patrick M. Reilly, "Smart Sets," *Wall Street Journal*, May 21, 1992, A1.

30. Brian Ek, "Background Information on the Prodigy Interactive Personal Service," Prodigy Press Release, February 12, 1990, 1.

31. Brian Ek, "Wall Street Journal Names Prodigy One of Leading Companies for the '90s," Prodigy Press Release, February 12, 1990, 1.

32. Dennis Lynch, "New Online Service Has More for Less," *Chicago Tribune*, January 26, 1990, B1.

33. Ibid.

34. L. R. Shannon, "Visiting a Mall, by Phone," *New York Times*, September 5, 1989, B1.

35. Alan Deutschman, "Bill Gates' Next Challenge," *Fortune*, December 28, 1992, 36.

36. Ibid., 31.

37. Ibid.

38. Ibid., 32.

39. Ibid., 31.

40. Maggie Topkis, "Six Images of the Future and the Faces Behind Them," *FW*, September 15, 1992, 41.

41. Patrick E. Cole, "The Next Magic Box?" *Time*, January 18, 1993, 47.

42. Paulette Dininny, "Black on Black," *US Air*, October 1989, 90.

43. Jim Impoco, "Technology Titans Sound Off on the Digital Future," *U.S. News & World Report*, May 3, 1993, 63.

44. Ibid.

45. Slutsker, "Tortoise and the Hare," 67.

46. Ibid.

47. Mark Landler, "Time Warner's Techie at the Top," *Business Week*, May 10, 1993, 60.

48. Impoco, "Technology Titans," 64.

49. Mark Lewyn, "This Isn't the Response TV Answer Expected," *Business Week*, June 29, 1992, 78.

50. Ibid.

4

• • • • •

The Coming of Interactive
Television

Whether talking about news, raw information, entertainment, advertising, or other applications, interactive television is seen as a vital part of the new technology puzzle. This chapter will look in more detail at this phenomenon, which is exciting so many communication engineers and entrepreneurs. It is currently only in the experimental stage, undergoing tests in several markets around the country, but many analysts believe it will be the standard for news and entertainment nationwide within a few years.

Newsweek reported in 1993, for instance, that "as the age of interactive media finally dawns, business people realize they are biting into something very tasty."[1] Estimates of the attractiveness of interactive media are coming fast and furious and, to a great extent, cover a wide range in terms of how much revenue might be derived from the dawning industry. One set of estimates ranges from $4 billion to $14 billion by 1995.[2]

VIEWER INVOLVEMENT

To a great extent, interactive TV is about getting the viewers more involved in their viewing of news and entertainment. It is an attempt to turn viewers into more than bored couch potatoes, not out of a sense of altruism, but because the backers of interactive TV think it will make viewing more enjoyable for the consumer, which will result in more TV use. Basically, interactive TV creates a two-way link between the viewer and the information or programs on television screens by allowing viewers to talk back to their sets. The promises of interactive TV are elaborate and include the claim that this system will learn individual viewers' tastes over time, filter their news for them, alert them to preferred types of upcoming movies, print coupons and tickets, let them play along with game shows, present fashion catalogs, and order virtually anything. They will also display a viewer's bank account and enable the viewer to make transactions right over the screen. Not only could the television offer all the customized information services of a computer (which is definitely more interactive than a television receiver), but it could deliver them on a grand scale. Writer Steve Rosenthal paints this scenario:

Viewers would plug into a global network with other viewers, with access to constantly updated information delivered through multiple media. Imagine a CompuServe or AppleLink in full motion video, with users deciding soap-opera plots, playing game shows, ordering obscure movies for instant viewing, and participating in cable TV special-interest clubs. Best of all, the consumer potato needn't even budge from the couch.[3]

More than a dozen mass communications-based, interactive services are on the drawing boards and should be appearing over the next few years. Financial backing is being provided by such giants as IBM, Sony, Philips, Time Warner, and other major communications and computer companies. Rosenthal notes that, drawing upon technological schemes ranging from fiber optics to pocket radio, these enterprises will involve consumers in interactive entertainment, education, banking, voting, shopping, and video on demand. "Each service will provide a somewhat different level of interactivity, using a variety of technological solutions," he explains.[4]

The market for such services, at this point, seems very large indeed. Market analysts Bain & Company, Inc. of Boston has predicted some 40 million households will subscribe to some sort of interactive TV by the year 2002. In addition, total industry annual revenues could rise about $6 billion. Another forecast, done by Frost & Sullivan International, predicts a $1.65 billion interactive television industry by 1996.[5]

To a basic degree, interactive media have been with us ever since the first radio station hit asked listeners to call in to play a contest or request a song. For television, the same holds true, and even today there are plenty of call-in television shows. *The Larry King Show* is one classic example, as are many interview programs on C-Span. Commercials across television stations and networks ask viewers to call in and provide direct-response 800 or 900 numbers to do so.

But these efforts at interaction pale in comparison to what lies ahead. Certainly a nationwide fiber optic highway may be a decade away, but some companies are planning innovative means that use less expensive, more widely available technology for networks that will be implemented by the mid-1990s. Two of those companies, Interactive Network and NTN

Communications, will be discussed later, as will two others, ACTV and EON Corp.

FCC CLEARS THE WAY

On January 16, 1992, the FCC set aside a special radio frequency for interactive, over-the-air television services. This action was among the first steps taken to pave the way for the introduction and implementation of interactive television. The FCC also decided to hand out two separate licenses for each of 734 markets across the country and to allocate those licenses by lottery rather than by judging applicants on their merits. The lottery has created intense interest among would-be license holders who are willing to pay the $1,400 entrance fee to try their luck at receiving one of the prized licenses.

In the near future, it may be possible for viewers to use their home television for a number of services that previously required them to leave home and drive to a town's business district. It is conceivable that viewers may be able to call up portions of an electronic newspaper or magazine they wish to read, pay credit card bills, make airline reservations, call up sports scores, or even order Chinese take-out dinners by pressing buttons on pistol-shaped remote-control devices.

In addition to their action, the FCC also voted unanimously to propose the opening of a large range of frequencies for use by emerging communications technologies, from tiny cellular telephones to satellite messaging systems and digital radio that offers sound as clear as that from CDs. The proposal would open a band more than four times the size of the one now used for cellular telephones.

In September 1993, the FCC issued rules to ensure that a broad range of contenders—from telephone and cable companies to other newcomers—would bid for licenses to offer new portable telephone services. Communications industry analysts have estimated that the emerging personal communications technology could attract nearly 30 million customers by 1998 and create more than 200,000 jobs in the next decade. Cellular service, which personal communications services (PCS) could supplant, had about 12 million subscribers in 1993.

Starting in May 1994, the government hoped to raise about $10 billion by auctioning off the portion of the radio spectrum that PCS uses. The FCC was charged with setting guidelines for just how that spectrum, which previously was under the domain of the Pentagon, would be divided and what industries would be able to bid for it.

The FCC premised its decisions on tests of a technology developed by TV Answer, Inc. (now EON Corp.). In that system, viewers would have a small box on top of their sets that could send and receive data to a nearby base station linked by satellite to a computer at the company's headquarters in Reston, Virginia.

HURDLES AND CRITICS

While most aspects of interactive TV seem to be going well for its proponents in the early 1990s, at least three key hurdles remain:

1. Increased competition.
2. Lags in certain technological developments and implementations, such as the laying of enough fiber optic cables.
3. Whether or not consumers will pay for these interactive services, and whether there will be enough consumer interest to generate the needed advertiser interest.

Critics of interactive TV point to the failed Warner Amex Cable Communications pioneering experiment, Qube, in Columbus, Ohio, which was downgraded into a much simpler cable and pay-per-view system in 1984 because of low consumer interest and high expenses. The primary goal in designing Qube was to allow Columbus television viewers the chance to tailor their cable viewing to match their own personal likes and dislikes. Qube offered all the cable programming options available at the time, but it also offered a pay-per-view option that broadened the viewer's program choices. The key feature of Qube, however, was its two-way, interactive capabilities. For instance, following a presidential speech, Qube subscribers were able to register their comments and feelings about the speech by way of their remote keypads and a series of numbered questions presented on the screen. Following these responses, Qube computers analyzed and presented the results over the screen to Qube subscribers. These same subscribers, by watching local government proceedings over the community access channel, could register their responses to issues and votes emanating from the television government meetings.

Assessing Qube's advantages, Michael M. Mirabito and Barbara L. Morgenstern write, "As an interactive service, the Qube system had great potential. Since it was a cable operation, Qube could have simultaneously supported television programming in addition to electronic transactions and information databases. . . . A single system would have delivered television programming and movies, and it could have supported a number of information retrieval operations."[6] Despite the outcome of this venture, other entrepreneurs are still working on true interactive TV. Many believe the adage that management guru Tom Peters put forth in his 1982 best-seller, *In Search of Excellence*: failure is the research and development of market capitalism. Peters noticed how excellent companies had learned to rapid-prototype—that is, build messy prototypes of products as fast as possible, then subject the prototypes to simulated market conditions, again as fast as possible. The point was to uncover fatal flaws before unhappy customers did it for them.[7]

Even the researchers at MIT Media Lab are working on new interactive systems that will put more control of programming and information into the viewer's hands. A fiber optic transmission line would be the workhorse vehicle for these new systems because of its ability to carry such a wide range of programming channels and electronic information services.

It seems clear that none of these hurdles nor the failed experiments of the past will derail the current communications industry momentum that is propelling it toward an ultimate confrontation with the issue of interactive TV's marketability to the general public. If it is feasible, a shakeout of competitors will ensue, and those with the most innovative ideas and resources will survive; the government will assist in the laying of a fiber optic highway, and the failed experiments of the past will disappear into the history books.

ADVANCES IN INTERACTIVE TV

This section will analyze some of the current advances made in the research and development of interactive TV. This interaction now exists on several levels, but true interactivity that calls for a higher breed of technology in signal sent and in the actual TV receiver is not yet operational on a large scale in the United States. Nevertheless, progress is being made toward interactive TV, and media companies—along with other telecommunications businesses—are banking on its wide-scale acceptance by American viewers.

One of the reasons why media seers of the 1990s are so sure that interactive TV will appeal to the public is that it will offer them more *choices per channel*. This is not to be confused with simply offering more channels for viewing, which is what current cable systems are doing. Technology marketers realize that simply sending 100 or more channels into a home is not the answer. True interactive television should allow viewers to become actively involved in the channel and its programming. Thus, there are more choices *within* each channel.

ACTV

Systems such as those devised by ACTV Interactive Response Television and tested in 1990 and 1991 would permit cable viewers multiple choices, both in camera angles and in entire programs, at the push of a button on a single channel. In a sense, interactive TV also tailors a show to the preferences indicated by viewers at home. William C. Samuels, president of ACTV, told the *Christian Science Monitor*:

We call this the new television because it changes all the rules of the game. We think this is the most important breakthrough in television since television itself was invented. Past breakthroughs related to signal distribution, to color, and to picture definition. ACTV actually could have a direct impact on the quality of programming. It's a technology that can talk back to you, the viewer, individually.[8]

The ACTV system, as do others like it, allows viewers to become actively involved in the programs they are watching. Tuning in to one channel, they can choose from an array of camera angles; they can actually respond to a person speaking to them from the screen; they can order a variety of shows on that same channel, and they can zero in on a specific program segment that they enjoy and would like to see more of. All that is needed to access these options is a box on top of the television set, about the size of a small stereo component, and a handheld remote-control unit with four buttons, corresponding to the four choices available to the viewer. Those four selections will probably expand to as many as 20, according to ACTV executives.

Technically, ACTV appears deceptively simple. Instead of a single signal on a cable channel, four signals are sent to the receiver box in the home. The viewer can tune in to any one of these four. Not only does ACTV technology put more directing control in the hands of the viewer, but it also has major implications for TV usage in schools, businesses, hotels, and worker training seminars. ACTV is owned by the Washington Post Company, so research and development resources should not be a major problem.

In 1990, ACTV experimented with some 300 cable subscribing homes in Springfield, Massachusetts, offering an eight-week test of interactive TV. Judging from some of the viewer reaction, the test looked promising. "It's a revolution," said James Demers, 53, who took part in the ACTV test. "You get the sensation that they geared (the programs) just to you."[9]

In particular, one group interested in the results of such tests is the advertising community. With this technology, ACTV can keep track of each household's programming choices, and this could enable advertisers to use the same interactive technology to target their commercials to a program's viewers who exhibit the right demographics for their client's products or services. "From a marketing perspective, everybody is trying to move to a more efficient media. I think [interactive TV] will be an important step in that direction," said Martin Nisenholtz, president of Interactive Marketing, a division of Ogilvy & Mather Advertising.[10]

Eon Corp.

This Reston, Virginia firm is vying for the same interactive market as several other competitors. The wireless system developed by Eon Corp. consists of a box, a four-inch antenna on the box, and a remote-control wand the needs no special programming. Viewers use the remote to move an on-screen cursor and click to select boxes or icons on the screen. The box transmits a signal to local antennas, or cell cites, serving 2,800 homes each. It is then relayed via satellite to the Eon Corp. control center that can handle 20,000 transactions a second. Like other systems, its applications include home banking, shopping, bill paying, long-distance learning, and playing along with game shows and sporting events, making the television set a hybrid between a TV and a computer.

Hewlett-Packard was selected by Eon Corp. to manufacture and market the TV control box and the remote control that resembles a video game joystick. The box, which can send and receive information by radio, is a personal computer in disguise, with an old 8088 microprocessor from Intel Corp. and four megabits of dynamic-random access memory, about twice the amount of memory standard for a personal computer. The expected cost of the initial equipment is $700 plus an expected monthly charge to customers of the service.[11] Interactive signals are transmitted from home by wireless transmitter, cable, or through telephone lines. Eon's cable-based competitor is ACTV.

As noted previously, the FCC announced in 1992 that it would hold lotteries to award operating licenses initially only for cell sites in the top 10 TV markets. The first lottery in New York attracted nearly 800 applications, and Eon Corp. was working to begin service there in 1993. But the company faces a barrage of competitors with differing technologies, and it may result in a battle over who controls the in-home box. If all the information is to be filtered through that one box on top of the television set, then a lot of companies will be going after the manufacture and marketing of that box.

Eon Corp. initially hoped it would get the FCC to award it a national allocation of radio frequencies for their pioneering interactive system. That didn't happen, since the FCC went with the lottery instead. Eon Corp. then shifted to an alternate plan of attack in which people across the country apply for licenses, then become Eon Corp. franchises.[12] But with other companies developing interactive systems that could also be franchised, there is no guarantee the license holders would choose to go with Eon Corp.

US West/Time Warner

Another example of a telephone company combining forces with a media company was the 1993 deal struck by US West and Time Warner.

Under the agreement, US West agreed to pay $2.5 billion for one-quarter of Time Warner's entertainment division, which owns cable TV networks, movie studios, and cable TV's HBO movie channel.[13] The purpose of the agreement was to provide cable TV customers in 32 states with an interactive TV system that could order movies for users, allow them to do banking, and carry out functions of other developing interactive systems.

It marked "the first time a regional telephone company and a cable TV and programming giant teamed up to put interactive information, entertainment and telephone services at cable customers' fingertips."[14] Under the arrangement, US West provides technology and management to help Time Warner build its high-tech, fiber optic cable TV and telephone system in Orlando, Florida. By 1994, Time Warner hoped the experimental system would deliver hundreds of channels, movies on demand, and a long line-up of home shopping channels and video games. It would also allow customers to make phone calls through the cable system if regulators were to allow it.

Services resulting from the partnership were expected to be available across the 32-state region by 1998, and the deal was predicted to put pressure on other regional Bell companies to make similar deals with other cable firms. Jerry Levin, chairman of Time Warner, has said repeatedly that no single company will be able to go it alone in the complex world of multimedia. He realizes he and other companies will have to seek alliances because companies such as Time Warner need both hardware and technical expertise to compete in multimedia. US West is only one of several companies with which Time Warner has forged ties. Others include AT&T, which supplies Time Warner with a high-speed digital switch to route programming to individual subscribers; Silicon Graphics, developing technology for a machine that could double as a video game player and an advanced cable converter box; Sega of America, teaming up with Time Warner and Tele-Communications to start a cable network that offers interactive video games, and Toshiba, which supplies advanced cable converter boxes to Time Warner's Orlando cable system and which already owns a 6.25 percent stake in the company's cable and film properties.

Federal law as of 1993 prohibits telephone companies from competing with cable firms in their own regions, but this deal skirted this law because Time Warner has few customers in territory served by the 14-state telephone power, US West.

Other Competitors

ACTV and Eon Corp. are not the only companies moving into the interactive TV field. Chapter 3 discussed some of the experiments being conducted by TCI, the nation's largest cable TV company, which has teamed up with AT&T and US West to test a $10 million hybrid system that combines telephone and cable technology. The 500-home Denver system, which offers video on demand, transmits signals part of the way on phone company fiber optics, then distributes the signal to users across the normal cable TV connections. Viacom International of New York, another large cable operator, was building test system in 1992 for its 12,500-subscriber Castro Valley, California, cable system that would use fiber optic lines for high-speed transmissions. The company plans to experiment with video on demand and various communications services.

IBM is another company which has invested more than $100 million in a new interactive TV company launched in 1993.

Not to be outdistanced, Microsoft also envisions a bright future in interactive TV and is trying to convince broadcasters, cable companies, developers, and CD-ROM player vendors that a common interface, namely Modular Windows, is the answer. "Modular Windows will act as the glue to tie all these receivers, CD players, and other TV-related boxes together," says Sanjay Parthasarathy, a Microsoft executive, "and the applications can be created by any Windows programmer."[15] In one scenario, cable companies could broadcast a signal in a format compatible with Modular Windows for providing text overlays and other additional media, possibly with local support in the form of CD-ROM card applications.

In addition, at least three California firms are highly interested in interactive TV. They are Interactive Network, Inc. (IN), of Mountain View, NTN Communications of Carlsbad, and ICTV of Santa Clara. The first two use telephone-based systems. IN is backed by NBC, United Artists, and A.C. Nielsen. During the 1992 Summer Olympics, subscribers to IN in Sacramento and San Francisco received statistics and athletes' histories in real time. IN sends signals by FM simulcast to an in-home receiver/keyboard/LCD (liquid crystal) display. To respond, viewers plug the unit into the phone line for 15 seconds. In 1993, the service was delivering from two to eight hours a day of TV-based play-along programming, plus news briefs, puzzles, and contests that users interacted with by using a two-pound control unit. The company planned to begin offering nationwide service later that year. Writer Steve Rosenthal notes that

IN is less a true interactive TV network than an FM radio-based data network equipped with TV-related programming. Subscribers can make choices and voice their opinions, but nothing they do individually or collectively has any direct influence over the program content or timing. All the technological interaction occurs completely separate from the television and its delivery mechanisms.[16]

Customers of IN purchase a $199 handheld data receiver with a small LCD screen, keyboard, antenna, memory, and built-in modem. There's a

$15 monthly charge for basic service; an optional $10 charge buys tokens for prize competitions.

So-called data jockeys at IN's studios in Mountain View piggyback part of their interactive signal on the subcarrier frequency of local FM stations. Text-based programs are broadcast to viewers and displayed on their laptop receiver as they watch "Jeopardy," "Wheel of Fortune," "60 Minutes," drama, and sporting events. As questions are asked on "Jeopardy," for example, viewers choose the correct answer from a multiple-choice menu on the receiver LCD. Pressing the right button before contestants triggers a tone and a CORRECT! message on the LCD. Viewers must train themselves to keep one eye on the set and the other on the LCD screen. At the end of the show, the viewer plugs the receiver into a phone jack and dumps the score into IN's central computer. Within about five minutes, a broadcasted graph appears on the LCD showing the viewer's rank compared with other home players.

IN had hopes of taking its interactive service national sometime in 1993. The system does have its problems, however. One is that users must plug their receivers into a phone jack in order to make the system two way. This may be too much work for confirmed couch potatoes. Also, the program content on the TV screen remains unchanged by anything the user does from the IN control receiver. Therefore, the interactivity has its limits.

ICTV, on the other hand, is a start-up company that favors a more direct approach to interactive TV. ICTV, in a converted warehouse near San Jose International Airport, calls that approach "cellular cable," and it uses coaxial cable TV coming into homes—upgraded when needed—as a bidirectional medium. Users would be able to alter programs and information on the screen as well as place orders. Advanced videocompression techniques are used to boost the signal-carrying capacity of standard cable. Each neighborhood would be divided into cells composed of about 150 homes linked by cable to a powerful PC or workstation.

The ICTV remote control pad has a two-inch-wide touch pad section as well as buttons. Sliding a finger across the pad will move a pointer on the TV screen to the desired option. In addition to standard basic and pay-cable channels, ICTV plans to fold several interactive channels into the system. The company expects that near-video-on-demand will be its most popular service. The idea, already in use on some high-capacity cable systems, provides a block of some 30 or so recent movies. With several copies of each movie and staggered starting times, the average delay for any film is only about 10 minutes. ICTV's system would provide previews, reviews, ordering, time-slot choice, VCR taping options, and even a simulated theater lobby where users can play video games before the movie begins. ICTV will also offer shopping opportunities. Twelve still frames of view will turn a model completely around, for example, so the user can see all sides of an outfit in an interactive catalog.

The system will also anticipate movies or products that might interest individual viewers. For instance, if a viewer has previously requested movies with particular actors his or her TV mailbox alerts him or her when upcoming films include these performers. ICTV could also carry classified advertising directed at each user.

NTN produces a football play-calling game and several trivia games. It has interactive game systems in several Denver bars, and its wireless key pad technology is in several California and Kentucky schools.

Yet another competitor is "The Box," a cable channel that lets viewers request music videos by telephone. In 1992, the large number of subscribers to The Box, after paying the cable fee, also were willing to pay for the call to request a song as well as $2.50 more for the music video.[17]

Analyst Rebecca Piirto notes there are still a few bugs in these and other interactive systems.

Most require special interactive programs, which cost more to produce. Telephone switching systems are prone to jam when confronted by mass responses. TV Answer's home transmitters will cost up to $700. And once these technological problems are solved, interactive businesses will confront the ultimate challenge: getting viewers to use the darn things. It's going to hinge on how easy the system is to use.[18]

Then, in October 1992, eleven major computer and communications companies organized an alliance, called First Cities, to probe the market for interactive TV services and maybe even lend their support and expertise to each other on joint projects. The consortium included Apple Computer, Inc., Eastman Kodak Co., Tandem Computers, North American Philips, Bellcore, Southwestern Bell, US West, and other companies, who together pledged to invest $5 million in the market study. If the results show promise, the plan is to wire 10,000 homes in a 1994 joint field test.

Experiments in interactive TV are not confined to the United States. In England, for example, Yorkshire Television has provided viewers with Britain's first do-it-yourself soap opera. In other words, they are invited to develop the story line and decide how the plot of the soap opera should go. About 1,200 viewers each week cast their votes by telephone, so there is nothing in the television signal or receiver that is interactive. It is simply an interactive form of viewership. Sarah Doole, the series producer, says she hopes the project will interest viewers more in the program and, at the same time, educate them on how difficult it is to make such a program.

People say that television is rubbish. . . . This is their chance to make it more interesting. We're saying to viewers that they can join in as much as they want. We are also saying that a lot goes into making soaps. . . . Viewers have to believe the drama.[19]

The producers explain that they also receive written suggestions and that the ideas come from a range of viewers, from children to aspiring scriptwriters. The television station offers to mail free to viewers helpful tips on scriptwriting.

Back in the United States, stations and networks have experimented with other forms of basic interaction with their audiences that does not involve interactive TV receivers. For instance, in 1989 NBC broadcast a two-part prime-time special on racial attitudes, asking viewers to use new live polling technology to access the answers to a quiz on racism. The program used an electronic system to conduct a live poll of studio audiences in four cities around the country. When asked a question, people in the four groups punched their replies into handheld devices with microprocessors. In five seconds, their responses were gathered and converted into charts and graphs on the screen.

In other semi-interactive settings, ABC's "Nightline" has used satellite technology to assemble a handful of individuals from around the world to debate various issues on the show. But Quick Tally Systems, the company making the handheld devices for the NBC special on racism, was trying to allow a "much larger group of scattered people to register their opinions collectively and quickly, making for unpredictable, highly topical television."[20] Eli Bleich, a former television producer who founded Quick Tally, said of the experiment:

You get an instant snapshot of a group's opinions, but it can also turn into a conversation. If the responses are really unexpected, the host can say, "Are you meaning this the way I take it? What if you were in this situation, what would you do?" A person operating a laptop computer during the session can instantly program in a new question and set it up for graphics.[21]

INTERACTIVE NEWS PROGRAMMING

Experiments such as these are noteworthy but really do not fall into the category of interactive TV as it is known in the industry today. Here, technology is used to assemble on-air participants for certain "Nightline" programs or—in the case of the network specials on public attitudes involving various issues—viewers are provided "900" numbers to cast their vote, but there is no vehicle for the average television viewer to talk back to his or her television set or tailor the program or programming to his or her taste.

In short, ever since the failed newspaper company-sponsored videotex experiments of the early 1980s, most of the interest in interactive TV has been evidenced by the entertainment and advertising industries. Among all the many headlines about interactive experiments in the late 1980s and early 1990s, stories about experiments involving interactive news programming are conspicuously missing. Whether it is because of a feeling that newscasts should be off-limits to public editing or whether producers of news shows have not discovered a demand for such a service, there have been only scant efforts at interactive TV news programming.

One such experiment did occur in July 1990, when Cable News Network (CNN) announced the first experiment in interactive news by a national television network. The experiment began on CNN's "Newsnight," an hour-long newscast at midnight. Viewer choices involved mostly secondary news or features. Viewers received a summary of headlines at the beginning of the show and, as anchors read the day's top news, viewers could dial a 900 telephone number to vote on which stories they would like to see. The stories that received the most votes were shown. Voting cost 95 cents a call. CNN officials said that viewers would not be dictating news value but would be telling the network what areas, outside of breaking news, interested them the most.[22]

INTERACTIVE TV IN SCHOOLS

Television—especially interactive TV—has potential educational applications in schools and universities for two-way communication between students and programs and for long-distance learning. A 1989 study by the federal Office of Technology Assessment found "distance-learning" projects—mostly for-credit video courses with a two-way hook-up between teacher and students—operating or planned in all 50 states, up from about 10 in 1987.[23] Later in this book, the potential changes in education as a result of such use of interactive TV will be discussed. Here, however, it should be noted that, while widely used, television as a teaching tool has yet to be proven effective, since research on such effectiveness remains inconclusive, much as with classroom use of computers.[24] Still, the number of long-distance learning courses for grades 1–12 offered in the United States by 1990 via satellite or other telecommunications links is impressive. The Office of Technology Assessment has reported some 350 courses that are taught in this manner nationwide. Of these, courses in foreign languages (119), mathematics and science (110), and the humanities, such as English, art, and composition (69) make up the lion's share.[25]

In another example of an educational application for interactive TV, a class of 18 second graders in Newark, New Jersey, donned earphones, stared at television screens, and responded to questions posed by colorful puppets by pressing buttons on remote-control units provided them. The *New York Times* reported in 1992 that the second graders were "completely absorbed in their interplay with the images on the screen, drawing words of praise from the images for correct answers and added instructions for wrong ones."[26] At this 13th Street School, the students are taking part in a new, individualized television teaching program that its developers (ACTV) call the first of its kind in America. Other experimental systems are now in operation, spurred on by the success of programs like the one in Newark. In this interactive program, however, the answers each student provides can show weaknesses and strengths in their knowledge and understanding. In turn, the system is intended to respond with instruction that is intended to meet the students' needs. In effect, the students design their own instruction program and learn at their own pace.[27] The federal government is helping on projects such as this. In Newark, for example, television rooms for the system have been installed in three other elementary schools and in the Montgomery Street High School with $1.5 million in federal funds provided under vocational and special education programs.

William C. Samuels, president for education and training of ACTV, asserts that the system installed in the 5 Newark schools could easily be expanded to the remaining 77 public schools in Newark, to other school districts around the state, or to districts across the country through satellite transmissions.[28] Eugene Campbell, executive superintendent of the Newark Board of Education added that the use of the system does not mean the schools will play down the need to learn to read, adding, "This is a strong oral program and many of our students come from a strong oral background."[29]

Bringing television into the classroom is a concept that faces tough hurdles, especially in light of the discussion generated in America about students spending too much time in front of the television set at home. Many parents are skeptical of its value in the classroom, others are against it totally, and still others support the experiments underway and are eager to see the results. Since school usage represents such a potential lucrative market—as Chris Whittle has shown with Whittle Communications Channel One, a daily news program with commercials that operates in thousands of schools around the country—there will undoubtedly be much interest shown by the television industry in this field.

SHOPPING VIA TELEVISION

Some possible lifestyle changes from shopping by television, over such home shopping channels as the Home Shopping Network (HSN) and the Quality Value Club (QVC) Network, are discussed later in the book. Some mention should be made here, however, of this utilization of interactive

TV that is already in existence and that has become very popular among many Americans. A quick look at the QVC Network, under its leadership of former Fox Television head Barry Diller, will show how this home shopping concept works.

In operation and format, QVC features one-hour time slots devoted to the promotion and sales of certain categories of products. One hour may feature women's fashions, the next may feature jewelry, and another may feature high-tech items. Viewers are provided extended descriptions and close-up views of the products and then are given a certain amount of time to call in and purchase the product. One QVC feature is to interview, by phone, viewers who have just purchased a product and ask them why it appealed to them. Products are then mailed to the viewers who provide their addresses to telephone operators at QVC. A mailing list is then compiled from these purchasers so the network can keep track of them for any promotional mailings.

Numerous testimonials exist to the success of such home shopping ventures. Entertainer and QVC clothing and jewelry designer Joan Rivers noted in 1993, "It gave me a business. . . . It's incredible what QVC has done for me."[30] Diller is not the least of the show's promoters either. "It's not broadcasting, not entertainment, it's not pure sales, it's not environment. It's all of those things in a different relationship to themselves. . . . When you see QVC on the selling floor, that's when you get it. You see the power," Diller says.[31] And that power is pretty amazing. For the first full quarter under Diller in 1993, QVC's net income was more than $21 million. In one hour alone, the first line of Saks clothing grossed $570,000 in sales with viewers. Million-dollar hours are not infrequent.[32]

The concept is so popular that Diller planned in 1993 to launch a Hispanic QVC in Mexico, Spain, and Latin America, and he predicted that it would go worldwide before too much longer.[33] Indeed, many analysts believe this is one proven use of interactive TV, and anything that can be done technologically to make it more convenient to interact with networks such as QVC or HSN will only increase the amount of business done in this personalized arena of shopping.

Still, even with the success of networks such as QVC, many are still wondering if there are enough similar uses that consumers will support enough to purchase the hardware and pay the subscription fees for truly interactive TV over the next several years.

DOES AMERICA REALLY WANT INTERACTIVE TV?

One of the key assumptions of those developing interactive TV is that Americans are going to want to spend a lot of time in front of their televisions—possibly even more than they are already doing. In 1993, Americans were spending between 3½ and 7 hours per day in front of their television sets, but there were indications that many viewers were nearing the saturation stage and starting to look elsewhere—outside the home—for leisure pursuits. For example, *Newsweek* reported in 1993 that the "adventure travel" industry was mushrooming in popularity as Americans were not only starting to spend more time outside their homes but in places like the jungles of Africa, the rainforests of South America, the mountains of the Pacific Northwest, and the rivers of the upper midwest and western states. The following are among the more popular adventure treks:[34]

- TransAmerica Trail Bike Route, a 4,500-mile ride over a two-month period from Astoria, Oregon, to Yorktown, Virginia.
- California Coast Route, a 990-mile bike trip along the Pacific coastal region.
- Grand Teton Mountain Trip, offering routes from simple hikes to advanced rock climbs.
- Colorado Ice Climbing Trips, from 2 to 5 days in length, teaching climbers how to handle cold-related perils.
- Colorado River Through Grand Canyon White-Water Rafting, taking from 5 to 15 days and covering some or all of the 240-mile route.
- Tatshenshini (Yukon/Alaska) White-Water Trip, lasting from 9 to 12 days and traveling through 180 miles of untouched wilderness.
- Amazon River Safaris, taking adventurers upriver in Brazil for a week of fishing and exploring the rainforest before returning to the city of Manous.

Once the province of only a few stronghearted trekkers, these adventure trips are becoming more popular as the following observations indicate:

Adventure travel, a loose designation more or less coterminous with "gentlemen not expected to shave," has grown in 20 years from a statistical footnote to an $8 billion business, perhaps as much as a fifth of the U.S. leisure-travel market. Nature stands at the intersection of practically every fashionable trend in American society—fitness, environmentalism, multiculturalism, western wear and, of course, affluence.[35]

With indicators such as this, the question logically arises as to whether a sufficient number of Americans will stay at home long enough to make the billions of dollars being invested in interactive TV pay off.

Commenting on interactive TV, Everette Dennis, executive director of the Gannett Center for Media Studies at Columbia University, says the potential is extraordinary. But he qualifies that observation by saying, "There's an assumption here that somehow the public wants to choose its own fare . . . like a book or magazine selection. Whether it applies to an electronic market isn't yet clear."[36] Not only is the audience demand unclear at this point, but the issue of whether or not a company can make a profit from interactive TV is also unclear. No one has done it so far, but all we have seen thus far have been localized experiments, and some of them are pretty rudimentary.

Dennis is not alone in questioning the marketability of interactive TV. Amidst all the news of technological advances and the hundreds of millions of dollars being poured into the development of interactive TV, which seems central to the whole multimedia concept, this question still confronts everyone associated with the industry: Is this a technology that the average American really wants and, if so, how much of it will he or she be willing to pay for? As this chapter has shown, there is a large number of companies and consortia who are working overtime to break through the technological glitches that still stand in the way of operational interactive TV. It is also important to remember, however, that often the most serious of these obstacles is posed not by technological challenges but by marketing challenges. The future may be coming into focus for communication technology, but it is still much more fuzzy when it comes to predicting what Americans will be willing to pay for and use in the way of interactive TV services. Chapter 2 discussed many of these marketing considerations, and it is wise to keep them in mind when trying to predict which of the technological advances discussed in these chapters will be a part of our lives in years to come. It is possible, as the failed videotex experiments of the 1980s showed, to have an interactive system offer too much in the way of services—services that the user does not feel important or worth the cost. David Serlin, executive vice president of ICTV has said, for instance, "When the only tool you have is a hammer, all your problems look like a nail."[37] Will Americans see the need to order a pizza from their television set when all they have to do is pick up the phone and call an advertised number? Will that and many other services be worth the few dollars a month that interactive TV companies will charge the user? If customer considerations are not brought into the equation—if the marketing department is not central to the development of technology—there could be a lot of money spent uselessly on products and services that the potential subscriber will not want.

It is also wise to remember that, as much in love with television as America seems to be, there may well be a point of saturation. Americans still like to pursue other leisure-time activities, often outside the home. To get full benefit of the many interactive TV services on the horizon, many Americans would have to confine most of these leisure-time pursuits to their living room or den in front of the television set. Some, obviously, would welcome this idea. But will enough people embrace it to make it worthwhile for companies to continue pouring hundreds of millions of dollars into the development of multimedia and interactive TV? A possible parallel example—not involving interactive television—

can be found in the 1993 Festival 500 Parade in downtown Indianapolis. This parade is held annually on the day before the running of the Indianapolis 500 and is touted as the second largest annual parade in America, ranking right behind the Rose Bowl Parade. The 1993 version of the parade, syndicated for television nationwide and co-hosted by Regis Philbin, was highly publicized as the first "interactive parade" in America. Each of the thousands of reserved-seat holders watching the parade was given a special "costume" (actually a newspaper-size paper American flag with a perforated hole to wear over the shoulders) and accessories bag containing such things as a kazoo, red clown nose, small American flag, and other items to wear or wave at the designated point of the parade. The idea was that television viewers would see these thousands of parade watchers join in the parade more closely by wearing the right items at the right times. As it turned out, however, very few people bothered to interact in these ways. They had come to watch a parade, not dress up themselves or look around in their bag for the right items of the right time. In short, the idea was a flop, despite the deft camerawork that tried to focus in on the few people who did interact.

Some industry and government experts say that companies such as Eon Corp. are going too far by implicitly promising overnight wealth to those Americans who win one of the licenses for interactive TV from the FCC. The *New York Times* reported in 1992 that "while the technology undoubtedly works, advertising experts say its profit potential is unclear."[38] Technology consultant Gary Arlen agrees saying, "There are lots and lots of questions about this [Eon Corp.] system. The biggest question I get is, 'Are they for real?' When you think about it, a lot of the pieces don't fit together perfectly."[39] One obstacle facing Eon Corp. and any other company trying to do what it is doing is the following: Will average Americans pay $500–$700 for a controller box that sits on top of their TV sets, while the transactions are expected to cost either advertisers or customers about $2 apiece, which will be split by Eon Corp. and the licensees? Even if the price of the controller were cut in half, won't many consumers be hesitant to pay for what, in large measure, amounts to just a new form of advertising?

Analyst Edmund L. Andrews notes:

Beyond that, advertising executives say other technologies can deliver similar services over phone lines, and cable television companies are preparing to introduce interactive features over coaxial cables. Consumers can already respond to many television commercials through the familiar—if slower—method of dialing toll-free "800" numbers.[40]

To be sure, the technological advances chronicled in this and other chapters are amazing, and many are piquing the interest of those people undergoing interactive tests around the country, as well as those who only read and hear about them. Many businesses that are developing the high-tech gadgetry are doing so in tandem with highly specialized marketing people and are trying to look at the failed experiments before them to get more of an idea of what will sell. Undoubtedly, much of the technology discussed here will become a reality within the decade, and there seems—at present—to be many more optimists in the interactive TV arena than pessimists. One such optimist, Michael Mascioni of Alexander & Associates, a New York consulting firm specializing in entertainment marketing has noted, "I would say there are substantial opportunities in interactive television."[41]

MediaWeek magazine, in a 1993 feature story on interactive TV, also questioned the marketability of the media, especially since it asks the viewer to change from a passive to an active role in watching television and demands that its viewers take part in choosing what comes over the screen. The article asks the following question:

But with half of America's VCRs still blinking "12:00" perpetually, will this technological tidal wave flood homes with too much information? Or will America surf that wave to TV utopia?[42]

Kay Koplovitz, president of USA Networks, says it is impossible to isolate the electronic superhighway that is being highly touted from the programming that will be delivered by it. In other words, just having the means for interactive TV is not enough—not by a long shot. Koplovitz states, "You can't think of this as just a superhighway, period. You want to know what the cars are going to look like."[43] And, one might add, whether the viewer will be willing to trade in his or her dependable model on the first in a wave of new and unproven models.

THE REVOLUTION IN COMPUTERS

One reason for criticism of interactive TV as the vehicle of access into multimedia is that personal computers are capable of delivering even more interactive services than any television set now can. Indeed, the personal computer industry is going through a revolution. PCs are now as powerful as many mainframe computers, and they can perform all the services and provide all the data that backers of interactive TV believe that medium can. Anyone truly interested in conversing with a television monitor can do so for start-up costs of less than $2,000, which includes a PC, basic software, and a personal laser printer. To take advantage of ongoing information and service providers, they may have to spend a few dollars a month in user fees, but that is generally the total cost.

Although the term *multimedia* is used generically at times to describe the entirety of the interactive media concept, those with PCs know it to denote the age in which a simple PC can gather, process, and assimilate information, sights, and sounds from a number of different media sources and enable the computer user to have mastery over all of them, mixing them together at will. In a real sense, PCs are becoming command centers in the office, home, and even the lap, pulling together material from both print and electronic sources. To the growing number of PC owners, it is the computer, unlike television as it currently operates, that provides the power to switch instantly between data, graphics, video, and audio, enabling them to control the content and form of information from a desktop or laptop.

Multimedia computing also enables users to experience and react to information instead of passively absorbing it. For instance, a student researching the history of Senator Robert Kennedy could use his computer to run videos of Kennedy's most popular speeches and then access transcripts of the same speeches and call them onto the screen, one after another. In short, multimedia technology is transforming computers from machines that only process pure data into powerful, interactive communications systems.

Multimedia is the next generation of the computer interface, which has evolved from switches and wires to teletypes, video terminals, and today's graphic user interface, popularized by the Apple Macintosh and, more recently, Microsoft Windows. As an enhancement to the interface, multimedia can add voice, animation, video, and other audiovisual information to electronic mail and other existing applications.[44] Backers of multimedia computers see the revolution as one that will enable individuals to take control of information in a way that was only recently possible by those with very large mainframe computers. The implications are huge. For instance, instead of using VCRs and remote controls to scan a relatively meager selection of broadcast TV, cable stations, and videos, computers will provide extensive selections of software options from which to choose.

There are some technical obstacles to overcome, however. While information services companies are focusing on new applications, computer and telecommunications companies are addressing the technical challenges created by those applications. For example, unlike paper media, the new media of animation, video, audio, and music must play on the computer screen or through a speaker. They must play at a constant speed in real time. Unfortunately, the architectures of PCs were not designed for such operation. So the challenge is to create a new operating system that can handle real-time data. Such an effort requires extensive software modification.[45]

A second technical challenge involves information overload. Audio can easily consume 24 kilobits of information per second—information that must be managed by the computer and stored on a disk. Video requires even more processing, which is usually well beyond the capabilities of PCs unless it is compressed dramatically.

The challenges are real but not insurmountable. To overcome these problems, data must be captured, processed, stored or transmitted, and played back. Each step often requires special components and software. Many multimedia hardware products provide the extra processing power needed to handle multimedia functions. For example, an audio card might include high-quality audio capture, a digital signal processor (DSP) to encode the audio, a port to connect a disk drive directly to the audio card and a digital-to-analog converter to play the sound. Multimedia video cards, such as those made by VideoLogic, can play video in a window on the computer screen.[46]

Adding CD-ROM technology to the growing power of PCs enhances the range of multimedia computers even further. Imagine that you are the owner of a firm called New Age Graphics and you are working on a project to create and mail an announcement for your firm that will include a promotional videotape. You are at your PC and one hand reaches out to pick up the entire type library available on Adobe software and another file containing 7,000 pieces of clip art. Next your hand lifts up every United States mailing address known to the U.S. Postal Service, and the names and phone numbers of 200,000 U.S. businesses. No, you don't need huge muscles; all of these items reside on CD-ROMs. Continuing the example, you make the promotional video using your computer and VCR, copy the Stone family of fonts from the Adobe disk for use in the flier. On the clip-art disc, you quickly find an attractive border, then search the disc of U.S. businesses and incorporate some into your mailing list. Finally, you run your list against the U.S. Postal Service database to make sure your mailing qualifies for discounts given to Post Office customers who presort their bulk mail. You have thus entered the world of computer multimedia, courtesy of your PC and CD-ROM technology.[47]

To enter this world, all you need aside from your PC is a CD-ROM drive, an audio board (which is built in if you have a Macintosh but which costs between $600–$1,300 otherwise), speakers (optional for the Macintosh), and the necessary software—either Quick Time for the Macintosh ($139) or Video for Windows ($199) for IBMs and computers compatible with them. There are even multimedia-ready PCs already on the market, and they are designated by the MPC logo. Examples of MPCs and Multimedia Macintosh computers are:[48]

- Tandy Sensation, costing about $2,200.
- Compaq ProLinea CDS, costing about $1,700.
- IBM PS/2 Ultimedia, costing between $3,600 and $4,825.

• Performa 600CD/llvx (a Macintosh computer), costing between $2,400 and $3,200.

If you invest in one of these systems, everything but the software is included. QuickTime is included with all Macintoshes that have a built-in CD-ROM drive, an item that costs between $500–$750.

To do production work, you will need additional hardware and software. To create a promotional videotape, you will need a video adapter board (costing between $1,200 and $2,400), a Hi-8 or S-VHS VCR ($1,500–$1,700), and presentation software ($300–$500). A color scanner ($1,000–$1,750) is also hard to do without.

Once you attach a CD-ROM drive to your PC, you will have an abundant supply of CD titles to choose from and interact with. The following is a brief listing of some titles available in 1993:

• **Art and Desktop Publishing:** *ArtRoom 5.2*, $699, by Image Club Graphics, containing nearly 7,000 high-quality clip-art images.

• **Education and Literature:** *Murmurs of Earth*, $59.99, from Warner NewMedia, containing the words and music spun into space aboard Voyager I and II. Also, *Poetry in Motion*, $29.95 by The Voyager Co., which contains contemporary poets who read their work via QuickTime movies.

• **Reference:** *Compton's Multimedia Encyclopedia*, $695, from Compton's New-media, containing the complete text of the 26-volume *Compton's Encyclopedia*, plus audio, animation, and illustrations. Also, *New Grolier Electronic Encyclopedia*, from Grolier Electronic Publishing, $259, containing 33,000 articles, 3,000 illustrations, plus audio, video, and animation.

• **Business:** *The American Business Phone Book*, $298, from American Business Information, with 9.2 million businesses on tap where you can access 5,000 names before you have to buy more credits. Also the *Business Yellow Pages of America*, $150, from Innotech, Inc., containing over 200,000 American businesses on one disc. Also the *1990 Census Data on CD-ROM*, from CD-ROM, Inc., $995, containing more than 100 key variables from the 1990 census by census tract, zip code, place, county, and state.

Obviously, some of this technology is out of range of the hobbyist, but for persons with small businesses who need to do a lot of multimedia work—which may in fact be in the home—it is very cost effective. Nevertheless, much of multimedia technology is inexpensive enough to interest even the hobbyist. Most of the desktop publishing hardware and software, for instance, is in the range of the average American who likes to work with graphics or maybe dreams of publishing his or her own newsletter or magazine. For everyone, however, the PC holds much promise as a working tool, enabling them to access the world of multimedia and do it sooner than they otherwise might with their conventional television sets.

SUMMARY

The decades of the 1980s and 1990s have become the digital decade in many ways as the older analog technology has given way to digital communications. The process of digital compression techniques, coupled with advances in fiber optics and even the carrying capacities of coaxial cable are helping to insure that the digital revolution will expand into the twenty-first century and ensure that massive amounts of information will be available to the public as never before in history. Not all of this communication will be land-based, however, as direct broadcast satellite technology continues to emerge and hopes rise with the launching of each new rocket carrying another direct broadcast satellite into space.

The decade of the 1990s has also seen great strides made in the development and marketing of wireless communication—the so-called PCS products of portable telephones, electronic notepads, fax machines, and computers. Additionally, not to be outdone by the television industry and its digitally-based HDTV experiments, the radio industry is tapping into the digital revolution with new developments in DAB systems to deliver sound quality as good as, if not superior to, CDs.

In short, what lies ahead in the communications field promises to be even more exciting than what has preceded it thus far, as media companies are gearing up and expanding to help get communications ideas off the drawing boards and into the nation's home entertainment centers.

NOTES

1. Jolie Solomon et al., "A Risky Revolution," *Newsweek*, April 26, 1993, 44.
2. Ibid.
3. Steve Rosenthal, "Interactive TV: The Gold Rush Is On," *New Media*, December 1992, 27.
4. Ibid.
5. Ibid.
6. Michael M. Mirabito and Barbara L. Morgenstern, *The New Communications Technologies* (Boston: Focal Press, 1990), 137.
7. Rich Karlgaard, "Fast Forward Forever," *Forbes ASAP*, June 7, 1993, 9.
8. Fred Hift, "Interactive TV Offers Viewers More Choices Per Channel," *The Christian Science Monitor*, December 24, 1990, 11.
9. Suzanne Alexander, "Interactive TV Test Is Watched to See Who's More Than Remotely Interested," *The Wall Street Journal*, May 10, 1990, B1.
10. Ibid.
11. G. Pascal Zachary, "HP is Building Gadget to Make TVs Interactive," *The Wall Street Journal*, February 27, 1992, B1.

12. Mark Lewyn, "This Isn't the Response TV Answer Expected," *Business Week*, June 29, 1992, 78.

13. John Schneidawind, "US West Plugging in to TV," *USA Today*, May 18, 1993, B1.

14. Ibid.

15. Gary Slutsker, "The Tortoise and the Hare," *Forbes*, February 1, 1993, 67.

16. Steve Rosenthal, "Interactive Network: Viewers Get Involved," *New Media*, December 1992, 30.

17. Rebecca Piirto, "Battle for the Black Box," *American Demographics*, November 1992, 6.

18. Ibid.

19. Sheila Rule, "Soaps with Sound and Fury: As They Like Them," *New York Times*, May 25, 1989, A4.

20. Meg Cox, "NBC Will Mix Tech and Talk with Live Poll," *Wall Street Journal*, August 28, 1989, B1.

21. Ibid.

22. Associated Press, "CNN Plans Experiments in Interactive News," *New York Times*, July 13, 1990, C28.

23. Gary Putka, "Schools Giving TV Warmer Reception," *Wall Street Journal*, December 26, 1989, B1.

24. Ibid.

25. Ibid.

26. Joseph F. Sullivan, "Second Graders Take to Interactive TV Teaching," *New York Times*, February 4, 1992, B5.

27. Ibid.

28. Ibid.

29. Ibid.

30. Katy Kelly, "Ex-Fox Chief Thinks Future Is in TV sales," *USA Today*, June 7, 1993, D2.

31. Ibid.

32. Ibid.

33. Ibid.

34. Jerry Ader et al., "Been There, Done That," *Newsweek*, July 19, 1993, 43ff.

35. Ibid.

36. Everette E. Dennis, "New News Technology," *Television Quarterly*, Winter 1990, 77.

37. Michael Antonoff, "Interactive Television," *Popular Science*, November 1992, 92.

38. Edmund A. Andrews, "TV Venture Is Criticized for Promises to Investors," *New York Times*, May 14, 1992, D5.

39. Ibid.

40. Ibid.

41. Ibid.

42. Michael Burgi, "No U Turn," *MediaWeek*, April 19, 1993, 28.

43. Ibid.

44. Nick Arnett, "Multimedia: Where Is the Industry Going?" *The World of MacIntosh Multimedia*, January 1991, 25–27.

45. Ibid.

46. Ibid.

47. Philip Bishop, "The World on a Silver Platter," *Home Office Computing*, June 1993, 61–62.

48. Ibid.

5

• • • • •

Electronic Publishing

Up to this point, most of the discussion has centered on interactive video. It is important to keep in mind, however, that in this electronic age, textual matter is still very much alive and is a growing part of the multimedia concept. Because of the economic difficulties, declining readership, and disappointing videotex experiments that the newspaper industry experienced during much of the 1980s, there is a tendency to think that print media will not be a major player in the era of multimedia. Nothing could be further from the truth, however, as several electronic publishing ventures are showing. It is true that the newspaper industry, as a whole, does not yet see a clear picture of its role in the ointeractive media. Still, most publishers realize that there is a role to be played by newspapers, and the Telecommunications Department of the NAA, along with other independent think tanks such as New Directions for News, are analyzing just what that role will be.

VIDEOTEX AND ITS APPLICATIONS

The term that has been most roundly substituted for electronic publishing is *videotex*, which refers to user-friendly, interactive electronic news and information services. These services in their various forms provide users with online access to information, entertainment, person-to-person communications, and several types of transactions. Most Americans access these videotex services by way of PCs, although users in other parts of the world, such as France, access videotex through specifically designed and dedicated terminals.

There are at least three broad applications of videotex at the present time:

1. The in-home consumer market for news, information, entertainment, and personal transactions.
2. The professional online database market that appeals to those involved in industry and commerce.
3. The in-store promotional or transactional market.

These services provide various specific functions within these broad categories. Some of these functions include:

- Information retrieval from a plethora of electronic databases.
- Communication services such as community bulletin boards, electronic mail, and group computer conferencing.
- Personal transactions such as making airline reservations, conducting banking tasks from the home, shopping electronically, and even ordering take-out food.
- Leisure-time pursuits such as interactive, electronic games and other contests.

All of these and other functions are operational today by way of videotex systems. Therefore, to define videotex as just electronic newspapers or magazines leaves out a whole array of other communications and information services. It also gives a false impression that videotex has been tried and found lacking via the Knight-Ridder and Times-Mirror experiments of the 1980s, when, in reality, the videotex concept is very much alive. A White Paper Report on videotex, prepared for the NAA in 1991, makes the following observation:

If videotex is defined as consumer's use of computers and modems to interact with a wide range of commercially marketed news, general interest information, computer software, communications, games, shopping, and other transactional services, the industry has some 1.7 million users in North America, many of them consumers with home offices or employees working at home.[1]

The report continues that, by adding other videotex services, such as electronic mail, computer conferencing, educational programs, hobbyist and special-interest bulletin boards, then that number of users rises sharply by thousands or possibly millions. For instance, there are now an estimated 10,000 to 16,000 public bulletin boards that are being used by owners of PCs with modems attached to telephone jacks.[2]
There are, in fact, at least four national associations existing that join users of videotex services: Electronic Networking Association in Allentown, Pennsylvania; the International FidoNet Association in St. Louis, Missouri; North American Association of Bulletin Board Operators in

Hartford, Connecticut; and the Videotex Industry Association, the largest of the four, headquartered in Silver Spring, Maryland. In addition to these associations, there are a half-dozen videotex service bureaus, such as the Genesys Group, Inc., and Tel-E-Tex, Inc., and another half-dozen or so videotex design, marketing, and consulting services, including J. Walter Thompson/Online and Interactive Marketing Group. Vendors of videotex data include Delphi, CompuServe, Genie, Gateway, Minitel, and Prodigy Services Co.

This chapter will focus on two of the broad applications of videotex: the in-home consumer market and the professional online database market. It will also look at some of the failed videotex experiments of the 1980s, and at how other countries—most notably France and Great Britain—have taken the lead in some applications of videotex.

THE EVOLUTION OF TELETEXT

One of the first forms of electronic publishing in the United States was the publishing of an electronic newspaper, or *print television* as some called it. What those in the industry called it was *teletext*, a system that the British developed that delivered print and graphic information on the TV screen. Unlike the later development of videotex, teletext is more of a one-way system of delivering text and graphics via a piggyback system on traditional broadcasting signals or by way of cable. A special decoder used with the television set unscrambles the teletext signal. Viewers do have some interaction with programming by way of a keypad controller, which they can use to call up certain sections of the electronic newspaper or certain categories of information.

The messages often come simultaneously with the regular television signal, squeezed into the vertical blanking interval (VBI) on the screen. Those older television viewers who used to spend a fair amount of time adjusting the vertical hold on their old sets will recognize the VBI as the black bar that went flipping by on the screen until they could get the scrolling to stop. The signals did not come via telephone lines, fiber optics, or satellites as they do today.

The interactive ability with teletext breaks down somewhat because the "frames" of textual and graphic material presented are part of a closed loop consisting possibly of 100 or more frames delivered in several repeat cycles. Additionally, there is some waiting time (although usually only several seconds) before the desired category of frames appears on the screen to begin its conveyor belt-like cycle.

Teletext first appeared experimentally in the United States in tests such as the one in 1978 in Salt Lake City, Utah. CBS-affiliate KSL-TV saw it as opening a new door to broadcasting and as a safeguard against what futurists predicted as an onslaught against TV by new and promising electronic wizardry from other segments of the communications industry. Viewers could access KSL's teletext by depressing buttons on a keypad and then viewing the "pages" of the electronic newspaper that would appear sequentially on the screen.

The KSL system was predated by Great Britain's 1972 start-up of the BBC teletext system, which engineers started by using two of the 20 unseen spare lines at the top of the television screen normally used only for sending test data.[3] The initial goal was to provide a means for delivering subtitles for the deaf, which is now a process called *closed captioning* and which is widely operational. Two years later, in 1974, the British Home Office granted a license to the BBC system, which had come to be named CEEFAX for "see facts," and another similar system operated by the Independent Broadcasting Authority (IBA). This second system was called ORACLE, for "optimal reception of announcements by coded line electronics. By the 1980s, the BBC was broadcasting 16 hours daily, every day of the week, on both its channels. BBC 1 delivered an electronic magazine of some 100 pages that changed often with updated reference information, while BBC 2 offered more static weekly pages.[4]

Several problems have plagued and thwarted the growth of teletext, but the most serious have been (1) the low level of interaction viewers have with the system and the need to allow "pages" of data to flow through on their own sequence; (2) the lack of an international transmission standard, especially since European and American television receivers have differing configurations (525-line screens in North America and 625-line screens in Europe); and (3) the relatively slow access time in calling up desired frames of information (although it may take only ten seconds or so, users report a high degree of impatience even with this lag time.) Nevertheless, many in the industry feel that teletext systems may still have their use in electronic data transmission because they can be updated continuously and almost immediately when new information becomes available.

EXPERIMENTS IN VIDEOTEX

Videotex offers more two-way capabilities than teletext. The interactive features are more pronounced and elaborate, and the Knight-Ridder videotex experiment called Viewtron, discussed in the next section, offers a good example of a videotex system. In general, with a videotex system, information does not scroll down or up a screen; users access different "pages" by depressing appropriate buttons on a remote-control keypad. Videotex, however, is generally not as simple to use as teletext, and it is a more expensive system. Videotex has been experimented with successfully in England and France, where it is now operational.

The American experiments, as will be seen later, have not been so positive. By the beginning of the 1990s, some five million French users and an increasing number of users in other European countries and North America accessed videotex through specially designed and dedicated terminals. The North American videotex industry has been growing at a rate of 25–35 percent annually for the past several years, but only about 1.7 million people now use commercial videotex services. This represents fewer than 10 percent of the installed base of PCs in homes.[5] Videotex via terminals is only available in a few metropolitan areas and the services offered, though plentiful, do not yet meet the full range of the public's interests.

Videotex, also generally referred to as *viewdata*, was originated in Great Britain at the then-British Post Office (now British Telecommunications) in the early 1970s. After successful field trials in the second half of that decade, the world's first fully operational, public videotex service opened in London. The year was 1979, and the system was called Prestel. By 1985, some 50,000 dedicated terminals were in use around the London area, with about 250,000 people using the service regularly. There were more than 500 information providers in use by the service.[6] Information providers are companies that provide a particular kind of information or entertainment feature or interactive service. Prestel users could access the system via a modem connected to their telephone lines. The capacity of the system could be counted in hundreds of thousands of pages of text, which ranged from news and feature stories, special-event calendars, business stories, entertainment listings, traffic reports, and so on. The specially designed Prestel terminals can be purchased or rented in England. Some users also can buy adapters that add the needed signal conversion feature to their conventional color TV sets.

Prestel received revenue from users through the purchase or rental of terminals and through per-page videotex charges. By the mid-1980s, however, Prestel was having trouble locating its proper market niche and was experimenting with the kind and range of services it offered users, trying to offer the mix that was in greatest demand.

In France, thing went more smoothly with videotex, possibly because of the way the country designed its system, which included creating a national system of videotex services that was linked to France's telephone service. As a result, the French videotex system was being utilized by more than one million private and commercial users, with that figure growing geometrically as the 1990s began.

Since the videotex service was part of the telephone service, all of France's millions of telephone subscribers could be found in an online, electronic phone book. Thus, callers could obtain these phone numbers anywhere in France by simply accessing them on their specially designed Minitel terminals. But that was just one feature installed in the French system. Users could also take advantage of some 2,000 providers of information and services over the system. A number of these were interactive services allowing users to conduct personal banking and shopping business from their homes or businesses.

Jerome Aumente points out that part of the success of the French videotex system is that it uses a flexible approach to payment of services that permits access to many databases and services without actual subscriptions. Callers simply tap into a KIOSK billing facility, use the specific service they desire, and are billed directly by the phone company, which, in turn, shares revenues with the service or information providers.[7] Another part of the system's popularity in France is that the Minitel terminals are offered free to anyone who subscribes to the videotex service. The terminals are used in conjunction with a telephone modem.

In America, it is to the credit of such media corporations as Knight-Ridder and Times-Mirror that they invested as much time, energy, and money into interactive field experiments as they did in the 1980s. Most of these experiments failed to produce solid enough results to mass market the services, but it is enlightening for future interactive projects to see some of the reasons for those failures.

Knight-Ridder is one of the largest newspaper companies in the United States. By the early 1990s, the company owned 28 dailies that were read by nearly four million subscribers and more than five million Sunday subscribers. Flagship newspapers of Knight-Ridder are the *Miami Herald* and the *Philadelphia Inquirer*. In fact, the entire company is visionary, and thus it was no surprise that executives of Knight-Ridder decided in the early 1980s to begin experimenting with some newer forms of news and information delivery.

Therefore, following tests in 1980–1981 in Coral Gables, Florida, it began in 1983 the first full-service commercial videotex operation in the United States. Basically, it was the kind of videotex service analogous to an electronic newspaper or magazine—complete with graphics—which is delivered over home television screens, designated video terminals, or PCs already in the home. Videotex operations are meant to be interactive, allowing users to call up the "pages" and kinds of information or graphics they want to view. Knight-Ridder created a subsidiary, Viewdata Corporation of America (VCA), to develop and operate the new service. Its product, called Viewtron, was a multifaceted and ambitious service. The experiment was confined to an area of south Florida, near Knight-Ridder's corporate headquarters in Miami. Included in Viewtron's menu of services were a variety of user services including:

• Some 750 topical service areas.

• Indexes to these topics.

- Keyword search capabilities. Users could access information about specific topics by inputting a key word or words involved in the desired topic.
- Full color capabilities.
- An attractive set of graphics integrated into the databases.
- The full text of the *Miami Herald* and news services such as the Associated Press, Dow-Jones, Knight-Ridder News Service, and others.
- Services such as home shopping and banking, games, sports updates, and online *Consumer Reports* stories.
- A classification system of news divided into local, national, international, and business categories.
- On the other end of the spectrum from world news, Viewtron also featured a form of "micronews" with such items as news about local school activities, honor rolls, and community activities.
- An array of educational services for youths and adults.
- A service whereby government officials could answer questions from the general public using the system.

In all, Viewtron began in 1983 to incorporate the services of some 50 IPs and a half-dozen "gateways," or switching points between service originators and users, into still more services and IPs.[8]

Accessing these various services was often expensive for the general consumer, however. To begin with, Viewtron required the home purchase of a specially designated terminal developed by AT&T and called the Sceptre. Originally these terminals sold for $900, but were discounted to $600 for users of the Viewtron experiment. In 1983, this terminal was the only way into the system of services and that proved to be a major problem for the success of the experiment.

In addition to the initial $600 cost for a Sceptre terminal, a monthly fee of $21 was charged for the basic videotex service. Southern Bell—which installed a special Local Area Data Transport network—charged subscribers $1 per hour access fee. So, if consumers went too deep into the menu of services to access more time-consuming features, the meter charge could climb to a fairly steep level.

VCA set a goal of having 5,000 subscribers online by the end of 1984. The result, however, was more like 3,000, causing the company to cut staff and even some user fees. It also caused the venture to start targeting owners of PCs to get more online subscribers, when it became apparent that there would be no more purchasers of the Sceptre terminal.

By the end of 1985, the future looked bleak for Viewtron. Despite some revenue from several thousand PC subscribers to add to the 3,000 Sceptre users, VCA was pumping tens of millions of dollars into the venture, and the bottom line was leaning heavily into the red. In 1986, VCA shut down Viewtron after spending some $45 million on the experiment. Then VCA disappeared, taking with it some promising joint ventures in other areas of interactive video. At closing, there were some 20,000 subscribers, with the vast majority of them owners of their own personal PCs, not the Sceptres.

In searching for causes of the collapsed venture, VCA and Knight-Ridder executives blamed the following:

1. Ingrained viewer habits that seemed to defy change in the early to mid-1980s.
2. The cost of the Viewtron service and accompanying Sceptre terminal.
3. The necessitated shift in focus toward owners of PCs and away from the planned Sceptre terminals.
4. A host of miscalculations about such things as consumer willingness to purchase a terminal to access the services, an overestimation of the number of homes with PCs and phone modems needed to access the system when the focus shifted to PC owners, soaring marketing costs to advertise the product and generate a need among consumers.
5. An overbuilding of the Viewtron system instead of approaching it more cautiously and bringing on new features and services gradually.
6. The more consistent use of the low-cost services of electronic messaging and electronic bulletin boards instead of the intriguing (and costly) sophisticated features and services.

In assessing the failure of the Viewtron venture, Aumente notes:

The failure of Viewtron was partly the problem of a public less attuned or even interested in being a part of the information age. They had to cross a low-cost threshold before they would even see what services were available. Some of the content simply duplicated what they had from other print and broadcast media more cheaply and more conveniently. The full range of interactive power of the new media was not fully exploited. People wanted value-added services and much more focused assistance. They were also buried under an information overload already and another product sold as offering more information was not attractive.[9]

It was also marketed as letting the consumer become a part of the future, but the consumer was obviously uncertain about whether he or she wanted to be a part of that future.

It should be noted that, even with these problems and miscalculations, Knight-Ridder did not abandon electronic publishing entirely. With its VU/TEXT service it has become the world's largest retrieval service of full-text regional newspapers with several thousand subscribers. Nevertheless, it is clear that several marketing miscalculations spelled doom for its home-targeted Viewtron.

Knight-Ridder was not alone in experiencing a videotex failure in the 1980s. The Times-Mirror's Gateway venture also failed in California, and the Field Enterprises Keycom operation dropped out of the general consumer videotex market in 1985. In the Gateway venture, some $30 million was pumped into a broad-based videotex service that utilized the specially designed Sceptre terminals.[10] The experiment began in 1984 and lasted two years. During that time, it had fewer than 2,000 subscribers, which was far too few for it to continue. In all, the Gateway system incorporated nearly 50 information providers when it began. Gateway carried an overall index to its contents, and this index included citations of top stories, summaries, and several special-topic features. A "Living" section covered such areas as travel, education, dining, health, and reviews. An entertainment section included the normal array of features found in that section. In addition to news and features, Gateway also offered electronic mail, games, home shopping, and basic transactional features, which allowed users to bank or invest from their terminals.

Users could either call up general headings in the index and browse, or they could look for specific data by way of keyword searches. The *Los Angeles Times*, flagship news operation of Times-Mirror, compiled an electronic edition of the newspaper daily and filed it with Gateway for users to access.

As with similar systems, however, the management at Gateway realized they were offering too many services and that the users did not want to pay for all these frills. So entire chunks of the offerings were dumped in an effort to hone the service to a more cost-effective level. Still a problem was the special terminal users had to buy or rent to access the data in Gateway. The service did make these terminals available for a $30 monthly rental fee, but that did not seem to help. As a result, Gateway decided to do some target marketing at the more than 125,000 PC owners in the Orange County area. It was thought that, since these people already had the necessary hardware and the interest to use it, they would represent fertile territory. By the time of its closing in 1986, PC owners represented half of the Gateway subscribers. Although advertising figured prominently in the Gateway service, advertisers did not see much benefit in paying to advertise over Gateway because of the small number of actual subscribers, coupled with their demographics.

Near the end, Gateway found that the features used most by subscribers was electronic mail, bulletin board, and video games. Walter S. Baer, director of advanced technology at Times-Mirror said the main lesson learned was that no one service stands out as a driving force to make a videotex service work.

And that makes the problem more difficult because you really have to put together a mix of services and price them in a way that together they do what individually they can't. I am confident that over time this will work out, but from our perspective it will take several years before the market is ready.[11]

VIDEOTEX IN THE 1990s

A summary of where videotex is in the 1990s can be seen in the White Paper Report on videotex, prepared by Conhaim Associates for the NAA. Among its observations are the following:[12]

• As a consumer medium, videotex is in the continuing stages of extended infancy on the product life-cycle curve.

• Videotex has a history of falling short of goals that are set too high for it to achieve.

• Videotex has been quite successful and profitable on a smaller scale, in meeting the needs of niche markets. This is an especially interesting and active area for videotex. Several online videotex systems are in existence solely to serve a particular target audience with specific needs or desires. Some examples of these special-interest videotex systems follow:

1. *Kids Network*: a project of the National Geographic Society that has received help from the Regional Bell Operating Companies, Apple, and IBM, and which now reaches classrooms in some 3,000 schools worldwide. It links students and teachers together for joint research that involves collecting and analyzing data.

2. *PeaceNet*: a California-based computer conferencing and database service connecting peace activists in the United States. By the 1990s, it had some 6,000 members who paid a $10 monthly subscription fee in addition to user charges to connect with their colleagues in other cities.

3. *HandsNet*: an outgrowth of the Hands Across America project and generates a great deal of nonprofit interest in telecommunications. There are now 750 organizations participating. It focuses on issues of hunger, welfare reform, homelessness, and other poverty-related issues.

4. *SeniorNet*: a subscription information and communications utility for senior citizens now publicly available on Delphi. It began as a closed-user research and demonstration project to see if online usage could improve the lives of the elderly and now has corporate sponsors in senior training and access sites across the country.

5. *PTI/VIA Project*: composed of nine municipalities and county governments developing models for civic videotex as part of a Videotex Industry Association project administered by Public Technology, Inc. The researchers are finding that many cities see providing information about videotex as a way of generating revenues while disseminating information. The project has identified 70 potential civic videotex applications, including voter registration information, volunteer and job opportunities, ordering materials, bidding on government auctions, and "mailboxes" for elected officials.

6. *Tri-State Online*: a free online service sponsored by Cincinnati Bell. It uses public domain Heartland Freenet software and features 35 public service information providers and forums on topics of public interest.

- A debate still exists in the videotex industry on alternative approaches to mass-market development. Some believe in going with the existing market of computer owners and developing computer software at the user end that will make videotex easier to use. Others believe in the telephone approach or distributing user-friendly but "dumb" terminals that have limited functionality with the intelligence residing in the network.

- Most recent videotex activity is in major markets, and the result is that competitors are fighting over mass market attention, offering the public a choice of services, philosophies, and payment schemes. In Dallas/Fort Worth, Texas, for example, the public can choose from StarText, the local tiered-free-structure service for computer owners featuring daily newspaper content operated by *The Fort Worth Star-Telegram*; Prodigy, the national flat-free service offered by IBM and Sears for computer owners that is strongly oriented toward merchandising; and U.S. videotex, the Minitel-based general audience service featuring interactive games, chatting, and community-based information along with national standards and Minitel Services from France.

- National services, such as CompuServe, Genie, and QuantumLink have primarily succeeded in attracting computer hobbyists first and then those using home computers for business purposes.

- Local information may be a magnetic feature for mass-market audiences, and this element is lacking in the national videotex services.

- The new videotex offerings look similar to the ones begun in the 1980s, only they are bigger and offer more services of different origins. There is now an infrastructure relying heavily on partnerships between large and small organizations, and this is undergirding industry development.

- The concept of inexpensive, "dumb" terminals is catching on. About two-thirds of the North American videotex gateway projects are using these terminals. The others are using PCs with specially developed software.

- Multifunctional services with flat rates of below $9.95 have been able to capture small, but loyal markets.

- A growing number of videotex services are featuring content that originated as a domestic service in another country (such as France's Telecom system) or was created especially for export.

- Although the market does appear to exist for videotex, there are several barriers on the horizon, including the following:

1. *Technology.* Despite attempts to make videotex easy to use, it is still confusing and difficult. And if the technology is simple, as it is with the Minitel-type terminal, access to services takes time, and important functions, such as the ability to work offline, are lacking.

2. *Market.* Only a small proportion of the population has workstations properly equipped to go online (5 percent with modems and software), although the installed base of computers is quite large (20 million in homes; 20 million in offices; 20 million computer game terminals).

3. *Content.* The key issue, most observers agree, is that videotex has not devel-

oped applications compelling enough for people to see as benefits for it to become a real, mass-market medium in the near future. Nor does videotex represent enough of an improvement over current methods of accomplishing the same purposes—reading newspapers, ordering from catalogs—to draw people in as steady users.

4. *Pricing.* Surveys of computer users and actual usage data indicate price sensitivity is an important constraint on the part of new as well as experienced online users. New online users will experiment with new services and stay online if paying flat rates or if services are free; experienced users are also reluctant to pay usage fees.

NEWSPAPER APPLICATIONS

There are several possible ways in which newspapers could become involved in videotex, and some newspaper companies are already participating. Among those newspaper companies involved in the early 1990s were the following:[13]

1. The *Atlanta Journal & Constitution* is an information provider on the Transtext Universal Gateway (TUG) that began with movie and restaurant reviews, newspaper archives, access to classified ads, and public forums. It also features the Associated Press newswire and local financial news.

2. Dow Jones News/Retrieval, begun in 1974, has moved from an information provider for consumers with heavy investment interests into a service targeted to businesses. The service features Dow Jones publications, but also includes a comprehensive range of other business and financial databases. Dow Jones is also an investor in one of its suppliers, Data Times, one of two large newspaper library archival services.

3. The *Fort Worth Star-Telegram* (Capital Cities/ABC) offers StarText. Mentioned earlier, this is an independent videotex operation that has gained more than 4,200 subscribers since it was started in 1982. For a flat fee of around $10, it provides unlimited access to current news stories and classified ads, electronic mail, *Grolier's Encyclopedia*, and a wide range of community information. It also has a "Business Edition" and a home banking service for which it charges additional monthly fees.

4. Knight-Ridder owns VU/TEXT, Dialog, and other database companies. Some of its business databases are also being used by general consumers. For instance, there is a gateway to Dialog on Delphi, a consumer videotex service with business and institutional private user groups.

5. *Newsday* (Times-Mirror) owns Newsday Online, an electronic edition of the newspaper appearing on NYNEX's Info-Look gateway.

6. The *Washington Post* offers access to its electronic library through several vendors, including VU/TEXT, DataTimes, and Compuserve. The *Post* also owns LEGI-SLATE, an online information service covering congressional activity and

voting records, federal regulatory activity, and other government-related matters.

7. The *Spokane Spokesman-Review* offers Electronic Editions, a bulletin board featuring searchable newspaper classified ads, educational quizzes, and electronic mail. Users pay a flat monthly fee of about $5.

Conhaim Associates believes the North American consumer videotex market may be divided into four distinct segments, each of which calls for a different market development strategy. Newspapers are active in all four segments. These four segments are illustrated in Figure 5.1.

Although newspaper companies such as Knight-Ridder and Times-Mirror were burned financially by the large-scale setbacks with Viewtron and Gateway, they realize that videotex services still may be profitable. Both companies are still producing videotex services on a more limited and targeted basis. As a whole, several top newspaper company executives are warning fellow owners and publishers that they need to heed the growing popularity of electronic, multimedia services. David Easterly, president of Cox Newspapers, advised newspaper company executives in 1993, "Now is the time to begin getting on the train. That train is going to be leaving the station."[14] Russell Neuman of Tufts University and MIT Media Lab told these same owners and publishers, "The electrons are coming. The electrons are coming. Be prepared to decouple from newsprint."[15]

The question facing most newspaper owners is how that decoupling should take place, and when. Several obstacles remain if newspapers are to begin publishing electronic editions, and the challenge will be adapting newspapers' news gathering, advertising, and distribution systems to these changes on the electronic landscape. Most newspaper consultants seem to feel that newspapers are safe in their present form for awhile, but the big question is how much time they have to adapt and to what extent they should adapt their formats. Some consultants are urging their newspaper executives to assimilate the skills and learn to use the tools of multimedia communication, so they can be ready to change formats from print to electronic signals quickly if the need comes. Other consultants are suggesting that newspaper companies form partnerships with telephone companies and become directors to other information services that might include electronic yellow pages. Still other consultants fear that newspapers are operating on a false sense of confidence that they alone can provide local news. They advise a gradual transition from an all-print newspaper to a print-and-electronic mix, and then to an all-electronic newspaper in the near future.

By mid-1992, the newspaper industry seemed to be entering a new era as the Tribune Co.'s Chicago Online became the first local electronic newspaper service available nationwide. A year later, Knight-Ridder's San

Figure 5.1
Videotex Market Segments

The North American consumer videotex market may be divided into four
distinct segments, each of which calls for a different market development
strategy.

	LOCAL Low, flat-rate subscription	*NATIONAL/INTERNATIONAL* Low, flat-rate subscription
FREE/ LOW-COST SPONSORED SERVICES	Private bulletin boards (BBS) Government-operated BBS *News/information* *Public service information* *Bulletin boards* *Conferencing* *Classifieds/Yellow Pages* *Software downloading* *Electronic mail* *Home banking* *Catalog shopping* *Live, real-time chat*	Private national BBS networks Government-operated free BBS *News/information* *Bulletin boards* *Conferencing* *Shopping services* *Electronic mail* *Home banking* *Grocery shopping*
FEE-BASED SERVICES	RBOC Gateways "Premium" Services on local subsistence *Pay-as-you-go services* *Local newspaper content* *Local classifieds* *Chat services* *E-Mail* *Home Banking* *Games*	General-interest subscription "Premium" services on national subscription videotex National videotex at hoc gateway Special-interest/niche videotex *Pay-as-you-go services* *Investor services* *Computer-hobbyist networks* *Other special interest groups* *Live, real time communications* *Publications archives*

1991 American Newspaper Publishers Association.

Jose Mercury Center became the second nationally available local service.
All of a sudden, newspapers were entering new territory by probing new
types of media services, and laying out huge sums of cash on research
and development; even cooperating with the competition if it seemed

expedient. Both Mercury Center and Chicago Online are being offered through America Online, a nationwide computer network based in Vienna, Virginia.

In the summer of 1993, some 19 news companies including Newhouse, the Globe Newspaper Co., Hearst, Knight-Ridder, Times-Mirror, the Tribune Co., and Gannett invested as much as $100,000 each to finance the development of the world's first "personalized" newspaper at MIT. The focus of this effort is on creating a kind of *Daily Me* newspaper, or one that is totally personalized to each reader's taste via a process of user modeling. This product could take several forms, including online news networks, or a tablet-sized, electronic flat panel product, or an electronically-displayed newspaper over a television or desktop computer.

In the race to develop electronic, flat panel newspapers, Knight-Ridder seems to be taking the lead in designing a product that would display an electronic image with similar features of a local newspaper. These would include most or all the articles and features that appeared that day as well as access to the archives of the newspaper. It would have the added benefit of continual updating and, along with still art, would also offer full-motion and full-color video. Knight-Ridder was speculating a launch date in 1995 for electronic editions of newspapers, cautioning however that the learning curve among users could slow down any widespread implementation.

One of the reasons that an electronic newspaper or magazine seems to make sense is that it is the easiest way to produce a personalized newspaper, and personalized newspapers are becoming the topic of much conversation among publishers. Newspaper companies have been moving toward this goal in various ways, from zoning newspapers to creating a plethora of special sections. In zoning, a newspaper tries to create separate editions for different geographical zones in its market. Typically there would be North, South, East, and West editions with a specially designated section for each zone contained in the main paper, which is the same for all zones. Some newspapers break this zoning into more geographical sections than four. But marketers are advising newspaper executives that, as good as geographical zoning might be, it does not compare to demographic zoning or—better yet—to producing a personalized newspaper that meets specific, individual needs. So, to move closer to that goal (which many publishers feel is unrealistic), newspapers are being divided into special-interest sections: business, arts and entertainment, sports, automotive, sci-tech, lifestyles, fashion and style, the home, food, travel, and any number of occasional special sections that might focus on specific events ranging from the Olympics to the Indianapolis 500, to the onset of winter, fall, spring, or summer seasons. In fact, newspaper historians refer to this new wave of sections as the sectional revolution in newspapers. Ironically, in their attempt to produce special-interest newspapers, they are also trying desperately to be all things to all readers. It is a mix that does not quite work. Newspaper readership is taking its licks from generation after generation who have been raised on an electronic media, and content cannot be personalized enough by zoning or by special sections to produce a truly personal newspaper.

Consultant Michael Conniff has noted the importance of a personal newspaper (PN) by stating the following:

The PN is the marriage of newspapers and direct marketing techniques, a process whereby newspapers are deploying new technologies—both print and electronic—to deliver a personal package of news and advertising as defined by each individual consumer. . . . The rise of the PN is analogous to the impact of the personal computer. . . . The PN will exert the same kind of pressure on the newspaper world.[16]

One current way newspapers are trying to offer personalized services are by providing *audiotex* services for readers wanting to know up-to-the-minute information about sports, finances, and weather, and other topics such as soap opera digests. The number of North American newspapers offering voice information services exploded during the 1980s and early 1990s to the point that about 1,200 newspapers were offering some form of them. One example of a newspaper audiotex service can be found in the *Seattle Times*' InfoLine, which is free to local callers. As of 1992, monthly volume was at 500,000 calls, and the callers were representing desirable demographics. For instance, nearly half of the callers to InfoLine financial and sports lines had household incomes of from $51,000 to $100,000. Although these callers were predominantly male, the InfoLine soap opera lines was used primarily by females, almost three-fourths of whom held college degrees. Some newspapers, such as *USA Today*, charge fees for using the "1-900" audiotex service, but callers use it by the thousands every day.

Some focus groups, such as one hosted by the Tribune Co., have shown that audiotex services rate high with readers. While they are open to the idea of sophisticated audiotex services, readers are not sure they want to have more advertising and technology pressed on them. In addition, they like the idea of obtaining personalized news summaries, but they also worry about their own privacy being violated.[17] They see this privacy being threatened by a newspaper audiotex service that wants to obtain personal information about readers so audiotex service in the future can be tailored to their needs. One such prototype audiotex service in 1992 was Call One, a service developed by the Tribune Co. that would collect a personalized daily briefing based on the caller's interest in news, features, and advertisements. In addition to presenting the information,

Call One would refer callers to articles and ads in the sponsor newspaper. A newspaper would love to have such information for future marketing and direct response uses, but readers are dubious about such databases involving personal information.

In addition to these kinds of audiotex information, both newspapers and magazines are offering voice personals in their classified sections where advertisers can create voice classified advertising.

Some newspapers have also begun fax editions as a way of getting up-to-the-minute, personalized information to certain types of business subscribers. Publishing by fax, however, means more than simply delivering newspapers and magazines at the speed of a phone call. Fax publishing has created a new type of publishing market of people who are interested in obtaining information rather than buying a product and of publishers who are desirous of creating new ways to sell. As far as advertisers are concerned, fax publishing means instant delivery of advertising and—frequently—instant responses as well. There were more than six million fax machines in operation nationwide in 1991, and another seven million are predicted to come in use by mid-decade.[18] Creative publishers see the marketing possibilities stemming from the fax machine. Facsimilies enhance the perceived value of the information by delivering it straight from the source in a convenient package. Fax publications also have a high pass-around rate, and they are easy to carry due to their small size. There is also a personal aspect to a fax newspaper that is not matched by a newspaper that is one out of a half-million that comes off a printing press and is sold out of a street-corner box. The downside to fax publishing is its expense to consumers. Subscription prices range from $1 per issue to hundreds of dollars per year, so subscribers must really want the information to pay that much for it. Two fax editions of newspapers being published in the early 1990s were:[19]

- The *Hartford Courant*'s Fax Paper, serving up abstracts of the next day's news and billed as "Ahead of Tomorrow." The paper promises delivery "on your desk weekdays by 4:30 P.M." The Fax Paper costs $500 a year by subscription and focuses on the *Courant*'s strengths of the local angle with a heavy emphasis on business news and news of Connecticut people.

- The *New York Times*' Japan edition TimesFax, written in English for Japanese readership. It beats other Western publications to press by using fax, and subscribers pay $1,600 annually for it.

For what they do, these fax papers seem to fill a niche. Because of their limitations and expense involved, however, it is doubtful they will fill the void that may exist in the near future for a personalized newspaper.

There are some more futuristic ideas on the drawing board that address the concept of the personalized newspaper, although their feasibility is still in question. One such proposal emanated from the MIT Media Lab in 1991 and was the product of research by Walter Bender, Hakon Lie, Jonathan Orwant, Laura Teodosio, and Nathan Abramson. Called Newspace, this idea is a broadsheet-sized electronic news presentation that uses paper-quality displays, coupled with personal computing technology to give users a range of new possibilities in content selection, imagery, typography, and human interaction. With Newspace, a "computational intermediary," acting in concert with—and on behalf of—the "reader" makes possible new publishing styles and forms and invites instant updates and spontaneous interaction while retaining the edition with a "front page," headlines, simultaneous presentations, and juxtapositions.[20]

In preparing the rationale of Newspace, the MIT group noted:

In the case of a newspaper, taking the ink off of the paper and sending it as bits is attractive; it is cost effective in terms of trees and trucks. The bits can be reassembled in the receiver, and displayed as it would have originally appeared. The final display could once again be ink on paper, such as a Fax paper, or displayed electronically. The essence of such a system is efficiency of distribution. Little would change in the use or content of the newspaper due to digital distribution.[21]

One of the inviting features of this form of electronic newspaper is that it looks like a newspaper with text, pictures, and headlines. Ironically, these features are almost universally absent from current online access to information via teletext of videotex systems. Because of recent advances in display technology, however, including the development of large and flat screen displays and clearer resolution, graphics are now much brighter, and text can be intermingled with other media, such as television, radio, and electronic mail. In Newspace, all of these elements can come together in a dynamic, personalized newspaper that still retains the looks of a newspaper.

Newspace is designed to be based on the user's interests and also takes into account the user's knowledge level and style preferences. This personalization is based on developing an implicit user model, wherein the user supplies the computer with personal data and preferences. As previously noted, however, this kind of personalization may be a disadvantage as users might perceive this as a threat to their privacy.

Newspace envisions a large number of information providers and sources in this electronic newspaper. These sources come from different media and are transmitted in different ways, but all are converted to a common format for use by the electronic newspaper. In return, the user supplies personal demographic and preference information, or such preferences are monitored by Newspace as the user accesses certain features of the system over time. In such a scenario, the user would not have to actively feed in personal preferences.

In describing Newspace, the MIT group explains:

> Our news system gathers information from other media than the traditional text wire services. . . . A compelling reason for using multiple modalities is that each form of media is inherently powerful in expressing different types of information. Quantitative information is best described graphically. The conceptual reasons behind a recent stock market crash may be better expounded by text. News of a speech or debate would be best presented by an audio clip. Pictures and video engender a certain reality about the existence of an event or a person. The digital domain provides us the ability to efficiently parse, search, compare and retrieve news information. We can then combine and transform stories in ways the editors never imagined. Linking is possible and so is the creation of composite forms. Graphics can be combined with the text or audio from a different news source.[22]

The resulting display of this data would appear on a large computer screen with both audio and video capabilities.

Regardless of the form these electronic newspapers might take in the future, the important point is that, even after the failures of Viewtron and Gateway in the 1980s, the newspaper industry is still looking at making the idea work again. With competition from the electronic media increasing in intensity, it is likely that we will see more electronic editions of newspapers in the near future.

ELECTRONIC DATABASES

One of the applications of videotex receiving widespread acceptance has been as an electronic database or information service of the kind found in university libraries or the kind available to businesses and to individual users as well. Among the many such databases in operation are the following:

- NEXIS, an electronic library containing more than 650 full-text publications and reports, selected full-text articles from publications, and abstracts of articles. This service is heavily subscribed to by business, libraries, and the news media. It is owned and operated by Mead Data Central with headquarters in Dayton, Ohio.
- LEXIS, a sister operation to NEXIS, which is an electronic law library containing publications, articles, and abstracts on legal issues and cases. It is heavily subscribed to by members of the legal profession.
- InfoTrac, subscribed to by many university libraries and offering citations and abstracts of articles from selected leading newspapers and magazines. There are two broad divisions of InfoTrac: a General Interest library, and a Business library.

- DataTimes, established by the *Daily Oklahoman* in Oklahoma City as a database of full-text articles from many daily newspapers around the country.
- VuText, established by Knight-Ridder as a database similar in design to DataTimes.
- Dialog Information Services, which is an electronic database similar to NEXIS and marketed to business clients.
- Prodigy, a home information and entertainment service offered by Sears and IBM.
- CompuServe, similar in design and offerings to Prodigy and marketed heavily to home consumers.

These are only some of the high-profile interactive databases. There are many more targeted to much narrower topical interests. In all these databases, however, time equals money and often a lot of it. In addition to paying a subscription fee to join the service, members are generally assessed charges based on the amount of time spent searching and using the library. Although home information services such as Prodigy charge only a few dollars a month for basic use of the service, more sophisticated services often charge as high as $300 per hour in connect-time charges.[23] Obviously these services are too expensive for home consumer use and are subscribed to by business and the media. At any rate, keeping costs down is a skill that comes from learning how best to search through the maze of information available in the database. Some services, such as Dialog and a similar one called BRS, offer supplemental services that are less expensive and that usually can be accessed only at night and on weekends. Dialog's service is called Knowledge Index, and the BRS service is called After Dark. Each contains more than 100 of their parent services' most popular databases. In 1992, Knowledge Index costs only $35 to set up and $24 per hour to use. On Dialog, the same files would often cost from $60 to $96 per hour, although some might run as high as $265 plus the network long-distance charge and the per-record cost. BRS After Dark costs $75 to set up, and each individual database has its own hourly charge from $10 up to $80.[24] LEXIS/NEXIS also has an off-hours option, marketed to schools and universities, with two alternative pricing structures: a flat monthly fee of $960, or an hourly rate of $80.[25]

These and many other electronic libraries offer timeliness and quick search and retrieval, often by entering a keyword or phrase. To access these services, users need a PC and a modem and sometimes special software that comes with a subscription to the service.

Many businesses, such as the news media, financial institutions, and financial planning specialists rely on up-to-the-minute information for background and/or decision making. For such companies, these electronic information services form a vital part of their day-to-day operations.

A much smaller, but growing market is found among individual consumers at home who use services such as Prodigy for anything from weather forecasts, to home shopping, to obtaining headline news or consumer report information, or videogames, electronic bulletin boards, and much more.

Communications scholar Frederick Williams envisions a public network information service in the near future. He sees the 1992 ruling allowing telephone companies to enter the information services business as providing great impetus to the creation of such a network, and he predicts that we will probably soon "see seven companies with combined annual revenues exceeding $85 billion become information providers or . . . electronic publishers."[26] He believes such a network should be directed at the entire American population, rich and poor, disabled and healthy, rural dweller and urbanite. Among the many information-exchange services that would benefit citizens most from such a network, Williams cites the following:[27]

• Booking medical appointments at health clinics or hospitals.

• Requesting information about a school district, including vacation schedules, menus, sporting events, dates and agendas of board meetings, budget summaries, or maybe even a record of one's child's class attendance.

• A national, electronic telephone directory such as the one France tried with its Minitel system.

• Making emergency calls for police, fire, or medical assistance with provisions for verification to prevent false alarms; location and other vital information such as medical data of family members or their bedrooms' location in the house.

• Simple information seeking or transaction uses of the telephone-based videotex system.

• Obtaining information about abortion rights and counseling or alcohol and drug abuse.

• Obtaining bilingual instruction.

• Obtaining bus or subway schedules and current conditions.

• Obtaining information on getting help for child or spousal abuse.

• Getting information on job listings.

• Browsing through the library's electronic card catalog or videotex system.

Using these information services should be no more complicated than exchanging simple combinations of voice, text, and graphics between the user and the upgraded telephone device, Williams says.[28] The device would be in the form of a "smart" telephone with visual display and touch-screen input capabilities. The technology for such a phone is already existent, although the price must come down to make it universally available to the public. Such an information network, although offering a wide range of services, could be tailored to individual needs by the users. In addition to some essential information services like those noted above, the network could also offer many commercial services for which users would be charged on a per-use basis, possibly accessing them with "900" numbers.

Whatever form the electronic information services take now and in the future, one thing appears certain: There is a market for the right mix of services and information, both in the commercial and home sectors.

ELECTRONIC MAIL

Once the exclusive domain of research scientists and computer hacks, electronic mail has now become widely used around North America and much of the rest of the world. This new form of communication, by which textual messages are created and sent to an individual's PC at home or work, is sweeping the country and has become one of the more popular features of videotex experiments. Electronic mail eliminates the painstaking task of finding an envelope and a stamp, putting the two together with an address, and then taking the finished product to a post office or mailbox. The exercise has become so tedious that many Americans now just pick up the phone and call, although they would rather put the message into writing.

Spurring the use of electronic mail, or E-mail as it is often called, was the creation in 1969 of the Internet, a global communication network started by the U.S. Department of Defense. Well over 10 million people around the world now have E-mail, and most of them live in the United States.[29] That number is rapidly rising, and the use is phenomenal. There is even an Electronic Mail Association in Arlington, Virginia, and it projects that the number of people using E-mail will increase exponentially in years to come. Even the Clinton administration, whose campaign used internal E-mail extensively during the 1992 campaign, was working on devising a system to allow any citizen to communicate electronically with the White House. E-mail networks have also been installed as part of some of the past and present commercial videotex services.

A great deal of the growth in E-mail popularity has occurred on college campuses where institutions pay a flat fee to connect to the Internet, and faculty, staff, and students receive free, unlimited E-mail. Even on business cards, E-mail addresses are taking their place next to phone and fax numbers. Many large corporations are on the network, and nearly all of the commercial information services link subscribers to the Internet. As far as cost is concerned, communicating via E-mail is cheaper than a long-distance telephone call or—often times—even a letter.

Among the disadvantages of E-mail is that this kind of mail can be lost, misdelivered, or opened by someone other than to whom it is sent. Additionally, some in the business community fear the loss of trade secrets through the careless use of E-mail to discuss design and implementation topics of products and services. Electronic junk mail has also surfaced as a problem. Individuals can get on mailing lists the same way as with conventional mail and find their E-mail files stuffed with electronic ads and flyers that they don't want.

Despite these problems, E-mail's popularity continues to increase, and it is one of the most viable applications of many videotex services on the market.

DESKTOP PUBLISHING

No discussion of electronic publishing would be complete without mentioning the great popularity of desktop publishing, which refers to the ability of anyone with a PC, inexpensive software, and a personal laser printer to publish newsletters, newspapers, or magazines. To be sure, many such efforts are fairly primitive when compared to established mass-circulation newspapers and magazines, but they often serve their purpose of enlightening smaller target audiences and getting messages out that home publishers want to deliver.

The advances in inexpensive desktop publishing equipment has also allowed many smaller newspapers—weeklies especially—to trim production costs and do more typesetting and composing work in-house by simply using a staff member sitting in front of a PC. Pages cannot only be designed electronically, but they can also be "pasted up" or composed electronically so that what comes out of the printer is the actual news page (or at least sections of it) that can be put in front of a camera, which will shoot a page negative from which a press plate is made. This efficiency is much less time consuming and much more cost effective, allowing these newspapers to put more money into the news gathering process and less into the production process.

Opening the door for this revolution in desktop publishing has been the PC, laser printer, and the plethora of word processing software programs on the market today. Leading the charge has been Apple Computers with its Macintosh line of computers and various upgrades of MacWrite word processing software programs. Microsoft is another popular word processing program, allowing users a number of applications. Graphics software such as Pagemaker makes desktop publishing a skill that is well within the reach of everyone who feels comfortable around a PC.

Such low-cost electronic capabilities take publishing out of the hands of wealthy companies and put it within reach of the average American who has something to say and an audience to say it to. It is a growing and important part of the electronic publishing industry.

SUMMARY

Teletext, videotex, electronic database services, electronic newspapers, audiotex, fax papers, E-mail, and desktop publishing are all key aspects of the emerging electronic publishing industry. The existence of these services reminds us that, although we are in the era of electronic information, that information can still take a written—as well as video—form. The text may appear on computer screens and may be mixed with other media forms, such as still and moving graphics and audio representations, but it will still be textual matter. The age of writing is not dead, nor is it ever likely to be so.

Two important implications of electronic publishing are that (1) we can get needed information faster and in more detail now than ever before, and (2) especially with the free database searches that many libraries offer, this information can be more widely obtained by more sectors of the public than ever before. Therefore, there is a certain egalitarian quality about the explosion of electronic database services, although—as later discussion in this book warns—there is also the possibility of creating a larger knowledge gap as certain information services become too expensive for the average American. Whether the future holds a society in which information is shared more democratically or whether a larger knowledge gap looms may depend on the costs associated with these information services, the kind of information policy the federal government creates, and the extent to which it may decide to subsidize some costs associated with accessing this knowledge.

NOTES

1. Wallys Conhaim, "Videotex: Growing Public Awareness," White Paper Report prepared for the Newspaper Association of America, Reston, VA, 1991, v.
2. Ibid., 3.
3. Milton Hollstein, "Teletext: 'Print' TV," *Grassroots Editor*, Spring, 1980, 15.
4. Ibid.
5. Conhaim, "Videotex," v.
6. Jerome Aumente, *New Electronic Pathways* (Newbury Park, CA: Sage, 1987), 28.
7. Ibid., 33.
8. Ibid., 57.
9. Ibid.
10. Ibid., 60.
11. Ibid., 62.
12. Conhaim, "Videotex," 3ff.
13. Ibid., 22–23.

14. George Garneau, "The New Media Landscape," *Editor & Publisher*, May 8, 1993, 14.

15. Ibid.

16. Michael Conniff, "Enter the Personal Newspaper," *Editor & Publisher*, January 16, 1993, 3.

17. Mark Fitzgerald, "What Do Callers Think?" *Editor & Publisher*, February 22, 1993, 14.

18. Rusty Weston, "Fast Fax Publishing," *Publish*, July 1991, 72.

19. Ibid.

20. Walter Bender et al., "Newspace: Mass Media and Personal Computing," *USENIX*, Nashville, June 1991.

21. Ibid.

22. Ibid.

23. Lawrence Krumenaker, "Get a Clue!" *Quill*, June 1992, 35.

24. Ibid.

25. Letter from Mead Data Central to the author, August 23, 1989.

26. Frederick Williams, "Network Information Services as a New Public Medium," *Media Studies Journal*, Winter 1991, 139.

27. Ibid., 140–143.

28. Ibid.

29. Robert Preer, "E-mail's Popularity Increases," *Boston Globe*, February 11, 1983, 1A.

6

. . . . .

Marketing the New Media

Creating the new media is one thing; getting consumers to use them is something else. Yet, because of the realities of the business world and the funding of research and development at the nation's top universities and corporations, there must be a fairly strong guarantee of usage before the experimentation proceeds very far. In the end, the shape that the media world of the twenty-first century takes will be determined to a large extent by consumers who are asked to purchase the hardware and software to access the new media and then pay monthly subscription or user fees. As the future unfolds, the companies supplying this hardware and programming will be watching to see which services initial users seem to want. If there is a demand for a lot of news, documentaries, and special-interest programming, then there will be an expansion of these kinds of offerings. On the other hand, if video on demand is a big crowd pleaser, then there will be more movies available than we know what to do with. In like manner, if interactive Yellow Pages, electronic town meetings, or videoconferencing are in demand, these will be services that become widespread. In a sense, it will be an election by viewers and their remote-control tuners. The companies that succeed will be those that correctly monitor users' wants and needs and then apply their products and services to those needs.

CORRECTING MARKETING MYOPIA

If media companies are ever going to get people to use their technology, they must pay attention to what those customers really want. That is not as easy as it seems because people do not always think or act rationally, and products they think they want end up not being used. Nevertheless, audience desires—as well as observed usage patterns—are vital in creating new media products. At the MIT Media Lab, staying close to the user is the chief guiding principle of their research. Officials at the Media Lab have noted:

[In the late 1970s] it was axiomatic among the movers and shakers in computer science that computing was not, could not, and maybe should not, be for people. As a result, computers were sensory-deprived . . . and those of us interested in computer sound and graphics were not taken seriously by mainstream computer scientists. Today, in startling contrast, such terms as "user-friendly" are worn out from repetition. It's old news now that the machines must be adapted to human ways, no matter how enormous a task that may be. Any academic, professional, or commercial undertaking that ignores this central fact of computing technology does so at its own imminent peril.[1]

In commenting on the success of the Media Lab, *Time* has noted that "the lab's unique mission is to transfer today's passive mass media, particularly TV, into flexible technologies that can respond to individual taste."[2]

These comments underscore the importance of designing products that satisfy consumer needs and usage patterns. Products should not be defined by what they do so much as by what need or desire they satisfy among the consuming public. Products that define themselves by what they do are defined too narrowly and run the risk of being surpassed in the marketplace by those that take their definitions from consumers' changing tastes and needs. Years ago, Harvard Business School Professor Theodore Levitt saw this principle as key to successful marketing of products and, thus, central to the continued life of the products. He felt that business executives who missed this point were guilty of what he called "marketing myopia." Using the example of the railroads, Levitt depicted their passing from the scene as principal people-movers in the United States because they perceived themselves as being in the railroad business rather than in the transportation business. They went on producing more trains, assuming people would always need trains for transportation. However, by failing to grow and diversify into other forms of transportation, the passenger train industry was overtaken by the airline industry, which adapted—and continues to adapt through innovative routing and fare structures—to passenger demands. Levitt notes:

They let others take customers away from them because they assumed themselves to be in the railroad business rather than in the transportation business. The reason they defined their industry wrong was because they were railroad-oriented instead of transportation-oriented; they were product-oriented instead of consumer-oriented.[3]

Like the railroad industry, it is still hard to get some newspaper publishers to consider that they are, in fact, in the information business and not in the business of producing newspapers. That is especially hard for publishers of small dailies and weeklies who may have gotten their start in the printing business. In a recent survey of newspaper editors, some took umbrage at the idea of newspapers being considered as part of "the media." This is changing, however, especially as the ranks of publishers are becoming filled with professional business and marketing managers. It is also changing out of necessity as other media companies spring up to take business away from more traditional newspapers via free-distribution weeklies, direct mail, and cable television.

The same kind of marketing myopia that infects some newspaper publishers today also affects some television executives. For decades, the television industry has been in the business of producing news and entertainment programming for the masses. As long as there were only three commercial networks, with programming going out through their affiliated stations across the country, this marketing approach seemed to work. With the rapid growth of competition, however, via cable and pay-per-view services, that mass-audience programming concept has become outdated and ineffective. The fact that audiences are now looking for narrower categories of programming and are becoming interested in programming on their timetable rather than the station's are challenges the television industry is scrambling to meet.

MEDIA MARKETING PRINCIPLES

Any successful marketing strategy must incorporate and integrate four components: (1) developing the right product, (2) at the right place [and time], (3) at the right price, and (4) with the right promotion. The failed videotex experiments of the 1980s were lacking in some of these basic principles. Involved in all of these steps is obtaining a greater understanding of the target customers and their information/entertainment needs. Harvard Business School Professor Benson Shapiro calls this "the new intimacy."[4] Rosabeth Kanter, in *The Harvard Business Review*, cites the following as key elements of a modern marketing strategy.[5]

1. *Understand who the customer is.* Managers have long differentiated between categories of recipients—the consumer versus customer. Traditionally, companies have favored one particular key relationship. Today, however, all relationships are important simultaneously; each influences the other. A

customer-oriented company must understand and involve the whole customer system.

2. *Turn customers into members.* Once the customers are identified, the effective companies are those that bring in a cross section of those customers to serve as members of focus groups. These groups, in turn, help influence any future revisions of the product. Another way of making customers into members is by doing things to increase loyalty among product users. In 1991, for example, *Time* began offering something called the *Time Insider* to subscribers. This was a special newsletter showing the story behind the story or how *Time* reporters go about getting a story.

3. *Make customers real to all employees.* Customers are largely an abstraction to employees whose jobs do not involve direct contact. This is a special problem in the news media, since reporters and editors are so often leery of making personal contact with readers and viewers because of potential conflict-of-interest situations that might arise with the need to cover stories on these people. This distancing may have contributed to some of the problems faced by the newspaper industry's fledgling videotex experiments of the early 1980s.

4. *Use customer data to benefit the customers.* Bell Atlantic's "intelligent network" strategy for basic telephone service involves storing customer preference information and automatically customizing the kind of local service the customer receives. The concept of "user modeling," long under study at places such as the MIT Media Lab, are focusing on this element by monitoring user habits and preferences and incorporating them into the design of a truly personalized electronic newspaper that may be different to each user.

5. *Keep promises by championing change.* Companies often promise to customize their products to customers or to offer special delivery or other related products. If these promises are kept, they help build customer loyalty. If they are not kept, customers will be lost. One way promises do not work is if a company jumps into a competitive war with another company without the financial ability to keep the customer service promises.

Harvard's Levitt cautions media managers and their technology supervisors against assuming that their newspaper or television station business will automatically continue to grow because they are the only ones in town who can provide information and entertainment. Levitt warns all managers:

In truth, there is no such thing as a growth industry, I believe. There are only companies organized and operated to create and capitalize on growth opportunities. Industries (or individual businesses) that assume themselves to be riding some automatic growth escalator invariably descend into stagnation. The history of every dead and dying "growth" industry shows a self-deceiving cycle of bountiful expansion and undetected decay.[6]

Levitt then identifies four conditions that usually guarantee this cycle:

1. The belief that growth is ensured by an expanding and more affluent population.
2. The belief that there is no competitive substitute for the industry's major product.
3. Too much faith in mass production and in the advantages of rapidly declining unit costs as output increases.
4. Preoccupation with a product that lends itself to carefully controlled scientific experimentation, improvement, and manufacturing cost reduction.

To any experienced media manager, Levitt's second condition—the belief there is no competition for the product in the marketplace—should come as absolutely no surprise. In an age when one hears so much about media monopolies and declining competition among daily newspapers, the larger and truer picture is that the mass media, and its more narrowly targeted units, is becoming a very crowded industry.

Levitt's third point—a love affair with research and development that is jealous of market considerations—is one that is worthy of strong consideration by media managers. He amplifies this point by noting that, in the electronics industry, the greatest danger facing executives producing the sexy new products is that infatuation with the sophisticated new products can—and does—blind managers to the fact that the consumer might not be ready for them, at least in the form developed. Again, one thinks of the failed videotex experiments of the 1980s. Such companies come perilously close to

creating the illusion that a superior product will sell itself . . . managements become top-heavy with engineers, scientists, and technical consultants. . . . Basic questions about customers and markets seldom get asked. The latter occupy a step-child status. They are recognized as existing, as having to be taken care of, but not worth very much real thought or dedicated attention. Nobody gets as excited about the customers in his own backyard as about the oil in the Sahara Desert.[7]

Lowell W. Steele, in his book *Managing Technology: The Strategic View* (McGraw-Hill, 1989), echoes this danger by citing it as a real misconception many managers have. The misconception is that technological advances have inherent value, when the reality is that the customer determines the value. Steele argues for a well-rounded, holistic view of technology within a corporation, asserting that technology managers cannot make such far-reaching decisions in isolation and that other executives, including the head of marketing, must be brought into the development process. He further warns against falling so in love with technology as to forget that customer service and profits are the basic reason for being in business.

One of the highest barriers to success in selling high-tech products is not the products, notes Alan M. Kantrow in *The Constraints of Corporate Tradition* (Harper & Row, 1988), but *paradigms* or ways of seeing the world. Innovations often require managers to rethink the way they view the world, to reconsider paradigms or develop new ones. Clearly, that is not easy. It is far easier, for example, to use 20/20 hindsight to explain why Knight-Ridder or Times-Mirror failed in their commercial videotex experiments, but it would not have been so easy to predict those failures ahead of time. Kantrow uses the example of Western Union and how it contributed to the fledgling Bell group's control of the telephone industry in 1879 by deeding over all of its telephone rights and patents to then-National Bell. An idiotic decision? Yes, in hindsight. But Western Union's paradigm in 1879 was that the pact did what it most wanted (ensuring its control of the telegraph) by guaranteeing that local telephone exchanges served a localized area and carried only voice messages—*personal* communications. All business messages that went by wire were to go by Western Union's telegraph, and all such messages did go by wire in 1879. Also, Bell agreed to pay Western Union a royalty on telephone rentals. Therefore, Bell took on all the risk and expense of a commercially unproven technology. Western Union cemented its mastery of an established and successful technology, eliminated a potential competitor, and took a nice cut off the top. A good move for Western Union— with its 1879 paradigm. The problem, notes high-tech business analyst Mark J. Estren, is that Kantrow offers no real solutions on how to break out of these constraining paradigms. Estren, however, suggests:

We cultivate our paradigms, too, and weed out the ideas we perceive as threatening them. It is from these apparent threats, however, that we will be better able to make our garden grow. High-tech managers who know this will be best poised to reap profits when they sow innovation.[8]

Estren also notes that some analysts, such as Karl and Steven Albrecht, have suggested other ways of approaching technological development to avoid at least some of the pitfalls created by faulty paradigms. The Albrechts' approach involves dividing corporate innovation into five stages: absorption, inspiration, testing, refinement, and selling. Each stage needs a role player to shepherd the new idea through that phase. So the spotter identifies the need for new responses to the environment. The inventor comes up with the creative options. The philosopher inputs the intellectual leadership needed to get the right people within the organization to sit up and take notice. The champion fights for the innovation as being useful, carrying the thinking into action. And the seller lobbies for the idea within the organization. Only if all these role players succeed will it be possible to introduce something new to the market.[9]

Donald McNamara, writing for the *Gannett Mass Media Journal*, also uses the concept of a new paradigm in describing how media managers must think in developing and marketing new technological products and services. He says this new paradigm features unparalleled consumer empowerment and choice—not just in content, but in time, place, and form. The twin elements of convergence and fragmentation have created fast-moving, dynamic media markets where the only constant is change and where traditional markets are shrinking and the real battles are for markets just beginning. "The new paradigm thus favors organizations that have the ability to adapt quickly to change, customize products, get to the market quickly and manage innovation. . . . Not surprising then that the entrepreneur is a driving force in today's media."[10] Among the modern-day entrepreneurs he cited are Ted Turner, who has led the development of the cable networks, and Chris Whittle, who has developed such innovative media services as the controversial Channel One for schools. McNamara concludes:

After operating in monopoly and quasi-monopoly markets, broadcasters, cable operators, and newspaper publishers now must face the discipline of the marketplace. For these media, the most important battles will be to revolutionize—reform is not a strong enough word—their corporate cultures and the ways they do business. They must take on entrepreneurial characteristics, not just to protect themselves from marauding entrepreneurs, but to match the newest invaders, the non-traditional media players. But in the age of star wars, many of the traditional media are still engaged in trench warfare.[11]

PROS AND CONS OF TECHNOLOGY CONSULTANTS

Because of the quickly changing technology scene, the level of existing production, and the many products to choose from and adapt, most major media are taking on technology consultants to help them navigate the waters of the high-tech world. Media managers rely on these technological soothsayers to help cut the risk involved in moving into a new venture and to choose the right equipment for their needs. When these forecasts prove accurate, the media company benefits greatly. When they are inaccurate, however, the media company suffers. Remember the Knight-Ridder example and the $55 million that company lost with its failed Viewtron venture. In 1983, the consulting firm Creative Strategies International forecast that the sale of videotex equipment and services would expand more than 90 percent annually, reaching $7 billion by 1987.[12] It did not happen, and Viewtron was abandoned by Knight-Ridder two years after commercial operations began in 1985.

Such miscalculations are more common than one might think. Analyst Herb Brody has noted that consultants often use projections provided by makers and/or sellers of the high-tech products, and those vendors routinely overstate their sales projections. "Extrapolated growth based on manufacturers' data will always be high," says Richard Arons, director of the market research firm Prognos.[13] In addition, inaccurate information also comes from scientific laboratories as well as from sales offices. "Scientists and engineers, infatuated with their technologies, sometimes delude themselves," Brody says.[14] Sometimes such false data can lead to tragedy. In the nonmedia world, for example, former Morton-Thiokol executive Roger Boisjoly has accused some top managers of his former company of intentionally misleading NASA into thinking the failed O-rings on the doomed space shuttle Challenger were safe in cold temperatures when they knew they might fail. Boisjoly said it was a management decision—not an engineering decision—to advise NASA to go ahead with the launch of the Challenger because management at Morton-Thiokol knew that was the advice NASA wanted to hear.[15]

Comments from consultants such as Ralph Finley, executive vice president of Dataquest in the late 1980s, support the belief that some managers will either hope—or even outright ask—to have the research data skewed to a position that supports their desire to proceed with risky ventures. "We regularly get pressure to say a market is bigger than it is," Finley told *High Technology Business* in 1988. "Bad news doesn't sell."[16] Other consultants have confided that self-delusion is as necessary in entering a risky business venture as it is in going into war. An army could not win, they say, unless every soldier is convinced that he is not going to be the one to get killed.

Some faulty forecasts result from consultants assuming that present conditions will continue into future years. In the case of satellite communications, most soothsayers predicted an explosion in that industry in the early 1980s, only to have the Challenger disaster put a long delay on the launching of new communications satellites. Obviously, some of these contaminating factors are out of the range of predictability, but still others are not. It is not unrealistic, for instance, to assume that market researchers should have foreseen the rampant spread of fiber optic telecommunications lines in the 1980s. These lines provide the same kind of service as communications satellites, and—starting in 1983 and 1984—the major long-distance telephone companies of MCI, AT&T, and GTE Sprint laid a nationwide web of fiber optics and took potential business away from direct broadcast satellite communications. Such developments led consultant John Varston, president of Technology Futures, to point out, "The best forecasting looks sideways as well as ahead. The things that traumatize business come from the outside."[17]

Nevertheless, technology consultants are deemed necessary, especially for managers who are not trained as engineers, as in the case of media executives who are considering ventures into the world of high-technology. In general, the better reports come from companies with full-time staff researchers, such as Dataquest, International Data Corp., and Arthur D. Little. Other companies in the high-tech consulting business include Business Communications, DataPro Research, the Gartner Group, Prognos, and the Yankee Group. In the newspaper industry, editors and publishers often seek advice on new products and systems integration from companies such as CNI Corp., Production Management Technologies, and Dewar Information Systems Corp. In addition, seminars like those sponsored by the Seybold Co. draw hundreds of media executives interested in computerized publishing systems. Industrywide, publishers, production directors, and technology supervisors attend the NNA Tech Convention held annually. This technology show and related workshops draw in newspaper executives who can huddle with hundreds of manufacturers, vendors, and consultants and hear about the wonders of assimilating high-tech products and services into the newspaper business.

THE CHALLENGE OF MANAGING CHANGE

Possibly the key challenge associated with researching, developing, and assimilating high-tech services into the news media—or any other industry—is that of managing change in an industry that would just as soon not change. Volumes have been written, and management consultants have grown rich delivering advice on how to manage change in a business. Change is a threat to many managers and workers because it represents the unknown, and people everywhere are apprehensive about the unknown. That is a fact of life from the boardrooms down to the workplace. Changes in routine, changes in the way business is conducted, changes in the way a product is defined—all these changes represent considerable discomfort for managers and employees.

In the news media, for example, anyone who worked in a newsroom during the 1970s and early 1980s saw the trepidation—and often outright anger and defiance—of reporters and editors who saw their trusty old manual typewriters (and then trusty new electric typewriters) taken away and replaced by electronic word processors, which newspeople still refer to as VDTs (video display terminals). Many journalists refused to be impressed by the future and chose instead to look backwards and long for their outmoded typing machines, which could not do half of what the new word processors could do. The same grief could be found in television newsrooms as late as the 1990s when their typewriters were also replaced by high-tech word processors. It is ironic that in a high-tech industry such as television such a scenario should occur.

A more problematic change for journalists—and many media managers—to assimilate has been in the shift from producing news content that reporters and editors feel is important for the readers to have to the concept of marketing the news. The program launched by Gannett called News 2000 is an example of the remolding of newspapers to respond better to perceived reader interests. In addition, Knight-Ridder has launched a kind of "customer- obsession" campaign that came to fruition in the experiment of a newly formatted and newly defined daily newspaper in Boca Raton, Florida, called the *News*. That newspaper may represent the state of the art in a reader-friendly newspaper that tries to deliver a quick read of the stories readers find interesting, in a full-color and easy-to-find fashion, and mix in some in-depth material on contemporary issues as well. Similar attention to reader interest has been shown by *USA Today* and the *Orange County Register*, both of which break the mold of traditional newspapers.

Such concepts have taken time for journalists to swallow, but there is evidence that attitudes are changing. For instance, Susan Miller, Scripps Howard's vice-president/editorial said in 1992 that many editors believe that reader-driven newspapers can be a "higher calling." She notes that the vast majority of staffers are becoming accustomed to the idea that "newspapers are to be of service to readers and are not staffed by a Brahmin class that was chosen to lecture the population."[18] The shift in thinking has taken its toll, however, and several top-drawer editors have quit in the process, often over disagreements with publishers on how far news marketing should go. Two such editors are Katharine Fanning, formerly of the *Christian Science Monitor*, and Bill Kovach, formerly of the *Atlanta Constitution*. Both stated publicly that when business and marketing executives start calling shots in the newsroom, then the journalistic product becomes compromised.

But when it comes to high-tech changes, media executives are often too quick to point to past failures such as Viewtron as proof that there is no future for electronic publishing of newspapers. One senses they breathe a sigh of great relief in the process, being as reluctant to turn loose of their newsprint products as their older reporters were to turn loose of their manual typewriters. Some editors, however, move beyond looking to history as the only guide to the future. Executives at the *Kansas City Star* and *Forth Worth Star-Telegram*, for instance, launched into high-tech ventures in the early 1990s despite the ghosts of Viewtron and Gateway. As mentioned earlier, the *Star-Telegram* calls its electronic information service StarText and targets it at the generation just coming out of school who are very computer literate. Gerry Barker, marketing director of StarText, says newspapers must keep advancing, building on the failures of the past instead of being scared off by them. He explains it this way:

People have misjudged it (the appetite for new technology among consumers). It's a social revolution that's happening out there. You can't throw dollars and technology at this and expect it to hatch. It's evolutionary. Just because we built a few Edsels doesn't mean the car is wrong.[19]

Media observer Doug Underwood notes that even Knight-Ridder executives are "planning for the day—which they see happening within this decade—when these multimedia newspapers will be available on portable, touch-sensitive, flat-panel displays."[20]

An example of a company that is more than one hundred years old and has channeled change for optimal results is the NCR Corporation. Since only one-half of 1 percent of all corporations 100 years old or more still survive, the age and continued existence of this company is significant.[21] NCR is thriving in a completely different environment from the one in which the company conducted most of its business over the decades. NCR has been called a "grand old sire in the youthful computer industry," but also a company for whom change is a challenge that is gladly embraced. This company that began making steel cash registers and then mechanical adding machines now is one of the top dozen computer makers in America. NCR chairman Charles Exley noted recently that his company has spent most of its years servicing the office equipment industry, yet has seen a big portion of that industry—the accounting machine business—go from a huge market representing more than half of NCR's business, to nothing. The reason: interactive direct-processing systems took the place of the old accounting machine.

Exley predicts that in the 1990s, America will see changes in computer software that are as dramatic as the hardware changes the country witnessed in the 1980s. Another change coming is that so-called fourth-generation computer languages will become a major factor in the marketplace. If this occurs, it will increase customers' ability to put products such as NCR's to work in their businesses. This new computer language will increase programmer productivity from four to ten times.[22]

Increasingly in the future, companies that fail to keep up with technological changes will disappear, probably becoming absorbed by other larger and more innovative companies. To keep this from happening, Exley urges companies to spend enough money on productive development and to be aware of what is happening and likely to happen in technology. Exley advises:

It's important to put research and development dollars into the right areas, first from the standpoint of market opportunity, and second from the standpoint of the right technology for that market opportunity. You also have to understand the implications the technology has for your customers. That's sometimes the greatest challenge—to know what will be the big opportunities for a client.[23]

Finding those "right areas," however, can be a full-time job for at least one or two managers in the corporation. Companies such as NCR also value decisions that are made at the lowest levels in the organization, where the information that bears on the decision is available and where the results of the decision can be measured. And they also value measured risk taking. Exley acknowledges that it is hard to balance the need to gamble on rapidly changing technology versus financial security, but he says the risk needs to be taken when it is perceived as having a good chance of success. And he warns, "Product development programs cannot be turned on and off and still be effective; once one is launched, you have to press ahead. A short-sighted management might attempt to cut back development programs quite dramatically in hard times."[24]

The best companies are those that value planned change, which always involves specific goals such as higher productivity, employee acceptance of new technology, greater employee motivation, more innovative employee behaviors, increased market share, and so on. Basic to these and other improvement goals are two underlying objectives: (1) to improve the ability of an organization to adapt to changes in its environment, and (2) to change patterns of managerial and employee thinking and behavior. To a great extent, a company's ability to move forward and embrace the challenge of change depends on the creativity of the organizational culture. It is no wonder that companies such as Apple, Microsoft, TCI, AT&T, and Hewlett-Packard have been at the leading edge of change over the past several years. Each of these companies has an organizational culture that not only accepts change, but actively pursues it. The following are a sample of the changes that today's media organizations are facing:[25]

1. Moving from an old emphasis on capital, low cost, volume, and automation to a new emphasis that values people, fast product change-over, quality, and responsiveness.

2. Moving from an old emphasis on mass markets, mass advertising, and lengthy market tests to a new emphasis on fragmented markets, market creation, small-scale testing, and speed.

3. Moving from centralized financial control to decentralized control with high spending authority at local levels.

4. Moving from centralized information control to decentralized data processing and personal computer proliferation.

5. Moving from centralized control on research and development with an emphasis on big projects to an emphasis on activities and functions as hotbeds for innovation, and on a "portfolio" of small projects and speed.

One of the most vexing problems of technological change is the rapid rate of high-tech product obsolescence. Fast-changing preferences by consumers, joined with so many technological changes and innovations, have shortened the life cycle of many goods and services in the high-tech field. It has been estimated that approximately 55 percent of the items sold today did not exist ten years ago, and that of the products sold then about 40 percent have been removed from the shelf. In the field of consumer electronics, a product often becomes obsolete in as little as six months. So, when product life cycles become shorter, organizations must be able to shorten production lead times. In the best of times, predicting which products a company should go forward with commercially represents a daunting challenge for company or project managers. When coupled with resistance to change, which is generally present in most organizations, managing change is not an easy task.

SUMMARY

Communications technology is advancing at an amazing speed. Were it left to technology alone, America's homes would now be using interactive, multimedia forms of media technology on a widespread basis and would be getting their news and information over the same kinds of vehicles. But technology alone is not enough to make the new electronic advances operational. Desires and needs of the marketplace, coupled with a familiarity with how to use the new technological gadgetry, are also necessary to get the products into the hands of the users. In fact, these marketplace considerations comprise the most daunting obstacle facing developers of the new communications products and services.

The past is littered with examples of failed services and products which did not adequately take into account the desires and needs of the target customers. Still among the unanswered questions, in fact, are just what types of communications products and services the public wants, what they want to do with them, and how much they would be willing to pay for them. These are the questions that companies—indeed the entire communications industry—are seeking to answer.

NOTES

1. *The Media Laboratory, 5th Anniversary* (Cambridge, MA: MIT, 1990), 5.
2. Ibid., 11.
3. Theodore Levitt, "Marketing Myopia," *Harvard Business Review*, September/October 1975, 1 of reprint.
4. Rosabeth Kanter, "Even Closer to the Customer," *Harvard Business Review*, January/February 1991, 9.
5. Kanter, "Closer to the Customer," 10.
6. Levitt, "Myopia," 1.
7. Ibid.

8. Mark J. Estren, "Escaping the Paradigm," essay review of *The Constraints of Corporate Tradition*, by Alan M. Kantrow, *High Technology Business*, July 1988, 18.

9. Ibid.

10. Donald McNamara, "At the Front: Clash of Cultures," *Media Studies Journal*, Spring 1992, 28.

11. Ibid., 35.

12. Herb Brody, "Sorry, Wrong Number," *High Technology Business*, September 1988, 25.

13. Ibid.

14. Ibid., 26.

15. "The Public Mind: The Truth About Lies," PBS Television Series reported by Bill Moyers, November 1989.

16. Brody, "Wrong Number," 26.

17. Ibid.

18. Doug Underwood, "Reinventing the Media: The Newspapers' Identity Crisis," *Columbia Journalism Review*, March/April 1992, 26.

19. Ibid.

20. Ibid.

21. Don Hellriegel, John W. Slocum, Jr., and Richard W. Woodman, *Organizational Behavior*, 5th ed. (St. Paul, MN: West Publishing, 1989), 536.

22. "NCR Chairman Charles Exley: On Managing Change," *High Technology Business*, May 1988, 46.

23. Ibid., 48.

24. Ibid., 49.

25. Hellriegel, *Organizational Behavior*, 535.

7
· · · · ·

Multimedia's Impact on Advertising

While a tremendous amount of research has gone into the development of interactive multimedia products and services, surprisingly little research has gone into how the new media will affect advertising and what role advertising will play in helping to finance the new media programming and services. Possibly this is because the advertising industry is so concerned with the here and now and with advertising response that can be measured. Multimedia is not yet upon us, and those portions of it that are do not necessarily lend themselves to the same kind of audience measurement that existing media advertising does.

An even larger question is how the relationship of advertising to consumers might be changed in an era when viewers can conveniently by-pass any form of programming—including commercials—that they do not want to see. Ever since the formidable advertising challenges of the remote-control unit, multichannel cable systems, and VCR came on the scene, the advertising industry has been responding to the new concepts of "zapping"—switching from commercials to other programming—and "zipping"—taping programs for later viewing and then fast-forwarding through commercials. The coming age of interactive multimedia promises to increase the viewer's ability to by-pass commercials to a new and threatening height for the advertising industry. For example, in the case of remote-control units, technology has now brought about a device called the *intelligent remote* or *universal remote*. This is a handheld unit that the viewer will actually be able to program to—among other things—automatically scan television channels like a radio scanner and to switch automatically to another channel when a commercial is encountered. Mitsubishi has already developed a VCR, called AutoCut, which can automatically edit out commercials. It utilizes a technique of audio signal differentiation. Devices such as this will make avoidance of commercials an easier task in the future, and advertisers are worried.

Nevertheless, the past few years have seen growing interest by advertising agencies in the developing new media and its impact on them. Agencies are starting to heed the warning of people such as Rick Parkhill, president of Infotext and a consultant on interactive media, who says, "Agencies that don't take the time to understand the new technologies are going to be woefully behind. Look what happened to agencies that ignored cable."[1] In another few years, however, most agencies—however reluctantly—will need to learn about and understand the new media because when this technology catches on, multimedia vehicles will be just another option in the media-buy mix that clients will want to consider.

SOME ADVERTISING SCENARIOS

Futurist Alvin Toffler paints a scenario of what advertising might look like in a few years as the age of interactive multimedia becomes operational:

You decide to purchase a camera. A small black box that sits atop your television set activates your idea and transmits it over a network. The box asks you to input some specifications that you require of this camera, and all the camera manufacturers who are interested in selling you one display their products to you. Through your remote-control keypad you are able to query the camera makers, scan the various cameras from a variety of angles on your screen, and read the information they provide over the screen. Then, possibly, the camera makers engage in a kind of electronic auction so you are ensured of getting the best price. It is comparable to what happens when governments take sealed bids for products and services. Should you decide to buy, you respond on your remote-control keypad, and your checking account or credit card is automatically debited. The production plant is then signaled electronically, and your camera is sent by a package delivery service so you receive it the next day, or if need be, your special-order camera is made for you and then sent to your home.[2]

How long it might take for such a scenario to take place is anyone's guess at this point. However, the technology required for such a transaction already exists. The popularity of such home shopping networks as QVC show that this type of purchasing strikes a responsive chord with viewers at home, and some elements of this scenario already exist on the QVC network. You don't even need a remote-control keypad to interact—just your telephone.

This kind of scenario focuses on the shopping process from the decision to purchase onward and on the means by which home shoppers might execute that decision. It undoubtedly involves either some shopping network or interactive computer software. But what about general advertising of products as we know it today on television? Will there be any room for it in the age of the new personalized media?

The Magazine Model

For a model on which multimedia advertising might be constructed, one could look at the specialized magazine that so dominates the industry today. Similarities between the specialized magazine industry and the coming age of multimedia include the following:

• Both serve highly fragmented audiences. There are thousands of specialized magazine titles in existence today, and most cater to a small, fine-tuned target audience. Such will be the case in the age of multimedia; this is already evident with the variety of cable channels and specialized networks. Magazine advertising is often built on the premise that a quality audience—one with appropriate demographics that is committed to the issue, profession, or avocation represented by the magazine—is as good or better to advertisers than a much larger audience that is, by and large, lukewarm to the issue and related advertising.

• Both focus on narrower audience demographics by presenting a media product totally devoted to a specific idea, interest, taste, vocation, or avocation. There are already medical channels, courtroom networks, learning networks, cooking channels, and nature channels and networks, and as time goes on, these special-interest channels and networks will be subdivided into even narrower interests just as the magazine industry has done over the years.

• As this kind of programming specialization matures and captivates viewers who hold deep interest in these subjects, advertising will become a complement to entertainment and information content of the program and will be responsible for bringing in a certain segment of the audience. It is no secret that avid readers of magazines such as *Popular Photography*, for instance, pay as much attention to the advertising in the magazine as they do the content. Additionally, the magazine—if the reader deems it an expert source on photography—will connect its editorial credibility with the credibility of the advertising in the publication. Thus, in several ways, the advertising in a well-respected, specialized magazine becomes an extension of the editorial content for the committed reader. One aspect of the magazine is almost as important as the other to many readers. There is no reason to think the same thing will not happen as multimedia channels continue to multiply, fragment audiences, and offer more narrow-interest programming.

What seems fairly apparent is that general-interest advertising will have a difficult time finding a niche in this new market of niches. Outside of the few broadcast networks that might remain and the local station affiliates, there may not be much room for the general, mass audience-oriented advertising that we know today. A comparison might be drawn between this era and that of the late 1960s when conditions began changing for the magazine industry, as it moved from a general-interest to special-interest medium. Since 1972, more magazines have sought more clearly defined reading publics than ever before. Even the remaining mass-circulation magazines such as *Woman's Day* and *Family Circle* have clearly defined target audiences and offer them appropriate content and advertising.

The television industry experienced this special-interest phenomenon as cable television grew from infancy to maturity in the 1980s. Over the past few years, the cable industry has logged double-digit increases in advertising revenues, and that growth is expected to continue.[3] Additionally, the cable networks have increased the number of categories they are selling. At the end of the 1980s, for instance, automotive advertising accounted for about 40 percent of all cable ad sales. By 1993, however, automotive ads made up only 15–20 percent of cable sales, while other categories such as health care, restaurants, and services such as legal and accounting began to dominate.[4] Cable networks offer their advertising clients something that broadcast networks cannot: sharply defined target audiences and micromarketing and target-audience delivery of commercials. One cable network, for instance, USA, is developing original programming that is targeted at adults aged 18 to 49, families, and working women. Another network, Lifetime, is exploiting its female demographics with appropriate programming. In one season in 1993, for example, Lifetime offered programming with a "women in politics" theme. This included a two-hour special on women's issues and an originally produced movie about a female president.

Buyers nationwide seem to be embracing special-interest programming, and that is just what multimedia can offer. With money tight, advertisers are looking at the narrowest and best audience demographics they can find, even if they can only access those targets via new, alternative media products.

At issue today is whether the traditional broadcast networks of ABC, NBC, and CBS can offer even the so-called critical mass many advertisers want. Some media observers believe advertisers still want network television's unique ability to reach a critical mass of viewers in one fell swoop. If total broadcast network share is hovering at 60 percent, as the industry claims, then advertisers are still interested in the networks, or so the thinking goes. Some observers, however, such as former ABC advertising executive Bill Sternberg, see the numbers and their implications for broadcasting differently. Sternberg writes, "the audiences that the (broadcast) networks now deliver are not a critical mass. The critical mass is the viewers the networks don't reach.[5]

Sternberg notes that between 1983 and 1993, the three networks' combined viewer average fell by 25.5 percent, although U.S. television households increased by 14.1 percent. How much more are advertisers going to be willing to pay to reach fewer and fewer viewers at any one time? Advertisers realize that a 60 percent *share* of the audience is not the same as a 60 percent *rating*. The latter refers to the percentage of homes with televisions, while the former refers to the percentage of viewers using their televisions. To get a critical mass of audience, advertisers are going to have to complement their commercials on the broadcast networks (with less money going to them as they continue to lose audience share) with advertising on the more specialized channels offered by cable and multimedia.

Interactive Adland?

Two studies conducted by advertising agencies early in the 1990s made a valiant attempt at demystifying the potential of multimedia and tried to predict what the new media will mean for advertising clients. One study was done by the Bozell agency, and the second came from Backer Spielvogel Bates.

The Backer study concluded that by the year 2002, advertising will have adapted to its new multimedia environments, but that it will be harder for a product to maintain a high profile in the marketplace.[6] Even though it will be simpler to identify target audiences and to discern which media are being used, the level of technology will make it equally as simple for viewers to tune out commercials. As a result, the Backer study notes, advertisers must become even more creative at getting viewers to interact with commercials. The study predicts that interactive television will appeal to about one-third of adults. Interestingly, about 20 percent of all adults would accept advertising on interactive TV systems, especially if such inclusion would help keep the costs down for subscribers.[7]

The Bozell study predicted that it will take about 5 to 10 years for interactive multimedia products to become part of the media landscape and, therefore, part of the media mix as advertising agencies view it. The study finds, however, that traditional media will continue to appeal to a sizeable section of the viewing audience.[8] Interactive television systems will have to provide added incentives to get viewers to watch the commercials they could just as easily zap. Coupons and promotions are two such incentives, and the Bozell study predicts they will be used heavily on the interactive channels.

According to Gary Arlen, president of Arlen Communications, Inc., a Bethesda, Maryland, research firm that specializes in interactive media, 15 percent of households will possess some kind of access to interactive TV by 1998.[9]

PPV AND VIDEO-ON-DEMAND CHALLENGES

Two high-profile features of interactive television are predicted to be pay-per-view (PPV) movies and special events and video-on-demand programming. PPV has already been introduced to American television viewers through such events as the 1992 Summer Olympics. Unfortunately for NBC, which offered the complementary PPV programming in addition to its regular network programming, not too many viewers were interested enough to pay the steep price NBC charged to view the events in their entirety over PPV cable. This has also been the case with other PPV ventures, as most of the events command only single-digit ratings and may come in below 1 percent.[10] But research indicates that if the right events are chosen for PPV and if the price is right viewers will be interested. As a result, PPV figures prominently in the minds of those companies developing interactive systems.

Incorporating advertising into movies and events that viewers pay premium prices for will not be easy. Some PPV executives, however, still think it can be done. Jim English, senior vice president of programming at Viewer's Choice, a PPV channel, believes sponsorships might be one answer. For instance, Time Warner Sports's TVKO PPV boxing company signed Kentucky Fried Chicken to sponsor a fight between George Foreman and Tommy Morrison in 1993. Sponsorship usually involves on-air billboards, signage at the event, and some value-added material, according to analyst Michael Burgi.[11] It may even involve a 30-second spot in the event, but not much more. Another PPV effort that Viewer's Choice has offered is "Princeton Review," which offers viewers study guides to the SAT exams taken by high schoolers. For $20, buyers can get a program that gives tips on how to improve SAT scores, and the program advertises a more expensive and complete course that viewers can purchase.[12]

Video-on-demand services offer viewers the ability to choose and control what they want to see and when they want to see it. In essence, this is the premise on which much of interactive television is based. The insertion of commercials into video-on-demand programming is problematic, but maybe not as much as some might think. For example, research conducted by the ElectroniCast Corporation in 1992 revealed that while 23 percent of U.S. households expressed extreme interest in subscribing to video-on-demand programming the interest level increased slightly to 24 percent with the introduction of a 30-second commercial. Viewers apparently felt that the addition of the advertising would help lower their own personal cost of subscribing to the video-on-demand service.[13] If commercials could be tailored to the suspected lifestyles and preferences of viewers watching particular kinds of specialized programming, then research shows that 53 percent of U.S. households would be likely to view such advertising.[14]

THE PROMISE AND CHALLENGE OF HDTV

At first glance, HDTV would offer nothing but opportunities for advertising. The sharper resolution and higher quality pictures enhances any visual presentation and will make commercials more pleasing to watch. Acceptance of HDTV is predicted to be especially noticeable among younger groups, and it is these groups who tend to be better educated and possess higher household income levels. In addition, acceptance of HDTV may be seen among the over 35 and over 55 age groupings.[15]

The impact of HDTV on advertising should be profound. With the additional bandwidth that digital transmission (HDTV signals will be digitally based) brings, there will probably be an increase in the number of cable networks, and each of them will be competing for viewers. For advertisers, this will mean more outlets, but also more competition. In addition, as mentioned before, these cable networks will be more specialized in programming focus and will appeal to narrow demographic audiences more effectively. Audiences, as a result, will fragment even further.

As to the challenge that HDTV will offer advertisers, it may surface in the production of television commercials.

Because HDTV offers vividly detailed images and delivers compact disc digital sound to television, creative personnel will have to be conscious of every detail of the commercial set and the required pros used in the production of the commercial. The same is true for audio. The slightest sniffle will be heard by viewers.[16]

In short, HDTV technology will require the highest quality standards of commercial production. This will mean more expense to produce television commercials in the future and those commercials seen by smaller audiences.

COMPUTERS AS AN ADVERTISING MEDIUM

At present, computer terminals are competing with television sets for the time of their users. One cannot view both screens at the same time. In the age of multimedia, however, the two media may be merged into one, and you will be able to run computer software in the television, or telecomputer. Either way, whether computers and television merge or not, computers and software have opened up a new medium for advertising. For example, Prodigy Services Co. joined *USA Today* in 1992 to become an online classified advertising service. To place an ad, advertisers simply type their copy directly into a PC. Advertisers may then use toll-free numbers, the mail, or their own online Prodigy mailbox to receive replies.[17] Other newspapers have been experimenting with electronic services, realizing that the Bell operating companies would be permitted to enter the electronic information publishing business.

Another unique form of computer advertising has been developed in Great Britain. Some observers refer to it as "invisible advertising" because it is so unobrusive. The medium is the computer video game, and advertising receives in-game exposure when a brand name is reduced to bits and bytes of memory to form the backdrop or even an integral part of the game. It could develop into an important outlet for advertising, especially children's advertising, since computer and video game penetration is so strong (in England PCS and video games are in 30 percent of all households).

In 1992, Coca-Cola teamed up with video-game giant Sega to appear on its video game Barcelona Olympics. The game features athletes running alongside Coke advertising signage and beneath a Coke blimp. In other game ventures, the linkage is taken even further. For instance, in the game James Pond II, the hero has to collect Penguin candy bars to proceed through the game. In another venture in England, Smith Crisps paid to have Colin Curly, the canine spokesman for its Quavers snack brand, play a starring role in the computer game Pushover. The game is being played by over one million children. Many of the players are among Quavers' core target market of 8 to 12 year olds.[18]

According to analysts of this type of advertising, the key is to weave in the advertising as part of the game, or at least the scenery, but not to make it obvious advertising. The other danger is to make it so subliminal that audiences will protest and accuse advertising of attempting to brainwash the young players.

THE POPULARITY OF HOME SHOPPING

Earlier in this book, home shopping networks were discussed. It is appropriate to again mention their popularity because these networks feature programming that is almost totally advertising. As such, the home shopping networks offer an expanding media outlet for advertising agencies and their clients. The degree of acceptance by viewers of such networks as QVC and the Home Shopping Network has risen dramatically over the past few years.

The concept has attained such a high profile that R. H. Macy & Co., the nation's 100-store retail giant, announced in 1993 that it would launch yet another retailing venture. Macy's announced it would team up with Don Hewitt, executive producer of "60 Minutes," and Tom Leahy, former CBS president, both of whom add a high degree of television expertise to the project. Still another partner is Cablevision Systems Corp., which brings the muscle needed to get the home shopping venture on good cable systems around the country. For Macy's it means that if the venture is successful it can hold the line on costs because it would probably not need to open more stores around the country in order to grow. It would simply use television to increase its profile and to move more products at the same time.

Macy's estimates that the channel will bring 15–20 million viewers into the television "stores" in the first year. Additionally, the concept of interactivity over television could mean that consumers can shop for any product line at any time and never leave their home.[19] There is a real challenge here for local advertising media, however. If the venture proves successful and if other large retail chains decide to sell merchandise over shopping channels instead of opening more local stores, then local media could lose a lot of future advertising.

It is still undetermined as to how successful home shopping via television will actually be in the future, but for now, the indicators appear positive as witnessed by the success of the QVC Network and Home Shopping Network. Within a few years, if these indicators continue, home shopping channels could change the way Americans shops and also how they watch television. At present, QVC is bringing in the biggest retailers and fashion designers, including Diane Von Furstenberg and Saks Fifth Avenue.[20]

In effect, QVC is the preliminary test program for video retailing. Obvious limitations for electronic shopping are that (1) one cannot try on a dress or suit when it appears on television, (2) there is an image problem for some more affluent demographics when it comes to home shopping channels because these channels have been appealing more to less affluent demographics; and (3) home shopping networks have a certain shelf life that is shorter than other forms of advertising.[21] There is also the reality that electronic shopping is such a new form of shopping that many Americans have yet to be introduced to it, and it will take some time before they feel comfortable with it. Shopping, too, has always been social outings for many people who enjoy getting out either alone or with a friend, mingling with others at the mall, and wandering through the brightly colored stores. Many stores, such as Brookstones and Sharper Image allow customers to try out innovative products right in the store, regardless of whether they buy them or not. These and other retailers are creating their own brand of interactivity, and for hands-on use of the product, it beats any interactivity television could offer.

Despite its current limitations, electronic shopping seems here to stay. The market could quadruple to sales of $10 billion by the year 2000.[22] More importantly, home shopping channels are forming the vanguard of wide-scale interactive television, albeit on a crude level. To interact, the viewer must pick up the telephone and call operators who are always standing by. But purer forms of interaction are just around the corner.

INFOMERCIALS

One way to avoid the viewer's predisposition to escape commercials is to make those commercials as interesting as other programming. Some producers have been trying to do just that, and there is growing evidence that their efforts are succeeding. They are succeeding with a kind of hybrid program that walks the line between a talk show format and an extended commercial. This type of commercial is known as an *infomercial*, and they are increasing in number and popularity. Some of the first infomercials were seen late at night in 30-minute time slots, which were purchased by promoters of the product or service. Most often, these infomercials sold seminars, books, and tapes of allegedly successful real estate entrepreneurs who wanted to show viewers how they could get rich quick with little or no investment (other than the few hundred dollars it took to purchase the complete instructional course). Today, these infomercials run the gamut from programs featuring well-known actors and actresses discussing the benefits of golf clubs, cosmetics, and psychic consultants, to seminars and books on how to enjoy more loving relationships.

As as medium, infomercials accounted for $750 million in sales in the early 1990s.[23] Even ABC TV experimented with a program called "Nitecap," a new late-night infomercial concept hosted by Robin Leach, popular host for "Lifestyles of the Rich and Famous." In "Nitecap," Leach presides over what has been called "a kind of transactional salon."[24] In this format, celebrities and other personalities promoting their products and services chat with Leach on an attractive set, while paid, attractive extras mill around in the background. In essence, viewers have been asked to attend a fashionable late night party where all the favors are on sale as the 800 numbers flash on the screen and coupons are offered as added viewing incentive. In early 1993, "Nitecap" was so popular in some of its test markets that it actually led the ratings for its time slots.[25] Other popular infomercial entries have been Tony Robbins's *PERSONAL POWER*, *The Principal Secret* with Victoria Principal, and *The Kathy Smith Fat Burning System*.

Possibly the secret of these newly formatted infomercials is that they combine elements of popular talk shows featuring well-known faces in beautiful settings and direct-market home television shopping, where ordering the products and services offered is as easy as picking up the phone. Like other types of late-night media programming, such as radio call-in shows, these social gabfests greet insomniacs and other night people with friendly faces and urge the viewer to join in the fun by using the telephone.

THE ROLE OF INFORMATION AGENT

Some prognosticators are boldly predicting the demise of advertising-financed media altogether. While traditionally mass media have consisted of editorial or entertainment content and advertising, some believe the new order will be to split these two types of content apart completely. The thinking is that, in an age of greater viewer control over programming, few if any would want to watch a commercial when they could watch something more entertaining or informative.

A question that arises from this type of prediction, however, is this: If many viewers no longer watch commercials, how will they learn about the advantages or disadvantages of products and services they wish to purchase? The answer, according to futurists such as James H. Snider is to be found in the *information agent*. Snider says this impartial information provider will benefit consumers greatly because the product information they receive today is biased because it is brought to them by the same people who make or promote the product. Therefore, it is promotional information instead of impartial consumer information.[26] With the advent of such technologies as multimedia and automatic billing, however, it will be possible for viewers to turn to an unbiased information source, as many do now with publications such as *Consumer's Digest* or *Consumer Reports*. The convergence of all major media into one digital medium could bring *Consumer Reports* and other publications like it online to the personal telecomputer, making the access product information convenient for the user. Automatic billing can also help users purchase information about products and services, since the telephone company provides an all-inclusive bill for information transactions each month. Many television viewers already take advantage of this kind of automatic billing, when they order PPV movies via the phone and then are billed by the telephone company, who then shares that revenue with the PPV network.

About the future of information agents, Snider observes:

Information Age shoppers will buy more products from their homes and fewer from retail stores. As the quality of information entering the home improves, consumers will feel more comfortable buying more things without leaving home. . . . More and more, the consumer will be purchasing directly from the manufacturer (over television) with the purchasing information gathered not from the local retailer, but from independent consumer advisers.[27]

SUMMARY

Like other pieces of the multimedia puzzle, the advertising piece is still being crafted to fit into place. At the present time, there is not enough information to know with any certainty what role advertising will play in interactive multimedia. One thing is certain, however: there should be a significant role for advertising. Creators of the new media products and services realize it is too valuable to leave out and that it will form much of the basis for financing the media, as it does today. It may form less of that basis than it does for current broadcast television, however. Instead, a more realistic assumption is that both advertising and subscription fees will together provide the financing base for the new media in much the same way as it does today for cable networks. In order to take advantage of the new media, however, advertising agencies must spend more time researching its capabilities and the best ways in which advertising can use the new media to deliver the demographics their clients want and need.

It is clear that the new media will fragment the media audience further than it ever has been fragmented before. This will be an opportunity as well as a challenge for advertisers who like the idea of narrow target audiences, but who also need to appeal to a large number of consumers. Still, with the specialized magazine industry as a model, there is no reason to assume that specialized television cannot become an advertising success as well.

Another challenge lies in the high-quality images that HDTV will provide: Commercials will have to be produced at high standards, and this will entail more funds spent on production. The results will be much more appealing for viewers, however, and it is hoped that the greater pulling power of these attractive commercials will make the higher production costs worth it.

NOTES

1. Hanna Liebman, "The Microchip Is the Message," *MediaWeek*, November 2, 1992, 29.
2. Ibid., 25.
3. Lisa Marie Petersen, "Cable: Targeted Audiences Help Break New Categories," *Media Outlook*, September 14, 1992, 50.
4. Ibid.
5. Bill Sternberg, "A Theory of Critical Mass," *MediaWeek*, May 10, 1993, 12.
6. Hanna Liebman, "2002: Interactive Adland?" *MediaWeek*, May 17, 1993, 14.
7. Ibid.
8. Ibid.
9. Ibid.

10. Michael Burgi, "Ads on Pay-Per-View? Maybe," *MediaWeek*, April 21, 1993, 27.

11. Ibid.

12. Ibid.

13. "Technology Projections: 2001 (Part 2)," *Direct Marketing*, June 1992, 45.

14. Ibid.

15. Ibid., 48.

16. Ibid.

17. "Technology Projections: 2001 (Part 1)," *Direct Marketing*, May 1992, 25.

18. Mat Toor, "When TV Advertising Means Playing the Game," *Marketing*, April 30, 1992, 24.

19. Hanna Liebman, "Macy's Decision to Try Home Shopping Viewed as a Worthy but Risky Venture," *MediaWeek*, June 7, 1993, 4.

20. Frederic M. Biddle, "Retailing's Future Vision?" *Boston Sunday Globe*, 78.

21. Ibid.

22. Ibid.

23. Andrew Susman, "Switching the Channel," *Direct Marketing*, January 1993, 44.

24. Ibid., 45.

25. Ibid.

26. James H. Snider, "Shopping in the Information Age," *The Futurist*, November-December 1992, 15.

27. Ibid., 15–16.

8
• • • • •

Legal and Ethical Implications

Since the new media that will deliver turbonews and entertainment fall under the heading of the electronic media, they are subject to the jurisdiction of the federal government and, in the case of the cable television industry, local governments, as well. The new media face certain operating restrictions and must deal within certain legal parameters that lawmakers have set for them. In addition to these existing laws, there are several sticky legal issues, such as a possible invasion of privacy, that lawmakers must deal with concerning the newer, more sophisticated forms of media. For example, television is able not only to deliver a huge supply of information as events are actually occurring, but also has the capability of monitoring the personal lifestyle patterns of individual viewers in order to create a more individualized product. As a result, the government is obliged to consider when and how it should step in with some form of regulation or else face a kind of Orwellian nightmare of Big Brother run amok. This chapter deals with how far technology and its marketers should be allowed to go in encroaching on rights that Americans have traditionally held sacred.

CURRENT BROADCAST AND CABLE LEGISLATION

From the early beginnings of radio and television, American lawmakers have believed that the broadcast industry should be regulated by the federal government. The Radio Act of 1927 was the first such regulation, followed seven years later by an expanded Communications Act of 1934, which created the FCC. That act was rewritten and updated in the 1970s to reflect more contemporary issues and the arrival of television as a powerful force in American society. Since that rewrite, some provisions, such as the so-called Fairness Doctrine requiring equal time for opposing views, have largely been gutted from the act.

The premise of the earlier regulatory acts has been that the radio and television industries utilize a precious, scarce, and public resource when they send their programming over the airwaves and a limited number of frequencies on the broadcast spectrum. Because this spectrum is in the public domain and because, without regulation, chaos would ensue among many would-be broadcasters, the feeling has been that the government should regulate this broadcast spectrum and issue licenses to those who would use it. Since the advent of cable and its growing popularity in America, however, the theory of the limited number of frequencies has been brought into question. Where there were only a few channels possible in a television market, now there is virtually an unlimited supply of channels because of coaxial cable and developing fiber optic technology. Should the assumptions used to create earlier broadcast legislation still be used today?

Throughout the 1970s and 1980s, debate has centered around the issue of regulation. On the one side are those lawmakers who favor regulation of the broadcast industry, and they cite the reasons traditionally given for such regulation: broadcast stations use free of charge a public commodity in the airwaves, and so these license holders should be required to operate "in the public interest." On the other side are those favoring deregulation, and they say that, ultimately, it should be the consumers of broadcast programming—the viewers and listeners—who define the "public interest." When consumers talk, by turning their dials, stations have to listen or face drops in ratings and resulting lower advertising revenues. The public thus makes up a powerful and influential group of regulators.

Thorny questions always arise, however, when contemplating deregulation of broadcasting: If the industry is deregulated, then who gets the licenses to operate broadcast stations? Who gives out those licenses and on what basis? It is a fact that there can only be a few broadcast operators in any television or radio market. In traditional broadcast stations, there are still a limited number of frequencies on the broadcast spectrum and someone must decide who gets to use them. So, if there is no regulation or requirements for operators to obtain and keep their licenses, how will they be handed out? One idea is to have an auction in which would-be license holders bid for the privilege of owning broadcast licenses (which often are seen as a license to make money because of the popularity of broadcasting). But if we are to say that only the wealthy should be allowed to receive broadcast licenses, doesn't that create a more serious ethical question about who is allowed to own television and radio stations?

The result of these issues and concerns is a rather fuzzy regulatory policy on the part of the federal government. The FCC supports deregulation with its rulings, while Congress—which must listen closer to voters—seems to be enacting regulation on some parts of the television industry, as with the Cable Act of 1992, discussed later. Add to this ambiguity the newer, more sophisticated media forms that are coming online and the uncertainty of lawmakers as to what kind of telecommunications policy to install, and one has a mixture of legal theories, rulings, and deregulation actions that will take some time to coalesce into a synergistic whole that makes sense—if that ever happens at all.

Nevertheless, there is an existing body of laws and regulations that the broadcast and cable industries must follow. Some of the major regulations are discussed in the following paragraphs.

BROADCAST REGULATIONS

The FCC is the federal agency charged with regulating the broadcast industry as well as the cable industry. Congress can still pass laws affecting the industry, but it is the FCC that has day-to-day regulatory control. Chief among its powers is the granting of operating licenses to those wishing to own radio or television stations. The FCC is composed of five commissioners, appointed by the president. In addition to Congress and the FCC, federal courts have influence in their interpretation of federal laws and in resolution of lawsuits. At lower levels of government, state and local governments make their influence felt at times, especially with locally operated cable companies.

In addition to these groups, the National Association of Broadcasters (NAB) is an industry watchdog with a multimillion dollar annual budget and a penchant for creating programming standards. The NAB also publishes and occasionally updates the *NAB Legal Guide to Broadcast Law and Regulation*. Among the legal issues for broadcasters cited in the 1988 edition of this guide are the following:

• *Obscene or indecent material.* The broadcast of obscene or indecent material is prohibited by law and carries a maximum penalty of a $10,000 fine or a two-year jail sentence, or both. It can also result in FCC administrative sanctions, including fines and the revocation of the broadcaster's license. This issue has undergone changes in thinking on the part of the FCC, however. For example, the FCC's new indecency policy has taken away much of the certainty in determining whether material is permissible for broadcast. Prior to 1987, the FCC limited enforcement of the indecency standard to repetition of the "seven dirty words" contained in the George Carlin "Filthy Words" monologue. The new policy utilizes the more general interpretation that language or material that depicts or describes sexual or excretory activities or organs, in terms patently offensive as measured by contemporary community standards for the broadcast medium, shall be deemed indecent if there is a reasonable risk that children may be in the audience. Additionally, the 10 P.M. "safe harbor" previously established by the FCC has been pushed back to midnight. Further, if the material appeals to the prurient interest of the audience, it may be deemed obscene and its broadcast is prohibited at any time.

News organizations have been interested in the FCC's refusal to exempt the airing of indecent language during coverage of a news event, although, again, the context in which the language is aired and the licensee's determination as to whether children may be in the audience are often considered. A warning that such material contains language that may be offensive to some segments of the audience is still a good practice, but may not provide a blanket shield from legal action.

* *Lotteries*. Broadcasting information about or promoting a lottery is a criminal offense under federal law and also a violation of FCC rules. There are only two exceptions: state-operated lotteries and fishing contests that are self-liquidating (all proceeds are consumed by prizes and operating expenses.) The three elements defining a lottery are (1) the awarding of a prize, (2) the selection of an ultimate winner by chance, and (3) payment, or other consideration, furnished to the promoter by anyone who wants to participate. This law also applies to print media.

* *Unauthorized communications and rebroadcasts*. The program of another broadcast station may not be rebroadcast without receiving the written consent of the originating station. If possible, this consent should first be obtained in writing. If not possible, oral consent should later be confirmed in writing.

* *Engineering operator licensing*. Persons operating AM or FM transmitters need only hold a Restricted Radiotelephone Operator Permit. No examination is required for a Restricted Permit.

* *Emergency Broadcast System (EBS)*. All operating personnel should be thoroughly familiar with EBS procedures, and these should be periodically reviewed.

* *Public inspection files*. The FCC requires licensees to maintain certain records in a file for public inspection during regular business hours. Upon request, stations are also required to make photocopies (at the requester's expense) of materials contained in the files.

* *Station logs*. Although the FCC has eliminated its program logging requirements, commission rules still mandate the maintenance of station operating (transmitter) logs.

Other laws and regulations are in effect concerning such things as "payola" and "plugola" (the acceptance of benefits in exchange for playing records or plugging products); rebroadcasting telephone conversations without prior notification; sponsorship identification; contests and promotions, station identification announcements, mechanical reproduction announcements, tower lights, and network clipping.

Federal law also prohibits individuals or groups from acquiring a radio or television station in the same market where they own a newspaper (a practice called cross-ownership), although several existing crossowner-ships were grandfathered when this ruling took effect. Additionally, the FCC prohibits the ownership of more than 12 AM and 12 FM radio licenses at any one time, or more than 12 television licenses, as long as the stations don't reach more than 25 percent of the nation's television homes. The FCC also keeps watch on the amount and kind of advertising targeted to children, especially those commercials contained in children's programs. If it dislikes what it sees, that displeasure may surface when a station applies to have its license renewed.

Cable Regulations

While cable television operators are subject to most of the same regulations that broadcast operators are, there is an additional set of regulations for them. The most recent act concerning the cable industry was the 1992 Cable Act, which Congress approved on September 22, 1992. In approving this act, the Senate ignored intense business lobbying and a threatened veto by President George Bush to give final congressional approval to reregulating the cable television industry. The act was an update—and in significant ways a reversal—of the 1984 Cable Act, which was instrumental in deregulating cable and freeing it from local government price controls. Highlights of the 1992 act are as follows:

- The FCC must determine "reasonable" rates for "basic" cable service, defined as public, educational, and government cable channels and local broadcast affiliates of ABC, CBS, NBC, Fox, and PBS.
- The FCC must ensure reasonable prices for installation and equipment needed to operate a cable-equipped television, including remote-control devices and converter boxes.
- Cable companies must not charge for services or equipment not explicitly requested by customers.
- The FCC must set service standards to protect against chronic outages and guarantee that customers receive a prompt telephone response to questions about billing, refunds, and service problems. Local communities would be allowed to set additional standards.
- After no more than 10 years, subscribers to basic cable would be allowed to purchase premium channels, such as HBO and Showtime, without first subscribing to an expanded tier of service giving them access to channels they had not specifically requested.
- Cable programming would have to be made available to competitors.
- Cable companies would have to negotiate with local broadcasters and get their permission before carrying their signals, but cannot refuse to carry the local signals.

These changes did not sit well with the cable industry. A closer look at the bill's highlights shows why. For instance, concerning the clause requiring cable programming to be made available to competitors, the bill has threatened the monopoly status that a large number of local cable companies enjoy. Only about 55 of the nation's 11,070 cable systems in 1993 had any competition. In the cases where competition does exist, rates are an average of 30 percent lower.[1] Lowering cable rates and bringing competition online were two areas that the new legislation intended to address. Critics of the act, however, said its emphasis on rates for basic cable guarantees that local operators will ignore their basic-service customers and concentrate instead on adding new pay channels such as Disney and HBO.

The requirement, labeled the "must carry" provision, that cable companies must carry the signals of any requesting television station in the area and also face the possibility of paying to carry those signals was a tough pill for the cable industry to swallow. Prior to the ruling, local cable operators paid nothing to carry a station's signal and were not required to get the station's permission to do so. Under the 1992 Cable Act, however, network affiliates and strong independent stations could demand royalties from cable operators or refuse to allow the operators to carry their broadcast signals. In addition, weak UHF stations, whose signals were not previously carried by local cable companies, could now demand that these companies carry their signals. For their part, cable operators responded that if they have to pay to carry stations' signals the cost will be passed through to the subscriber, and cable bills could jump from $23 to $51 annually.[2]

A third provision, which causes problems for cable programmers such as Turner Broadcasting, would force programmers in which cable-system operators have equity stakes to sell their programs to noncable rivals for 10 years. This means telephone companies, satellite broadcasters, and other developing technology that compete with cable TV will have guaranteed access to CNN, TBS, ESPN, and other popular cable programming. The argument against this provision from cable companies such as Tele-Communications and Time Warner is that they have made huge, risky investments in Turner and other companies so they could develop a steady supply of programming. Why should they have to share that programming with noncable competitors who contributed nothing?

In another of the bill's attempts to encourage competition, there is a prohibition against local governments awarding exclusive franchises to cable companies, although fewer than 1 percent of American cable systems have cable competitors because operators do not feel there is enough profit potential in a market where one cable company already exists.[3]

In the year following the act's approval, numerous local battles ensued between cable operators and local broadcast stations over the provisions of the 1992 Cable Act.

TELEPHONE COMPANY DEREGULATION

As has been shown in previous chapters, the broadcast and cable industries are not the only major players in the age of multimedia. They have been joined by the nation's telephone companies, most notably AT&T and the regional Bell companies, whose business used to lie exclusively in telephone services but which is now encroaching into supplying information to travel across those phone lines. The transformation of the telephone companies into information providers is one of the key regulatory stories of the twentieth century as far as the new information age is concerned.

Legal status of the monopoly position held by AT&T was provided by the Communications Act of 1934. AT&T built and operated the nation's basic telecommunication system, and the federal government provided it with certain wide operating parameters in order to prevent the development of a nationalized telephone company. This favored status came to an end in 1982, however, when its protection was removed by the government. AT&T was required to divest itself of many of its subsidiary operations including the regional Bell telephone companies. AT&T received something in return, however, as it was permitted for the first time to compete in communications and information services.

Initial government action took the form of regulations that curtailed AT&T's near-monopoly status in the areas of equipment supply and long-distance service. As early as 1968, the FCC allowed the first piece of competitive equipment not manufactured by AT&T, known as the Carterphone, into the Bell network. This ended the AT&T restriction that only Western Electric equipment could be used in the Bell network.[4] The next attack on AT&T's monopoly focused on long-distance services. In 1970, the FCC voted to allow other companies to compete with AT&T in intercity long-distance service, opening the door to companies such as MCI and GTE-Sprint. Other regulations followed, and opinion grew that no company should be allowed to hold such a monopoly—or even near-monopoly position—that AT&T held. The Justice Department took the lead in splitting up AT&T's huge operation, and in 1982, the efforts proved successful with the divestiture of AT&T.[5] The court ordered the divestiture to be completed by 1984. By that year, AT&T had reorganized into the following units:[6]

- *AT&T Communications*, which was the largest of the units and which managed the traditional long-distance phone business.

- *AT&T Information Systems*, which was charged with moving the firm into data-related equipment and services.
- *Western Electric and the Bell Laboratories*, charged with product development and marketing, both directly and through third parties such as Sears.
- *AT&T International*, which was responsible for global marketing of products and services.

In 1983, the 22 local Bell telephone companies that were now independent of AT&T organized themselves into seven regional Bell holding companies. Each of the companies was large enough to be included immediately in the top 10 percent of the Fortune 500 firms.[7]

In return for this divestiture, AT&T was given a chance to compete in the new and growing telecommunications and information services markets. It was this privilege, however, that angered the media industry, most notably the newspaper industry, which over the course of the next several years, spent millions of dollars to lobby against implementation of AT&T's right to enter the information services market. While the 1982 divestiture order did keep the RBOCs from entering into development of information services, the Department of Justice proposed, in 1987, the lifting of these restrictions. It was then that the newspaper lobbying efforts went into high gear, as did those of the phone companies. In the summer of 1991, U.S. District Judge Harold H. Greene lifted all remaining restrictions on the expansion of the RBOCs into information services. The newspaper and television industries did not take this order easily and immediately began appealing and lobbying Congress to have Greene's order reversed and keep the phone companies, who own a key means of transmission, from also being able to supply news and information over those same lines. Judge Greene did place a stay on his ruling, pending the outcome of expected appeals. But in May 1993, the U.S. Court of Appeals and then the Supreme Court supported Greene's ruling and decided that the Bell companies should be allowed to expand into information services. The court dismissed the arguments that the Bell companies could discriminate against competing information service providers. Cathleen Black, president and CEO of the NNA, noted that her group believes the decision "is erroneous and unfortunate. We are analyzing our remaining legal options." She continued, "If nothing else, however, this decision underscores the urgent need for Congress to move forward quickly with comprehensive telecommunications legislation."[8]

PRIVACY, ACCESS, AND SECURITY ISSUES

Three multimedia issues that have ethical and legal implications, especially given the advanced stage of development of many new media technologies, are (1) individual privacy, (2) public access to the wealth of information made possible by the new media, and (3) national security considerations which arise from a media that is able to provide sensitive information immediately around the world to any governmental power that might be tuning in.

Individual Privacy

Alexander Solzhenitsyn may have put the issue of loss of privacy, resulting from the collection of too much information by others, best when he wrote:

As every man goes through life he fills in a number of forms for the record, each containing a number of questions. A man's answer to one question on one form becomes a little thread. . . . There are hundreds of little threads radiating from every man, millions of threads in all. . . . They are not visible, they are not material, but every man is constantly aware of their existence. . . . Each man, permanently aware of his own invisible threads, naturally develops a respect for the people who manipulate the threads . . . and for those people's authority.[9]

In today's multimedia era, it is the computer that is collecting and keeping track of these threads, and the storage capacity for this kind of information is virtually limitless. We have all seen evidence of this kind of information keeping. Every time we get a mail-order catalog, whose subject piques our interest—but which we did not order—or receive an unsolicited phone call from a telemarketer who somehow knows we have a certain credit card—and wonder how he or she got that information or our phone number—we realize there is a great deal of information floating around out there about us already. But it is not just finding that our name, phone number—and maybe some key behavior or buying preferences—is in someone's database that is disconcerting. During the activist era of the 1960s and 1970s, many people in America realized that the FBI and CIA were keeping files on them and even monitoring some of their political activities if they appeared in the least bit suspicious. There is even a joke, which may be truer than we care to admit, that the best way to get the government to start a file on you is to call or write them and ask to see your file; if there is no file, then they will probably start one, based on your curiosity.

Add to these concerns the fact that advertising and marketing are now based largely on the collection and use of demographic and psychographic (personality/lifestyle/behavior) information about individuals, and one wonders if anything is really private anymore. Earlier in this book the concept of user modeling was discussed. User modeling is a concept where the television set is programmed to watch the viewer even as the viewer is watching it. In so doing, it records and keeps track of viewer behavior and may even ask the viewer to help out by inputting certain lifestyle characteristics or preferences for types of information and entertainment. Then, on the premise that what we all want is a highly tailored, individualized media program menu, it uses that information to captivate us and have us spend longer hours in front of a television screen than we are already doing.

In all of this, the loss of privacy looms as a large concern; the use of the collected information to form a persuasive and manipulative assault on our senses is an even deeper concern for many. How concerned are Americans about the loss of privacy? In 1990, the Louis Harris organization conducted a study on the subject and reported that 80 percent of Americans are concerned about their privacy, and 70 percent believe that consumers have lost control over how companies use the information they have collected on individuals.[10] In 1986, the Office of Technology Assessment found that "technological advances have opened up many new possibilities for improving the efficiency of government record-keeping; the detection and prevention of fraud, waste, and abuse; and law enforcement investigations. At the same time, the opportunities for inappropriate, unauthorized, or illegal access to and use of personal information have expanded."[11]

The government has not been totally immobile on this issue of privacy in the computer age. Existing privacy laws are intact that make it dangerous for the media to do the following:

1. Intrude on a person's solitude.
2. Make public disclosure of embarrassing facts about a person if that information is not judged by a court to be newsworthy.
3. Cast a person in a false light.
4. Misappropriate a person's name or likeness without permission, especially if that misappropriation is part of a sales or marketing effort.

There is also privacy legislation protecting the unauthorized public disclosure of information about students and their school records.

Several bills have been passed by Congress since 1970 to help curtail loss of privacy, including the following:

- The Fair Credit Reporting Act of 1970
- The Privacy Act of 1974
- The Family Education and Right to Privacy Act of 1974
- The Cable Communication Policy Act of 1984
- The Electronic Communications Privacy Act of 1986

• The Computer Matching and Privacy Protection Act of 1988
• The Video Privacy Act of 1988

Louise M. Benjamin notes that these acts focus on three objectives:[12]

1. Creating a balance between what an individual is expected to divulge to a record-keeping organization and what benefit he or she expects in return.
2. Opening up record-keeping operations so recorded information is not a source of unfairness in decisions made about an individual.
3. Creating legitimate expectations of confidentiality in the record-keeping process.

Among the principles in the previously mentioned legislation that reflect these goals are the following:[13]

• Storing personal information is prohibited.
• Information should be appropriate and relevant to the purpose for which it has been collected.
• Information should not be obtained by fraudulent or unfair means.
• Individuals should have prescribed ways of accessing information that is kept about them.
• Individuals should have a prescribed way of correcting, erasing, or amending inaccurate, obsolete, or irrelevant information.
• Organizations collecting, maintaining, using, or disseminating personal information should ensure its reliability and take precautions to prevent its misuse.
• Federal, state, and local governments should not collect personal information except as expressly authorized by law.

Even with these principles in place, however, the amount of unauthorized information collected by private industry about individuals seems to continue growing. Several of the privacy acts are out of date and do not deal with the new means by which businesses can gather and use information about individuals and their buying behaviors. Additionally, most Americans seem uninformed that these various pieces of privacy legislation exist, so they don't realize they have legal recourse should their privacy be violated in an unauthorized manner.

One such example of information that is hard to keep private are the messages entrusted to E-mail. Anyone who assumes that information traveling by electronic mail is more private than a phone call, letter, or face-to-face meeting may be sadly mistaken. There are no clear rules that govern E-mail, and the question of E-mail's privacy is now one of the thorniest legal issues of the electronic age. The Electronic Communications Privacy Act of 1986 prohibits "outside" interception of E-mail by a third party (such as the government, police, or an individual) without proper authorization, such as a search warrant. But this law does not cover internal interception of these messages, such as sneaking a peek at the office gossip's E-mail.[14] Historically, the courts have ruled that such interoffice memoranda is private only if workers had a "reasonable expectation" of privacy when they sent it. Many employees hold no such expectation as far as the courts are concerned.

Philip Elmer-Dewitt notes the following about E-mail's privacy problems:

The fact is no absolute privacy exists in a computer system. . . . System administrators need to have access to everything in a computer in order to maintain it. Moreover, every piece of E-mail leaves an electronic trail. Though Oliver North tried to delete all his electronic notes in order to conceal the Iran-contra deal, copies of his secret memos ended up in the back-up tapes made every night by White House system operators.[15]

With these kinds of potential privacy problems developing along with the new age of computerized information and record-keeping, newer and more relevant laws are needed to plug any loss-of-privacy holes left by existing regulations.

Public Access to Information

There is always a possibility—many say probability—that the new media era will result in an even greater knowledge gap than exists today. For many Americans, information may be in abundant supply, but it may be difficult to access. That difficulty for many could lie in the expenses associated with subscribing to basic electronic information services, not to mention being able to afford the hardware and software needed to access the data. So the question of how to avoid creating an information elite in America is a good one and a timely one.

A significant part of the Clinton administration's agenda has been to seek a national information infrastructure, designed to connect every home, school, college, and business in an electronic communications network. Such a network, at least in partial form, is operating as the Internet system, mentioned in chapter 5. Internet is now serving up to 30 million computer users with more logging on daily. It currently handles scientific communication, electronic mail, data transmission, and bibliographic material.[16] The problem with Internet, however, according to Kevin Cooke and Dan Lehrer, is that it is a "network of networks (where) no one group or person is in charge. It's definitely out of control."[17] Another network proposed by the government is the National Research and Education Network (NREN) discussed later in this chapter. NREN is another initial step at forming an all-inclusive information network.

Some observers warn, however, that if networks such as Internet become privatized, then the government would be giving the private sector unregulated and monopolistic control over its electronic connections, allowing huge companies such as Time Warner or AT&T to decide what goes on the system and who can access the information, not to mention how much they would have to pay.[18] For all the comparisons between the nation's interstate highway system and an information highway, consumers must remember that what is being discussed is, in actuality, a highway of the mind, as technology analyst Roger Karraker calls it. Since it is such, then control of it becomes of paramount importance because of its potential for setting personal agendas and, to some degree, controlling the kinds of things we think about.

National Security

The new media technology and its ability to bring in news from virtually anywhere at any time brings up the possibility of breaches in national security. Ever since the years of the Nixon administration, national security considerations have been greeted with ambivalence by many people because of the potential for abuse by the government—as well as the media. Even as vice-president Spiro T. Agnew was taking the news media to task for distorting too much information, his own president was distorting and concealing information about Watergate and trying to use national security as a reason to keep from divulging the extent of his involvement in this and other misdoings. Judge John J. Sirica had to point out to Nixon—and to the American public—the difference between true national security considerations and considerations of political expediency. Since President Nixon left office, other presidents have used national security considerations less vociferously to keep the media from discovering truths, for example, in judging how reporters may or may not cover wars. It is unlikely that any war will ever be covered as exhaustively as Vietnam, and every skirmish the United States has engaged in since has been fought under tight media access restrictions. The official reason has been national security considerations, and often that is a real consideration. The unofficial reason is that it is very hard to sustain unified public support of a war effort if Americans at home are watching the true horrors of war on the field as U.S. soldiers fight, are wounded, and die.

Chapter 9 discusses some of the considerations involved in Operation Desert Storm and Operation Rolling Thunder in the Middle East. Here was the media's opportunity to cover war in real-time fashion, with reporters doing live stand-ups as bombs, rockets, and missiles were exploding behind them in the distance. It was a kind of "gas mask reporting"; Americans watched reporters don masks during their stand-ups, fearing chemical warfare. It was a time when CNN earned its stripes for overseas reporting, and Americans sat glued to their sets to listen to Peter Arnett report on the bombing of Baghdad from a hotel in the midst of the city as the Allied bombs were falling. With only a couple of exceptions, however, this real-time reporting was tightly controlled under an Allied media pool system controlled by Allied officers. Reporters were told where they could go and where they could not go. Public affairs officers accompanied reporters as they did their interviews. Daily briefings were structured so as to keep sensitive information away from the media as much as possible.

From the point of view of the U.S. military, an uncensored media is an uncontrollable media. Reporters are not the best judges of what is sensitive material and what is not. The possibility of having a reporter air information live exacerbates the problem, especially since the enemy could see the same live, real-time newscasts. An uncensored and uncontrolled media could give the enemy the advantage. To many in the media, however, the danger is always present that military censorship, based on real issues of national security, might translate into political censorship, based on political expediency and perceived image of the administration.

In large measure, this issue is an old one. It raises the dilemma of confidentiality, which is necessary to defend the United States, in a democracy where citizens need to be informed so they can make intelligent decisions. The new age of instantaneous, real-time reporting is causing both lawmakers and journalists to rethink this vexing issue.

VISUAL SLEIGHTS OF HAND

Most of us seem to be convinced of the truth about a phenomenon only if we can see it occurring. Think of the two adages, "A picture is worth a thousand words," and "I'll believe it when I see it." One state, Missouri, is even called the "Show Me State." But what if a situation arises in which we cannot believe our eyes? What if a form of visual manipulation exists that is able to distort what we see so that we can no longer trust visual forms of evidence? That kind of capability has long existed for still photography, and creative geniuses such as Hollywood's Industrial Light and Magic have given us all kinds of special effects in movies from *Star Wars* to *Jurassic Park*. But computerization has opened the door even further on the ability to manipulate visual images, and even some respected news media, such as *National Geographic*, have fallen prey to the temptation of distorting reality with a photograph to present a more aesthetically pleasing scene. (In the case of *National Geographic*, it was a seemingly harmless enough distortion: moving a pyramid for a more pleasing setting in Egypt.)

Photography is being transformed from a chemical-based medium to an electronic one, and pictures may never be the same again. Filmless cameras, now being used by many journalists, record images on small computer discs, which are then fed into a PC for processing and then printed out. Sometimes, however, there is an additional step taken that is often euphemistically called "image enhancement." Image distortion is sometimes a more accurate description of this step. Electronic still photography offers many positive rewards to the industry but, like other new media technology, relies on the ethics of the user to produce accurate portrayals.

As the 1990s began, Eastman Kodak Co. introduced the Photo CD, which puts a photographer's portfolio or an amateur's collection of snapshots on a CD-ROM instead of film. In reality, those photographers who participate in this electronic still photography are moving into the realm of computing instead of photography as it has been known. In the process, it may be computer skills—more than photographic talent—that results in some of the most dramatic photographs. Will these photographs be accurate depictions of reality? Michael Mauney, a former staffer for *Life* magazine who now shoots corporate annual reports, told *Forbes* magazine: "It's getting to the point where any 20-year-old wunderkind at an ad agency will be able to sit down at the computer and realize the wildest idea. It will be great for business, but not for photographers.[19]

This capability would not necessarily be good for consumers of news who look to the media for a picture of reality, not fantasy. As for the world of advertising, this is just one more opportunity for professional marketers to persuade consumers of the value of their client's product, despite the faultiness of that product. Today, as journalist Sean Callahan notes, assigning a commercial photographer to shoot original material is only one of several options—and usually the most expensive—for the increasing number of clients needing photography work done. Increasingly, images are available on CD-ROMs as well as online from many different sources. Once purchased, these digital image files can be enhanced, refined, and even combined with elements of other images to create substantially new images.[20]

As the 1980s drew to a close, increased computer speeds and new software for Macintosh computers developed by firms such as Adobe Systems, allowed this graphics technology to move from large, mainframe systems to the PC and into desktop publishing. This allowed graphic artists, art directors, and photographers to manipulate images with unprecedented facility and precision. Image processing now routinely accomplishes tasks ranging from the mundane, such as removing a blemish from a portrait, to the mischievous, such as the *Spy* magazine cover in 1992 showing a beaming Hillary Clinton dressed as a dominatrix, or *Texas Monthly's* montage of Governor Ann Richards as a biker.[21] In television commercials we see bizarre but seemingly real images of Paula Abdul dancing with Gene Kelly and other deceased actors and actresses showing up in new commercials that tout the value of present-day products.

But it is in the news media where distortion of photographic images—whether still or moving—is most troublesome. With a system such as Adobe's Photoshop, which has emerged as the standard photo-processing package for PCs and which retails for about $900, putting it in reach of all newspapers and magazines, an editor can be tempted to create all kinds of image enhancement or even brand new images that none of his or her photographers ever shot. The prize could be increased readership, since it is a well-documented fact that it is the photographs and other newspaper graphics that pull in the most readers.

In one small instance of computerized distortion of a newspaper photograph in 1989, a Coca-Cola can was removed from a shot of a photographer on the paper who had just won a Pultizer Prize. Following a growing number of cases of digital alteration of photographs, the National Press Photographers Association (NPPA) developed a statement of principle that states, "Altering the content of a photograph in any degree is a breach of the ethical standards recognized by NPPA." In the end, the realization must occur to news photographers and their editors that the same standards of accuracy and ethics that apply to writing and reporting the news must also apply to depicting it visually.

TOWARD A NEW MEDIA POLICY

Two of the key issues confronting Congress and the FCC over the next several years will be (1) what kind of controls should exist for the new, so-called information highway and (2) who should be given the power to control that highway. The significance of this highway and its control is hard to understate. Futurist Alvin Toffler writes that the future of America depends on the creation of electronic communication networks.

Because so much of business now depends on getting and sending information, companies around the world have been rushing to link their employees through electronic networks. These networks form the key infrastructure of the 21st Century, as critical to business success and national economic development as the railroads were in [Samuel] Morse's era.[22]

Roger Karraker notes that these data highways, which could connect schools, colleges, universities, researchers, industry (and eventually the general public) could help create high-quality education in the smallest schools or start a societywide revolution as important as the invention of printing. On the other hand, if the public and certain other sectors of the nation are denied access to these highways—and only the wealthy and powerful can tap in—then these networks might become nothing more than a classic case of economic imperialism, a kind of taxation without communication. One critic has even called the resulting product "toll roads between information castles."[23]

As noted earlier in this chapter, lawmakers are still debating the value— or at least the priority—of this high-bandwidth electronic network. That debate threatens to slow down progress toward creating a unified, national media policy to decide issues relating to this information highway. Unlike the speed and intensity with which Japan is approaching the issue, American lawmakers are engaged in turf battles and spats over who should do what, how, and when. In the meantime, at least four crucial questions remain unanswered regarding this new data highway:

1. *Who will—or should—construct the highway?* Should this be a project that the government takes on, or should it be left to private industry to build and maintain? Or should a combination of public and private ingenuity be used?

2. *Who will the highway serve?* Stated another way, who will have access to it? This is an important question, given the knowledge gap and power gap potentials that exist from limiting access to this network.

3. *Where will the funds come from to construct and maintain the highway?* This is the question that concerns lawmakers the most, especially in light of the need to curtail government spending. Most experts agree that regardless of national economic goals the federal government will have to somehow pay the lion's share of the cost of the new fiber optic highway because the expense is too great for private industry to shoulder on its own. Nevertheless, private companies such as TCI and Time Warner have already announced intentions to spend billions in helping to construct portions of this highway that would serve their interests and other companies will probably follow suit.

4. *What kind of information will—or should—be allowed to travel this highway?* As Karraker notes, if the federal government owns the network, then the First Amendment is in place and unpopular speech and art would probably be protected. On the other hand, if the highway belongs to private industry, the future of freedom of electronic speech is not so clear, as a company owning the network could censor discussion of controversial topics.[24]

In general, there are two models that this new information highway might follow. One is based on the model of the nation's interstate highway system, the funding of which is heavily subsidized by the federal government. In this model, which has been supported by such lawmakers as Vice-President Al Gore, the federal government would become a sort of catalyst, the highway would be a public resource, and taxes would be used to build it.

A second model is more like that of the railroad system in which private industry receives government protection of a near-monopoly status to own and operate the information highway, and in return, they supply the capital and labor needed to build the network. This is also the model upon which the nation's telephone system was built. Not surprisingly, companies such as IBM and MCI are backing this model. In 1990, these two companies along with Merit, an agency of the state of Michigan, formed ANS (Advanced Network Services), a not-for-profit joint venture that proposed to build, finance, maintain, and operate a private network if the federal government would guarantee that research institutions had annual budgets sufficient to pay their ANS bills.[25] Although, on the surface, it might seem Americans would be reluctant to allow private industry to control the information highway, it does have its appeal in an era of record budget deficits at the national level. If someone other than the government is willing to pick up the tab for the multibillion dollar project, the argument goes, why not let them and give them a wide degree of operating latitude as part of the deal? Still others fear what might happen if this highway is not treated as a public resource with equal access for all and First Amendment protections in place.

Because this information highway is already in its initial stages of construction, decisions on these and other issues should be reached soon. In 1991, Congress passed a $3 billion High-Performance Computing Act, and President Bush signed it into law. In effect, the act gave approval to paving the first several miles of the fiber optic highway that one day will be constructed across the nation. The money from the act was to be used to develop and install computer hardware that would help propel data among several of the nation's leading research centers. The connected centers would form the first pieces of the NREN network, which is seen as the start of this national information highway.

Many media observers such as Leo Bogart believe that any national media policy should reaffirm the doctrine of public responsibility as the price for private use of any public property such as the airwaves and should also establish criteria of acceptable performance. Bogart adds:

The requirement of the 1934 Communications Act that broadcast stations operate in the public interest should be revived and extended to cable system operators and program providers. If broadcasters were once again made to acknowledge that they have a social duty, the subject might at least move higher up on their own agendas.[26]

Another observer of the information age, Wilson P. Dizard, believes that the answer to the regulatory puzzle does not lie in any master plan so much as in a range of "general approaches, each of which advances the prospect of making adjustments to the new information environment within a democratic framework."[27] The common thread stitching all of these approaches together is the premise of creating a workable balance between public and private sector roles and responsibilities. Dizard outlines two approaches as follows:

The facile approach is simply to do more of what we have been doing. . . . The federal government would continue to act as a regulatory balance, brokering between the major economic interests involved and buffering the present communications structure against the instabilities of too rapid change. . . . The second, and more radical, approach is to make the public sector a more active participant. . . . The few proponents of this idea argue that only direct public intervention can create an integrated, full-service network operated as a publicly owned utility. The problem with this alternative is that it is politically impractical. . . . Justified or not, the idea raises the specter of domination by government in an area where it has up to now largely been excluded, both by law and custom.[28]

A third approach would be to establish a solid commitment to a full-service national information grid, augmenting the present fragmentary system in stages. The basic construction and management of the completed system would be a job handed to private industry, which would develop the grid in as many competitive modes as technology and market considerations would allow. Then the government would monitor its performance, based on agreed-upon social goals.[29] In short, it would be a model based on the present regulatory structure whereby the FCC and Congress supervise the broadcast and cable industries. Certainly one key responsibility and role of the government under this approach should be to ensure widespread public access to this information grid. Another governmental role would be to ensure individual privacy as much as is possible in the new age of electronic databases.

Dizard concludes:

Given the economic and political stakes involved, the (current) regulatory structure cannot be phased out immediately. But there is no reason why a national commitment, based on a new pattern of public- and private-sector cooperation, could not be made now to carry us through the transitional phase to a full-service information grid providing low-cost, high-capacity services to every sector of American society.[30]

By late 1993, two bills designed to remove several competitive restrictions, including a ban on electronic publishing, on the seven RBOCs were introduced in the House of Representatives. Earlier that year, the Senate Commerce, Science and Transportation Committee's Communications Subcommittee held hearings on S. 1086, the Telecommunications Infrastructure Act of 1993, which focused on several issues involving telephone companies.

One of the House bills, H.R. 3626, addresses both the 1982 Modification of Final Judgment (which resulted in the creation of the seven

RBOCs) and the Communications Act of 1934. The bill's first title section is known as the Antitrust Reform Act of 1993, and the second is the Communications Reform Act of 1993. Also known as the Brooks-Dingell bill, named for its co-sponsors Representatives Jack Brooks (D-Tex.) and John Dingell (D-Mich.), was introduced a week after the U.S. Supreme Court upheld the decision allowing the RBOCs to expand into electronic publishing.

The Brooks-Dingell bill was designed to offer a level playing field as the RBOCs move into electronic publishing. The bill received different degrees of support from the newspaper industry, which favored it, and the RBOCs, which saw in its provisions too much possible regulation of the telephone companies regarding electronic publishing. Nevertheless, the RBOCs seemed to approve of the introduction of such a bill to offer some consistent telecommunications policy and prevent chaos from ensuing in the highly competitive electronic publishing field.

Several newspaper companies are already involved in joint ventures with telephone companies in their own local markets in developing electronic news and information products. Under the Brooks-Dingell Bill, these ventures are allowable if the RBOCs keep their financial interests below 50 percent.

The Brooks-Dingell bill includes safeguards in the form of mandatory equal access to local networks, with nondiscriminatory pricing; the stipulation that the RBOCs operate electronic publishing businesses as ventures separate from their telephone operations; a ban on the RBOCs using revenue from their telephone networks to provide an unfair advantage to their electronic publishing businesses, and a requirement that the RBOCs undergo an annual independent audit.

The second House bill, H.R. 3636, was introduced the same day as H.R. 3626 by Representative Edward Markey (D-Mass.). Called the National Communications Competition and Information Infrastructure Act of 1993, it included provisions allowing the telephone companies to purchase cable systems outside their service areas, open up local telephone service to competition, establish a joint federal-state board to guarantee universal access to services, and establish services at affordable rates. Its co-sponsors included Representatives Jack Fields (R-Tex.), Rich Boucher (D-Va.), and Michael Oxley (R-Ohio). It quickly became known as the Markey-Fields bill and drew hearty support from the NAA.

Not to be outdone, the White House offered its own proposal for telecommunications legislation in December 1993. Vice President Al Gore said the Clinton administration wants to tear down regulatory hurdles in the communications industry, unleashing private enterprise to build the high-speed networks of the twenty-first century. Gore said the White House supports the gradual removal of restrictions that separate the cable television and telephone industries and keep local phone companies from offering long-distance service. He added that the White House wanted to sweep away the regulations that cross-industry mergers and technical developments are making obsolete. Major communications companies, including the RBOCs and AT&T, immediately applauded Gore's statement.

Gore explained that loosening the restrictions would encourage business to build a national information infrastructure, bringing the nation's communications network into the next century. This is the network commonly called the electronic superhighway or data highway and consisting of thousands of miles of fiber optic cables linking homes, schools, businesses, and government.

Gore said the White House proposals would require both legislative and administrative action but would be made in consultation with Congress and both the public and private sectors.

SUMMARY

Clearly there is a need for a new uniform, national communications policy that reaches out and addresses all of the societal implications inherent in this new age of interactive multimedia. The fragmentary, often inconsistent, and hopelessly outdated current set of regulations will not suffice in a time where the attainment of knowledge and the loss of individual privacy are threatened for large sectors of American society. Creating a national media policy may be one of the most difficult tasks federal lawmakers have ever had to tackle, given the intense lobbying efforts, often seeking contradictory goals, that are coming from private industry and special-interest groups. It will take courage for Congress to stand in the face of such political pressure and do the right thing for America by ensuring public access to what will probably be a largely privatized national—and even international—information highway.

NOTES

1. James Cox, "Regulation Bill Sets Off Lobbying Brawl," *USA Today*, September 17, 1992, 2B.
2. Ibid.
3. Ibid.
4. Wilson P. Dizard, Jr., *The Coming Information Age*, 3rd ed. (New York: Longman, 1989), 129.
5. Ibid., 134.
6. Ibid.
7. Ibid., 141.
8. Debra Gersh, "Court Ruling Favors the RBOCs," *Editor & Publisher*, June 5, 1993, 43.

9. Alexander Solzhenitsyn as quoted by Louis M. Benjamin, "Privacy, Computers, and Personal Information," *Communications and the Law*, June 1991, 3.

10. Ibid., 4.

11. Ibid.

12. Ibid., 8.

13. Ibid., 8–9.

14. Philip Elmer-Dewitt, "Who's Reading Your Screen?" *Time*, January 18, 1993, 46.

15. Ibid.

16. Kevin Cooke and Dan Lehrer, "The Whole World Is Talking," *The Nation*, July 12, 1993, 61.

17. Ibid.

18. Ibid., 62.

19. Sean Callahan, "Eye Tech," *Forbes ASAP*, June 1993, 60.

20. Ibid.

21. Ibid., 64.

22. Roger Karraker, "Highways of the Mind," *Whole Earth Review*, Spring 1991, 4.

23. Ibid., 8.

24. Ibid., 5.

25. Ibid., 6.

26. Leo Bogart, "Shaping a New Media Policy," *The Nation*, July 12, 1993, 59.

27. Dizard, "Information Age," 170–171.

28. Ibid.

29. Ibid., 174.

9
. . . . .

Journalism: Changes in Nature and Effect

Harold Innis and Marshall McLuhan showed the world years ago that the news and entertainment media are anything but neutral in terms of the effects they have on the content presented and the effect that content and presentation style have on the consumer. This is not to say that reporters do not exercise objectivity in their reporting; it is the type of media they work for which often determines what will be covered, how it will be covered, and what effect that coverage will have on the viewer or reader. McLuhan went so far as to proclaim that the medium is the message and then went further to assert that the medium is the *massage*. That is, every new form of media takes our senses and roughs them up a bit, alters our sensory perceptions, and—often—leaves us in a bit of a fog about what was just presented. Writing in the 1960s and early 1970s, McLuhan—who drew on many of the ideas of fellow-Canadian communication theorist Innis—focused most of his attention on broadcast television (cable television was only in its infancy).

A few passages from McLuhan's *Understanding Media* provide deeper insight into his thesis about changes resulting from different modes of learning and communication:

A Passage to India by E. M. Forster is a dramatic study of the inability of oral and intuitive Oriental culture to meet with the rational, visual European patterns of experience. "Rational," of course, has for the West long meant "uniform and continuous and sequential." In other words, we have confused reason with literacy, and rationalism with a single technology. Thus in the electric (read electronic) age man seems to the conventional West to become irrational.[1]

McLuhan goes on to describe how, in the Forster novel, the moment of truth and dislocation from the typographic trance of the West comes in the Marabar Caves where Adela Quested's reasoning powers "cannot cope with the total inclusive field of resonance that is India." Forster adds, "Life went on as usual, but had no consequences. That is to say, sounds did not echo nor thought develop. Everything seemed cut off at its root and therefore infected with illusion."² Says McLuhan:

A *Passage to India* is a parable of Western man in the electric age, and is only incidentally related to Europe or the Orient. The ultimate conflict between sight and sound, between written and oral kinds of perception and organization of existence is upon us. Since understanding stops action, as Nietzsche observed, we can moderate the fierceness of this conflict by understanding the media that extend us and raise these wars within and without us.³

McLuhan is well known for his separation of various media into "hot" or "cool" categories, depending on how much information they provide and how much they expect the viewer, listener, or reader to search for. To him, a hot medium is one that "extends one single sense in high definition."⁴ High definition is the state of being well filled with data. Therefore, the print media—newspapers, magazines, and books—are hot media. McLuhan feels that a photograph is, visually, high definition and so is hot. On the other hand, a cartoon is relatively low definition because very little visual information is provided. The telephone is a cool medium, or one of low definition, because the ear is given a meager amount of information. Interestingly, he also puts television into the "cool" category, and that seems especially appropriate when it comes to the nightly newscasts on a local station that generally features only a scant 12 or 13 minutes of actual news as opposed to weather, sports, anchor chit chat, and commercials.

McLuhan extends his thinking to assert that it makes all the difference in the world whether a hot medium or cool medium is matched with a hot or cool culture (one of low or high involvement).

The hot radio medium used in cool or nonliterate cultures has a violent effect, quite unlike its effect, say, in England or America, where radio is felt as entertainment. A cool or low literacy culture cannot accept hot media like movies or radio as entertainment. They are, at least, as radically upsetting for them as the cool TV medium has proved to be for our high literacy world.⁵

This may be one reason why radio has become the chief mass medium of information for most countries in Africa, who look to it to find out what is happening at home and around the world. As an entertainment medium, radio takes a back seat there.

Hot media are, therefore, low in participation, and cool media are high in participation (involvement or completion) by the audience. What happens with television viewing, however, is that if the viewer does not choose to participate, to complete the thought or involve himself or herself enough to understand what is being presented, then they may well receive only the most superficial report of the day's activities and the actors and actresses behind them. Most Americans, at one time or another, fall into this trap of passivity, highly vulnerable to manipulation either by the station or the politicians, business executives, and others who use the media to manipulate audiences. At times, it is simply the saturated bombardment on our senses of various unrelated bits and pieces of information, folklore, and entertainment that saps our ability to concentrate on what we are viewing and leaves us feeling numbed when we switch off the set and go to bed.

THE THEATER OF TELEVISION

This saturated bombardment of the senses is a result of the "theater of television." Elements of this theater include the following:

1. An abiding interest in how a story is told as much—or more—as what is told.
2. A story focus on individual people as representative types of much larger population groups.
3. Attention to the emotional impact of the story as well as the actual content.
4. A story structure that includes an identifiable beginning, middle, and end, even though the story may be an ongoing one whose conclusion is far down the road.
5. A report where the story is written to the available video instead of vice versa. In other words, the video comes first in a very real sense and is deemed more important than the content. (How else do you explain taking up precious airtime with a story on the San Diego Chicken or having the sports anchor wrestle a bear in a fishing and hunting exhibition that has come to town?)
6. Attractive and focus-group-tested anchors leading the narration of the stories, along with equally engaging on-air reporters.
7. Stories that often deal with "hot topics," as defined by television news consultants, previous ratings, and what has worked in other markets. In one of innumerable cases, for instance, a Boston television station aired a five-part series on the youthful musical group, New Kids on the Block, and another Boston station aired a five-part series on cats largely because it proved successful at a Phoenix, Arizona, station a few months before.

When a news director comes into the newsroom and congratulates a reporter for his or her story by saying, "That was great television!" what he or she is really saying is that most of the above elements were present in the story. The news director is not saying that it was a great piece of American journalism; only that it had great video and emotional impact on the audience and did its job in keeping them tuned in for what was to follow.

Michael Deaver, former media aide to President Ronald Reagan, openly acknowledged the existence of the theater of television in the late 1980s. He told documentarian Bill Moyers that television networks are eager to receive and use any White House video they receive, even though they understand that it is propaganda. Deaver went even further in saying that the viewers generally buy the illusions this video is selling, even though the audio—or reporter voice-over—is saying something totally different. "In the battle between the eye and the ear, the eye wins everytime," Deaver said.[6] To show what he meant, Deaver referred to a video of President Reagan touring a home under construction in Fort Worth on a day when the economic news of new housing starts was depressing for the administration. To give the public a sense that there was a housing boom, Deaver decided to fly the president to Texas where a new subdivision was under construction. The reporter voice-over delivered the depressing housing starts report, and the video the network used was Reagan walking through a framed-up house. Viewer reaction, Deaver said, was to virtually ignore the audio and focus instead on the video which gave the illusion that new housing starts were up.

CBS reporter Leslie Stahl has also acknowledged the importance of video. In an interview during the initial year of the Bush administration, she recalled how one network producer would only permit her to report critical remarks of the immensely popular Ronald Reagan if it could be tempered with pleasing video casting the former president in a more favorable light. She also said that, "even though I know it's not right, I like to wallpaper my pieces with pretty pictures."[7] Right or wrong, this is the essence of television. It is a visual medium, and it is only becoming more so as time goes on.

Television, then, has a vastly different effect on the news and consumers than does the print media. Although newspapers are becoming more colorfully visual, they will never be a true visual medium. Their stock in trade is still written text, although those stories are becoming shorter and shorter to make room for more graphics and white space and to accommodate the ever-shortening attention span of a decreasing number of regular readers. Nevertheless, newspapers are not as plagued with media-determined restrictions as is television. News stories are not written to available video, and the pictures that are used are meant to amplify the content of the story. In other words, more than television at least, form still follows function in the newspaper world. Newspaper and magazine reporters have more time to devote to their reporting than do television reporters. Therefore, the stories generally emerge more complete and detailed. Even a 15-inch story in print—an average story for most newspapers—is twice as long as an average 90-second reporter package on television. During the 1970s, when the networks were experimenting with hour-long newscasts, one analyst discovered that the entire content of one of these newscasts could fit nicely into only two-thirds of the front page of the *New York Times*.

In addition to having an effect on the amount of information conveyed, however, the different natures of television and print media also affect the way in which it is conveyed and how it is received and decoded. By and large, the print medium conveys its stories in a linear fashion; one point follows another, one observation follows another. While it may seem the same for television reporters, the same is not true for the reader versus the viewer. The print medium requires more patience of their readers, who are often content to absorb the information in a linear fashion. Television, however, makes a different appeal. It is an appeal to the growing desire among many news consumers for the all-at-once experience that live video, tape, and jarring pictures bring to the learning experience. Then, it is often this video that is most readily recalled by the viewer, as Deaver pointed out earlier. This is not only true in news stories, by the way. It is true for commercials as well. All of us can recall commercials that were so entertaining that we remember the production but forget which product or service it was touting.

But it is news reporting on which we base our view of the world, and when something happens to the nature of this reporting, it often happens to us as well. Television is a shocking medium. It has the power to deliver the experience itself, not just a report of the experience. In so doing, it affects a different part of our brain than does simple linear reporting. Certainly the Vietnam War comes to mind when thinking about this idea. One wonders if America would have become so outraged over the length of the war and the ferocity of it had it not been for television's nightly film of the carnage. Television delivered the shock of the killing and brutality in very graphic terms; much more than print could have done.

A more recent and curious example of television's shocking power was seen in the live—or real-time—coverage of the bombing of Baghdad and the ensuing war in the Persian Gulf. Most adult Americans, who were not raised on live television violence as their children have been, found this live video and real-time reporting an exhaustingly gripping experience. Adjectives that many television viewers used to describe their feelings as they saw the Iraqi capital being bombed ranged from deeply involved to uncomfortable, to extremely afraid. Along with these feelings was a deep sense of concern for those innocent civilians who—at the time of viewing—were in peril for their lives and who could have been killed even while the cameras were rolling and sending the live transmission back to American living rooms. It was, many said, a kind of surreal experience;

as if they were there; as if Baghdad were only a block or so away from their own homes. Psychologists warned of the effect of this real-time coverage on children and cautioned parents to guard their television viewing and explain to their children in nonthreatening language what was occurring and why. In short, for weeks on end, television delivered the experience and the shock of real war in a way that had never happened before. The viewing public saw news being made as field correspondents delivered rumors along with facts and had to wait until later to find out what was true and what was not because real-time reporting does not allow time to discern the difference.

Commenting on the coverage as it was airing, ABC correspondent Jeff Greenfield wrote:

We watch almost hypnotically; a Times-Mirror survey revealed that half of us literally cannot turn the TV set off. And yet we watch with a growing sense of frustration, a hunger to hear every fragment of information linked with the knowledge that much of what we learn we will unlearn in the next half hour. And this, perhaps, is the most significant, most troublesome aspect of television's first "real-time" war; the uneasy blend of instant, immediate, round-the-clock access to information that is inherently incomplete, fragmented, or downright wrong. Both in terms of what we are learning and what this kind of access may be doing to us, it may well prove to be immeasurably more important than any other question about television's impact on the war—and on ourselves.[8]

Analysts such as Greenfield agree that when rumor is allowed to parade as fact before the public, it may result in more harm than good. Add to these rumors the huge amount of information dumped on the American television viewer during the Gulf War by television alone, and some very real problems become apparent. There may simply be more information available than most viewers can feasibly assimilate without, as Greenfield warns, "succumbing to an overwhelming sense of stress and confusion and frustration and exhaustion."[9] Seeing that a solution to the problem cannot possibly lie in having the networks cut back on their reporting (for which of them would do that, anyway), Greenfield concludes that the next best solution would be to have the correspondents and their editors back home acknowledge the simple truth of the matter by saying, "I don't know what is happening right now, or what it means."

In writing about the effects on the audience caused by television, Edmund Carpenter notes that television combines many different elements of the communication experience into one, creating this seemingly more involved viewing experience. It combines music and art, language and gesture, rhetoric and color. It also favors simultaneous visual and auditory images.[10]

Cameras focus not on speakers but on persons spoken to or about; the audience hears the accuser but watches the accused. In a single impression it hears the prosecutor, watches the trembling hands of the big-town crook, and sees the look of moral indignation on Senator Tobey's face. This is real drama, in process, with the outcome uncertain. Print can't do this. . . . Books and movies only pretend uncertainty, but live TV retains this vital aspect of life.[11]

Perhaps it is this element of uncertainty—of not knowing how a live, real- time event is going to turn out—that makes us uncomfortable or a little more apprehensive when we watch such live events as the beginning of a war in which our country is involved, or the eruption in flames of the Branch Davidian Complex in Waco, Texas, with many women and children still alive inside the flaming buildings. This uncertainty is a narcotic that keeps many viewers tuned in, when we otherwise might tune out if it were on tape or film.

As to the element of involvement, no medium does it better than television. Part of the reason is it is such an up-close and personal medium, and in combining the various communication elements noted earlier, it seems to bring us into relationships as we watch them unfold on the screen. Carpenter describes it this way: "In television, you can dig into the most humble, ordinary relationships; the relationship of the bourgeois children to their mother, of middle-class husband to his wife, of white-collar father to his secretary.[12]

Other analysts have described this property of television as that which makes television a sensual and erotic medium because it brings people and relationships so close to the viewer. And again, this eroticism is an addictive element that other media seem to be incapable of producing. It is an emotional dimension, and television delivers it well. Carpenter notes:

The gestures of visual man are not intended to convey concepts that can be expressed in words, but inner experiences, nonrational emotions which would still remain unexpressed when everything that can be told has been told. Such emotions lie in the deepest levels. They cannot be approached by words that are mere reflections of concepts, any more than musical experiences can be expressed in rational concepts. Facial expression is a human experience rendered immediately visible without the intermediary of word. It is Turgenev's "living truth of the human face"[13]

Asa Berger reminds us that "news isn't so much a report of reality as a form of 'created reality.'"[14] It is a reality created by the person aiming the camera and deciding what scenes or people we should see. It is not their intent to dupe or manipulate us necessarily, but we must remember that this is a mediated reality and someone's interpretation of reality. Berger concludes, "Each medium has a kind of logic inherent in it and

news people—without necessarily being conscious of this—are profoundly affected by the medium they use."[15] This is certainly the case
with Leslie Stahl's comment earlier, and it is true for all television reporters. Thus, the sense of reality that people get from television may
well differ from the sense of reality they get from the print media.

> We now have begun to see television news stories . . . as dramas—or to recognize
> that journalists cast a dramatic form upon stories, which leads to interesting ques-
> tions about what news is and how it functions. When we see news as a narrative
> or story, news no longer seems to be a simple report about reality. The fact that
> news stories have a strong dramatic aspect to them may offer an insight into why
> so many people seem to be almost addicted to news programs on TV. News, we
> now recognize, is not just information; it has become a form of theater.[16]

One of the chief differences between television and print media is that
in television a teller and a listener have been added to the tale. This is
the news anchor who frames, reads, and reviews each story and who is
clearly the one in command of the storytelling. S. Sperry explains that
the role of the anchor is to "move the program along, linking story to
story according to some larger pattern of meaning, as if the stories of the
half-hour were thoughts from a single mind, ordered and moving in rational progression." Sperry continues, "The tale is narrated not merely
to provide information but also to affect the listener in some way: to
persuade or change him, to evoke an emotional response, or simply to
interest him."[17]

When it comes to the property of immediacy, which traditional television and its newer forms are able to deliver, we can see another effect
on the kind and validity of information presented. It is a general truism
in newsrooms that the longer a reporter has to work on a story, the more
complete and accurate it may be. Truth seldom emerges in a hurry. *Time*
essayist Roger Rosenblatt once noted that, like a growing fern, truth re-
veals itself only in stages.[18] The history of journalism is littered with examples of stories that would have been great, if only they had been true.
More often than not, entries are inserted into the corrections and clari-
fications column of daily newspapers because some reporter or editor
rushed too quickly to get a story into print without having adequate time
to check on its accuracy and completeness.

When talking about accuracy, we must remember there are at least
three kinds:

1. *Factual accuracy*, which is what we most often think of. A thing either is or
   it is not. Someone said something or they did not; something happened or it
   did not. This kind of accuracy is often the easiest of the three to achieve because many distinct facts are often easy to discover and are indisputable.

2. *Contextual accuracy*, which is the focus of most critical attacks on news stories. If getting facts straight is possible on deadline, getting the context right is often not possible. It takes time to develop context—to put ideas, statements, and events into their historical perspective. A journalist once observed that daily reporting is so much a matter of reporting who hit someone's jaw that there is seldom time to ask what the victim was doing sticking his jaw out in the first place. Journalism has come a long way, both in print and television, in pursuing the context of the story and the reasons behind the actions, but the daily deadline leaves only so much room for this type of insight, and it is seldom enough time.

3. *Linguistic accuracy*, which is the nuance and connotative meaning in which the report is couched. MIT linguist Noam Chomsky and the late semanticist S. I. Hayakawa have made careers of studying this type of accuracy in all kinds of communications. They concluded that the way in which something is said is often more important than what is said. Linguistic accuracy, like contextual accuracy, does not play well on deadline except with the most literate of journalistic writers who understand the nuances of vocabulary and phraseology.

The reality is, however, that with real-time reporting becoming likely for both electronic and print journalists because of the merging of the two media into one that is instantaneously accessible by consumers, these types of accuracy could suffer. It was hard enough for a television camera crew to show up minutes after an eye-popping event occurred and deliver an accurate story a half-hour later on the 6 o'clock news. But with real-time reporting, the reporter cannot even wait that half-hour because the story may be viewed or read even as it is being assembled and written. In an arena such as this, rumor and fact command equal attention, and it is not clear until later which is truth.

THE NEWSPAPER EFFECT

The newspaper delivers a different format of news, with differing effects on the consumer. As a print medium, it demands a little more of the news consumer because reading is a more difficult process than watching television, but also because the points made are revealed more slowly, in a more linear, one-at-a-time fashion. Often, points are made more subtly than on television, where there is little time for subtleties. Thus, patience and a higher degree of discernment—if not actual intelligence—is needed to process news stories in print as opposed to television stories in which someone else is reading the story and delivering it in an animated manner.

Research also indicates that many people feel they trust television news more than print news for many types of news stories. While that may seem odd, based on the amount of research and space given to an average newspaper story versus a 90-second TV news package, the results seem to be consistent throughout the variety of credibility surveys. Attaching such credibility to television may not seem so odd, however, if one looks at what constitutes credibility: familiarity, liking, trustworthiness, and expertise. It is much easier for most people to attach such factors to a television anchor or on-air reporter—who has been coached on how to appear more credible—than to a print story written by someone the reader has no way of knowing or seeing. In other words, there is no visible teller in newspaper stories, and the teller may well be the most important element in any narrative. In the movie *Broadcast News*, for example, the highly talented reporter and writer, played by Albert Brooks, found that no amount of moving prose could elevate his career at the network as quickly as the poised and suave news anchor, played by William Hurt, despite the fact that the anchor was a near-failure as an actual journalist. Those who work in television news know that, while this example comes from the world of fiction, it is not far-removed from the conditions in real life. Staff cutbacks at all three major networks in the 1980s that jettisoned several solid journalists and left the more appealing personalities in place show this to be true. Thus, in television news, credibility is not so much a function of good writing—or even good reporting—as it is of carefully constructed illusions of familiarity, likability, expertise, and trustworthiness of the anchors. "Television is a world of mirrors," says one Indianapolis news anchor for the ABC affiliate. "Consultants and focus groups are often more important in deciding a journalist's credibility than the journalist's own credentials and abilities."[19]

Historian Elizabeth Eisenstein notes, "History bears witness to the cataclysmic effect on society of inventions of new media for the transmission of information among persons. The development of writing and later the development of printing are examples."[20] She notes further that all of anthropology—as well as casual observations of children—"reminds us of the gulf that exists between oral and literate cultures."[21] If television—in whatever form—is to replace the print medium as our chief storyteller and teacher, then we should be aware of the consequences that are likely to occur. Some of these changes will be discussed in the next chapter, and they include loss of individuality and—according to McLuhan and Innis—the loss of literacy and a return to a sort of modern tribalism. There is always a danger of overstating a thesis, and many researchers and casual observers feel that McLuhan overstated his, glossing over the differences between people and cultures and assuming that a sort of bullet theory of mass media effects is valid. Communications research over the past two decades has cast doubts on such a theory of blanket, uniform effects and has, in its place, championed more of a diffusion theory of media effects that takes into account such influences as peer groups and families. Research has also focused on uses and gratification theory, which take into account the functions that news serves for individual consumers. Nevertheless, McLuhan does provide food for thought, and there is a lot of anecdotal evidence to back up his views on the changes wrought by television over print. For instance, regarding the loss of individuality and private identity, consider that hearing a speech or watching a television program bring people together. To read a newspaper, book or magazine, however, people are encouraged to draw apart, even though they may be in the same room. They are drawing apart to immerse themselves in the stories they are reading, from which they may draw different interpretations and impressions because of the subtleties present in the writing. Eisenstein notes, "By its very nature, a reading public (is) not only more dispersed; it (is) also more atomistic and individualistic than a hearing one."[22] In looking at the rise of reading in civilizations, she concludes:

Even while communal solidarity was diminished, vicarious participation in more distant events was also enhanced; and even while local ties were loosened, links to larger collective units were being forged. Printed materials encouraged silent adherence to causes whose advocates could not be found in any one parish and who addressed an invisible public from afar. New forms of group identity began to compete with an older, more localized, nexus of loyalties. Urban populations were not only pulled apart, they were also linked in new communication. Personal attendance was increasingly supplemented by vicarious participation in civic functions and municipal affairs.[23]

Continuing to look back in an attempt to understand the different effects of an oral (today, a television) culture and a written culture, Walter Ong states that the print medium removed the ancient art of orally based rhetoric from the center of education and encouraged the quantification of knowledge, through the use of thematical analysis, diagrams, and charts. Like McLuhan, he feels that print was a prime factor in helping people to establish personal identities and personal privacy. "It produced books . . . setting the stage psychologically for solo reading . . . and eventually for completely silent reading. . . . Print created a new sense of the private ownership of words . . . [and it] encouraged human beings to think of their own interior conscious and unconscious resources as more and more thing like, impersonal and religiously neutral. Print encouraged the mind to sense that its possessions were held in some sort of inert mental state."[24]

Many linguists, communication theorists, and historians also believe that the print medium provides a sense of closure. This can be described as a feeling that what one reads in a newspaper or book is in its final state; that it has reached a sense of completion. A newspaper, for instance, does not accommodate changes as quickly as does a television news report, which can come on at any time, be updated even while the anchor is reading the story, and can appear, as in the case of the television coverage of the Gulf War, to go on endlessly.

While it may seem a strange example, think of how a key religious text such as the Bible might affect you if it were produced only as a video and not as written text. Would it have the sense of closure that Ong talks about? Would it have the same authority? What if you did not like the looks of the characters on the screen? Would that detract from the truthfulness of their statements? Would you even pay attention to the spoken text, or would you (as Michael Deaver insists) be swept away by the video and forget about what is said? And would it be as personal an inspirational medium as the Bible is today? Could you pull out a pocket version of it on a hike in the mountains or late at night in a hotel room when you are in need of encouragement and hope? In answering such questions, possibly an understanding of the differences between the effects of written texts and visual texts will begin to emerge. They are important differences, and the age of visual information is changing a lot about the way we learn and the effects that learning has on us.

There are, however, those communications scholars who disagree that television clouds or detracts from the literacy rate of Americans. Usually these researchers point to the lack of empirical research done on television's effect on literacy and assert that because of this paucity of research any conclusion ascribing a negative effect by television on literacy is unfounded. One of these researchers is Susan Neuman who, in her book *Literacy in the Television Age*, attempts to debunk three popularly held theories regarding television's effects. These theories are that (1) television is entertainment without intentional learning goals, and reading has been displaced by it; (2) television communicates through analogical forms—direct symbols—while schools rely on digital forms, or words and numbers; and (3) television exposure rewards only immediate benefits and its rapid fragmentation induces short attention spans, which work against any logical learning by print in schools. But the proof these researchers offer is an absence of empirical proof rather than an impressive array of actual research results that might confirm their conclusions. One theory that Neuman does seem to support, at least in some degree, is that television enhances children's learning by stimulating new interests. Therefore, television can play a positive role in educational achievement if not in literacy training particularly. As Clifford G. Christians notes, "Neuman offers a different understanding of television's educational value. She advocates a theory of synergy in which 'the skills acquired from media act conjointly in helping children construct meaning and generate inferences in new contexts.'. . . Neuman's research suggests that there may be a 'spiraling effect' in which television serves as a constructive intellectual stimulant."[25]

Although Neuman and others who rely so heavily on empirical research acknowledge that there may be a good deal of anecdotal evidence supporting the view that television diminishes literacy—and that indeed there is some evidence of that also from reading achievement scores—they feel that this is not evidence enough to confirm the three theories that she attempts to contradict. The empirical data, however, that these researchers need is extremely hard to come by. Practically, conducting studies over time and involving a large enough sampling of subjects is beyond the reach of most communications researchers. Christians concludes about the work of Neuman and others, "While valuable in their own right, these books will not serve as much of a catalyst for long-term resolution of literacy as will philosophical anthropology."[26]

So it is with some sense of concern and apprehension that one realizes the print tradition has become at least challenged—if not irrevocably diminished—by the new oral and visual traditions of television. Television (see the discussion of Channel One in chapter 4) has become such an omnipresent education tool in secondary school classrooms, which shows that this diminishment is only increasing, as does the research indicating that the average American watches almost 7 hours of television each day. It appears to be the passing of an era—the era of literacy that replaced the first oral tradition several hundred years ago. It began with the rising popularity of television in the 1960s and 1970s, and it is about to enter a new era with the coming age of interactive TV.

THE MERGING OF PRINT AND ELECTRONIC MEDIA

The tradition of print has not been totally wiped out by television and computers. As we have seen, some of the new media forms that will be part of the multimedia blitz are the electronic newspaper, magazine, and book. Even though the pressroom-produced newspaper may become a dinosaur in the twenty-first century, we will still be able to read printed text across the face of our PC or television set. HDTV or extensible television will make this reading more resolute and easier on the eyes than it currently is, and there will always be a home printer available to produce a hard-copy version of the newspaper. Nevertheless, it will be interesting to see—in light of failed videotex and teletext experiments of the past—how much this written-text format of the multimedia menu is accessed and used versus how many subscribers will turn to a channel where they can still have a pleasing personality tell them a story.

In addition, part of the multimedia allure is the actual mixing of video with text. Photographs on a newspaper no longer have to be stills; they can be moving even while you are reading the text that wraps around the video frame. Once again, however, one hears the assertion of Michael Deaver. If, in the battle between the eye and the ear, the eye wins every time, one wonders if the eye will not be constantly drawn to these colorful, dramatic video frames instead of the written text around them. Several tests run by such think tanks as the Poynter Institute for Media Studies show that even with traditional newspapers, the eye spends more time on visual elements than on printed matter.

Newspapers are also offering electronic databases, discussed in chapter 5, to be accessed via personal home computers. This, too, is a further merging of the textual and visual fields of information. Once a newspaper has an electronic library, it is a relatively small step to sell the archival information to outsiders. The resulting databases from different newspapers are made available to consumers through one or more of several established consumer databases such as CompuServe, Nexis, Vu/Text or DataTimes. These services offer customers fast access to interesting pieces of information from a large memory bank of data. Most such databases are priced so high today that they are beyond the reach of most would-be individual subscribers. Instead, they are marketed mostly to other news media and to businesses who want to stay abreast of the latest developments in news.

Newspapers are also mixing audio with their print services via *audiotex*, the offering of information over the telephone, such as updated weather and sports information as well as the latest news briefs and stock quotations. *USA Today* is a classic example of how this service is offered via 1-900 phone numbers in which callers are assessed charges for this latest information. New technology has made it possible to offer telephone information services like this unburdened by the cost of providing banks of human operators and not limited to the confines of prerecorded tapes. Customers with push-button phones can make simple choices and quickly get back tailored information from stored digitized data. A study done by the American Society of Newspaper Editors (ASNE) notes the following about audiotex services:

Much of this traffic has no obvious tie-in to traditional journalism, but there may be niche markets for newspapers. To be a viable product, the information would have to be of interest in small nuggets, because of the inefficiency of the spoken word in communicating complex information. It would have to be easily specified, and it would have to satisfy an urgent need, especially if the same information already is scrolling across the screen of a financial or weather or sports service on cable TV and the only cost is having to wait a minute or two for it to come around.[27]

Of course, a much discussed mixing of news media formats exists with videotex and teletext, detailed in chapter 5. Schemes to provide interactive news have used a variety of delivery techniques: PCs already owned by the customers, special terminals provided with the service (for free or for a cost), data over telephone wires, data over cable TV, data sandwiched between the pictures on the broadcast TV signal; information displayed on a screen, information printed on a computer printer, and pages rolling out of a fax machine. Few stones have been left unturned in the search for development of the electronic newspaper.

The ASNE notes that "the most successful formula, so far, has been broad-based services linked to home computers over telephone lines."[28] Offerings on these services include breaking news, electronic shopping, service information such as airline schedules and movie times, bulletin boards, and database search and retrieval. "In terms of current volume, material generated by journalists is only a small fraction of the total," the ASNE observed in 1989.[29]

At a conference entitled "The Cost of Technology" held at Columbia University, Anthony Smith described the new technologies' effect on information:

The same thing is happening to information today that happened to land during the Enclosure movement in the history of England, when common pastures were appropriated by the lords, privatized and, of course, became instruments of the wool and textile industry. Information that has been common property is increasingly being privatized, appropriated in value-added networks, and is being sold.[30]

As the next chapter will show, the selling of what used to be free information has some huge implications when it comes to creating a knowledge gap in America. We all are familiar with the old adage "information is power." When information lies in the hands of only those who can afford it, as is increasingly becoming the case, then the foundation of an informed citizenry making appropriate decisions in a democracy is undermined.

In another assessment of the effects of today's information revolution, David Crowley and Paul Heyer comment:

We can draw on insights from past media revolutions. We know, for instance, that new media frequently bypass difficulties, bottlenecks or barriers engendered in the use or control of older media. In the later middle ages, print helped democratize the reading public in Europe. It lessened the control over literacy exercised by church scribes. The resulting changes profoundly reorganized the ways in which knowledge circulated in society. Likewise, in the promotion of electronic communications such as broadcasting, analysts have seen an equivalent bypassing of the institution of the book and newspaper in accessing information.[31]

Derrick de Kerckhove refers to the new information age as the era of psychotechnologies. A *psychotechnology* is any "technical device which extends or emulates one human psychological feature or another, or a group of them."[32] Psychotechnologies include "live" information-processing devices and networks, public and domestic, such as the telephone, radio, television, computers, or satellites. Explaining this concept further, de Kerckhove says that at the simplest level we must be seated in front of a television to watch the programming. Similarly, we must call on our memory and creative imagination differently when we read a newspaper, magazine, or book page, or even when we listen to the radio. Then, at a higher and more speculative level, "our exposure to largely distributed media such as books or television may actually have secondary effects well beyond the time of the exposure itself, and entrain us both socially and psychologically to respond according to technological rather than exclusively psychological criteria."[33] For instance, the meaning that we infer from information is often predicated on how images play in our minds. We must turn words into visual images in our head if a novel is to be interesting or come alive to us. Such translation is necessary if what we are reading makes any sense or connects with anything within.

Both McLuhan and de Kerckhove agree that private identity and individuality is wrapped up in reading because reading mirrors the activity of an autonomous mind and the evolution of one's perception of his or her own personal identity.[34] In short, while reading invites a person to make sense within, television invites him or her to make sense without by weaving us into a "mass psychology," which chooses issues for us and unifies us in "soul-searching predicaments. . . . Public morality is worked out live on TV." De Kerckhove calls this "the new electronic common sense . . . cautious . . . bland [and not taking] chances with public morality or sides on issues."[35]

Assessing what information overload, via television and the new media, can do to the viewer, the *Washington Post's* Meg Greenfield has offered warnings of "misreading the shorthand," but concludes that, in the end, having more information is better than having less.

[With TV], time and space as we once knew them in my lifetime are obliterated. And so too are psychic distance and political solitude. Politicians, when they are not themselves seeking to manipulate their television personas, are forever worrying that the rest of us will be manipulated by seeing something we won't understand. . . . The danger is, of course, that by seeing so much more we will believe we have seen and known everything and that we understand much more than we do. But that is surely no reason for trying to curtail what we do see. . . . I can think of circumstances where individuals, as in criminal trials, may be hurt and circumstances in which a premium may be put on political misbehavior because the camera is rolling. But I can't think of any in which the viewing public has been one whit harmed by the presence of the force—TV—which has been the real revolution in our time.[36]

With the addition of the interactive dimension, the lines between television and print will become blurred in this new age of multimedia and videotex. In the same way, the grounds of human psychology will also be blurred once again. We will be reading, if we choose to, but we will also be distracted by all the pretty, moving pictures and graphics. We will also get a chance at becoming not only the news show's own director but also its editor, as more and more power and control passes into our hands by way of the two-way remote-control device. Not everyone is thrilled about this new consumer control, however.

Writing an op-ed piece for the *New York Times*, Peter M. Herford noted in 1990 that an interactive experiment by CNN that year which allowed its viewers to select all but the lead story in its newscasts was badly misguided. Under the experiment, viewers could call in and vote on story selections from a sort of broadcast menu of news stories available for airing. "What happens when the choice of stories is left up to a public vote? The results can be disastrous," writes Herford, director of the Benton Fellowships in Journalism at the University of Chicago. "Mass audience surveys always show a preference for domestic news over international news, entertainment news over news of government and economics, news of Donald Trump over news of the homeless. The best news organizations offer a balance."[37] It is a complaint that editors have lodged many times against news by viewer or reader consensus: in turning over the editing controls to the public, the editor foregoes his or her responsibility in deciding which, among the many stories available, are significant enough to have an impact on the news consumers. It is the old debate of giving the public what they say they want versus giving them what the editors feel they need to have in order to be informed citizens in a democracy. Taking the one side casts one as a mere marketer of information; taking the other view casts one as an arrogant journalist who distrusts and belittles the public he or she is called on to serve.

In the uniting of television with interactive computer technology lies the basis for something else, discussed in greater detail in chapter 2: artificial intelligence, or AI. This is the attempt to simulate some of the most useful cognitive abilities which our psyches, supported by literacy, has provided us. Already there is a vast amount of computer software that goes beyond the parameters of a single mind and extends many mental processes such as thinking, reading, sorting, storing, judging, imagining, designing, planning, overviewing, analyzing, and creating.[38] In short, machines are being designed to do much of the cognitive work that was once reserved solely for humans. At least such computers will be able to extend our powers; our job may simply be to think something; the computer's job will be to get it done. De Kerckhove describes it this way:

The new media are striving to become intermediate environments accessing the intimate reality of our private psyche and bridging it with the outside world. They effect a kind of social mediation in a single continuous extension of our personal powers of imagination, concentration and action. They function largely like a second mind, soon to be endowed with more autonomy than we may care to give it.[39]

If live television sped up the deadline demands on reporters—and on the accuracy of their reports—we can expect only more such pressure from the new multimedia formats. Tom Brokaw, managing editor and anchor of the NBC *Nightly News*, has noted that "the essence of this new technology is speed. But if journalism is reduced simply to an exercise in swiftness then we will have become hostages to the new technology; not the masters of it."[40] Brokaw goes on to say that this speed also provides newsmakers with instant access to the American people. As a result, a lot of foreign policy is being conducted on television in programs like *Today* and *Nightline*. Brokaw warns:

The obvious danger here is that with the access made possible by the new technology, television journalists will be tempted to become negotiators and arbiters and not merely reporters. Our mission, really, is to examine and to explain policy, not to formulate it. Moreover, we must be especially vigilant that satellites do not become merely expensive megaphones with which foreign leaders offer their views to the world in an unexamined fashion. . . . The test for all of us . . . is how to strike the balance between form and content, how to use the new technology to enhance the fundamental tenets of journalism without surrendering them.[41]

Jon Katz, a former executive producer of the CBS "Morning News," believes that journalism—especially broadcast journalism—is being redefined by the new advances in communications technologies. He describes these changes as follows:[42]

1. *Local cable news*. When Time Warner plugged in its 24-hour cable news operation, called New York One News, in New York City in 1992, "a new age of truly local television news dawned." The New York City venture was not the first of its kind, but it is the largest profile operation in existence—or at least it was in the early 1990s. According to Katz, this operation seemed to have much more of a local focus than other local cable operations. And with this amount of time to fill, there is not much significant local news that will not get covered, especially if Time Warner funds it to the point where enough reporters and camera crews can be put into the field. This focus on local news is good because most news should be localized. Local operations such as New York One will put the heat on traditional local network affiliates who promise local news but deliver very little of it. Katz believes these operations must "contend with live news not just from Moscow but from Main Street. Television will be able to tell you where all those sirens are headed, and show you the fire as well."[43]

2. *Video culture*. More than 40 million home entertainment systems

are now installed in American homes, which use Nintendo, Sega, Genesis and the like. New services such as the Miami-based Video Jukebox network permit subscribers to dial up their own music videos. Some 13 million homes already subscribe to this network. Sports channels are also experimenting with interactive controls that allow viewers to select a variety of camera angles, turning each viewer into a kind of director. Specialized programming will connect with Bell Company computer systems and home entertainment programs to trap any person who owns a television. In 1992, the FCC designated a special radio frequency for interactive, over-the-air television services, allowing users to order take-out food from restaurants, pay bills, and call up sports scores via their remote-control devices.

3. *Pay-per-view*. In 1992, NBC made broadcasting history by showing more than 1,000 hours of the Summer Olympics from Barcelona by way of PPV. Although an ambitious experiment, the viewer demand was not great, and subscriber rates had to be cut to attract more viewers. Nevertheless, PPV presents a serious challenge to the already-squeezed broadcast networks.

4. *C-SPAN*. Cable's public service channel will become one of the most significant sources of government and political news in America, according to Katz. During the 1992 presidential campaign, C-SPAN aired 24-hour press conferences, call-ins, debates, and the like. No other news network, not even CNN, did that.

5. *The Baby Bells*. "Calling them babies is like calling the Terminator 'Toodles,'" quips Katz.[44] The Bell companies can now enter the information market with computers that access financial and other information and with message systems that will expand Americans' ability to chat electronically with people nationwide.

6. *Live, real-time, coverage*. The Gulf War, the Clarence Thomas-Anita Hill hearings, and the aborted coup in the former Soviet Union were covered in real time by live television. All connected the viewer in unprecedented ways. On this point, Katz notes:

The challenge for broadcast news has never seemed more fundamental: at a time when television technology can take us almost everywhere to cover almost anything, what precisely is the new role of the broadcast journalist? To introduce live coverage? Or to explain, shape, and comment on it? . . . Like much of the mainstream print media it has challenged and in some ways supplanted, broadcast journalism tends to equate the status quo with responsible, ethical journalism and to view the new video culture as a cross between prostitution and Armageddon . . . broadcast journalism has allowed itself to be perceived as dying, in a constant state of retrenchment and cutback. Yet television news is hardly becoming extinct; it is spreading all over the place. In one sense, commercial broadcast journalism is freer to experiment and innovate than at any time since its inception.[45]

SUMMARY

The precision of speculation on the future of the media and its impact on definitions of news is somewhat hazy. It is not yet known which of the many media forms discussed in this book will even be implemented on a large-scale, commercial basis. We have some sense from history how prognosticators have been wrong about the shape of the future, despite an abundant amount of current information that seems to indicate what that future will look like. Popular CBS radio commentator Charles Osgood, for instance, once looked back at an early twentieth century World's Fair in which a large-model exhibit of a small city under a glass dome was said to be the way the city of tomorrow would be constructed to ensure proper climate year-round. His observation on the exhibit? "The future is not what it used to be."

Another example, although closer to the mark, is found in Newton Minnow's famed "Vast Wasteland" speech delivered May 9, 1961. Looking to the future of television, Minnow called UHF television a "sleeping giant" that would one day revolutionize the industry and that could provide a half-dozen broadcast networks like ABC, CBS, and NBC.[46] Well, UHF television did become a reality, although it has not exactly proven to be the future of television nor the sleeping giant that Minnow predicted. And, as for a half-dozen broadcast networks, most analysts now believe television will be lucky to retain all of the big three. Probably more interesting than what he did predict was what Minnow did not foresee in the explosion of cable TV, which has truly been the story of the 1970s and 1980s. Nor did he—or could he have been expected to—see the dawning of multimedia forms and interactive TV by way of fiber optics and/or direct broadcast satellites.

Obviously, much of what the future has in store lies just beyond the pale of current information or even speculation. One thing is clear, however, the decade of the 1990s will probably witness more changes in media forms and their effects on journalism and on news consumers than any decade since the founding of the printing press. At the risk of appearing too much a foolish prophet, the next chapter will look at some of the possible lifestyle changes that could be brought by the new media.

NOTES

1. Marshall McLuhan, *Understanding Media* (New York: Mentor), 1964, 30.
2. Ibid.
3. Ibid.
4. Ibid., 36.
5. Ibid., 37.

6. Comments by Michael Deaver to Bill Moyers on PBS series, *The Public Mind: Illusions of News*, November 1989.

7. Comments by Leslie Stahl to Bill Moyers on PBS Series, *The Public Mind: Illusions of News*, November 1989.

8. Jeff Greenfield, "America Rallies 'Round the TV Set," *TV Guide*, February 16–22, 1991, 5.

9. Ibid., 7.

10. Edmund Carpenter, "The New Languages," in *Communication in History*, ed. David Crowley and Paul Heyer (New York: Longman, 1991), 218.

11. Ibid.

12. Ibid., 219.

13. Ibid.

14. Arthur Asa Berger, ed. *Media USA: Process and Effect* (New York: Longman, 1988), 149.

15. Ibid.

16. Ibid.

17. Sharon Sperry as quoted in Dan Nimmo and James E. Combs, "The Nature of Television News," in *Media USA: Process and Effect*, ed. Arthur Asa Berger (New York: Longman, 1988), 150.

18. Roger Rosenblatt, "Journalism and the Larger Truth," *Time*, July 2, 1984, 88.

19. Personal interview with Diane Willis, news anchor for WRTV, Indianapolis, IN, July 10, 1993.

20. Elizabeth Eisenstein, "The Rise of the Reading Public," in *Communication in History*, ed. David Crowley and Paul Heyer (New York: Longman, 1991), 94.

21. Ibid., 96.

22. Ibid., 100.

23. Ibid.

24. Walter Ong, "Print, Space, and Closure," in *Communication in History*, ed. David Crowley and Paul Heyer (New York: Longman, 1991), 109–110.

25. Clifford Christians, book review of *Literacy in the Television Age*, by Susan Neuman, *Quill*, April 1992, 26.

26. Ibid.

27. "ASNE Studies Audiotext," *Editor & Publisher*, April 28, 1989, 32.

28. "ASNE Studies Audiotext," 33.

29. Ibid.

30. Anthony Smith, comments made in "The Cost of Technology," Columbia University Seminar, April 1990, New York City.

31. David Crowley and Paul Heyer, *Communication in History* (New York: Longman, 1991), 246.

32. Derrick de Kerckhove, "The New Psychotechnologies," in *Communication in History*, ed. David Crowley and Paul Heyer (New York: Longman, 1991), 267.

33. Ibid.

34. Ibid.

35. Ibid., 268.

36. Meg Greenfield, "Misled by the Facts," *Newsweek*, June 26, 1989, 76.

37. Peter M. Herford, "Experiment in Interactive News," *New York Times* March 21, 1990, 12A.

38. Ibid.

39. de Kerckhove, "New Psychotechnologies," 269.

40. Tom Brokaw, comments made in "The Cost of Technology," Columbia University Seminar, April 1990, New York City.

41. Ibid.

42. Jon Katz, "New World of TV," *Washington Journalism Review*, February 1993, 11.

43. Ibid.

44. Ibid., 12.

45. Ibid.

46. Newton Minnow, "Television as a Vast Wasteland," speech delivered at FCC Convention, May 9, 1961, Washington, D.C.

10
• • • • •

Lifestyle Implications of Multimedia

This chapter examines some of the changes in lifestyles that are being predicted if multimedia—and its resulting turbonews—becomes a regular feature of our daily lives. Included in these changes could be the following:

1. An increasing awareness among people of their world, but also an extension of the knowledge gap among different economic classes in society.
2. A greater degree of instruction and socialization by television in schools.
3. A tremendous impact on the ways companies conduct business, especially on a global scale.
4. Vast differences in the way Americans go shopping and make purchasing decisions.
5. Differences in the way Americans structure their work habits, for example, an increasing use of the home as the workplace.
6. The creation of a global community linked by multimedia.
7. The threatened loss of individual privacy resulting from larger and more extensive consumer databases.
8. The ability to receive more tailored information from a much more segmented—indeed individualized—media.
9. The loss of individual identity and saturation of media images.
10. The rise of computer crime as more and more of the nation comes online.
11. An acceleration of the pace of politics, as office-seekers can reach voters faster and in a more saturated manner than ever before.
12. A growing "technification" and possible dehumanization of people as they are reduced to numbers in huge consumer databases.

13. A rise in our vulnerability to sophisticated marketing and advertising techniques, especially as we input more and more information about ourselves and personal preferences into huge databases.

14. An overlapping of job functions and a blurring of lines of authority as computer information systems are integrated more and more into the various aspects of business.

15. Differences in social relations as electronic bulletin boards and E-mail replace more face-to-face contact among people, and the threatened decline and fall of personality as we interact more with different facets of multimedia.

The following sections will analyze some of the changes on the horizon that have just been listed. Keep in mind that these are speculative in nature, based on the evidence that is available now in the fast-changing world of communications technologies, and that several years from now some future Charles Osgood might look back at these predictions and note, "The future is not what it used to be." With these caveats in mind, here are the predictions.

THE KNOWLEDGE GAP

The new media have the potential of providing more knowledge and awareness, but they also can further extend a knowledge gap in America and in many other parts of the world. In some countries—most notably Third World countries—this gap is very wide, as few people possess the means to obtain information about what is going on in their countries and around the world. But to add America to the list of African, Asian, and Middle Eastern countries experiencing such an information drought is alarming to many people. After all, isn't everyone talking about what a glut of information there is in the United States? Indeed, aren't we living in the much ballyhooed Information Age? The answer is yes—and no. There is a growing information gap or knowledge gap in this country that will only get wider when information that is now available in a rather inexpensive form will one day cost a lot more to obtain and will require certain equipment to do so.

Such a knowledge gap will also help to develop more distinct class lines rather than the hoped-for classless society. Some researchers, such as Cecile Gaziano, believe that these classes will polarize, reversing the trends of the past five decades.[1] This polarization could result in the following:

1. A decline in the quality and degree of education and educational opportunities.

2. Changes in the way we work and the structure of the economy.

3. A widening gap between the rich and the poor.

These changes are likely to be felt and seen more in the large urban centers of America, but they will affect all Americans to one degree or another.

The knowledge-gap hypothesis suggests that a rising diffusion of information in a society will lead to increasing knowledge gaps among individuals who live in different socioeconomic sectors of society. The hypothesis further predicts that social groups occupying lower-strata positions may gain information but not as fast as those people in higher-strata groups. Therefore, the predictive element here is socioeconomic class: the richer classes will be able to receive more information than the poorer classes. Studies have focused on different educational phenomena in this country to help confirm the knowledge-gap hypothesis. Several years ago, one such study focused on the degree to which the PBS program "Sesame Street" enabled children to gain more knowledge than children who grew up prior to the program's creation. The study indicated that, while post-Sesame Street children acquired more knowledge as children than did pre-Sesame Street children, there was a fairly wide knowledge gap created by those children who did not have access to a television set in the first place and those that did and who, hence, could watch "Sesame Street."[2]

Researchers know that the chief sources of knowledge in America are interpersonal relationships, formal schooling, organizational memberships (including church and family groups), and the mass media. It is well known that all of these methods of learning and socialization are distributed unevenly among members of the population. Some children and adults circulate in peer groups in which education and knowledge are not a high priority; some children grow up in broken families without a mother or father; not all children are able to attend good schools, and not all people are able to afford newspapers, books or magazines, or subscribe to cable television—even if they can afford to purchase a television set.

With the expense associated with the new multimedia systems, it seems likely that the exposure to knowledge gleaned from mass media will only decline for those who cannot afford the necessary electronic components of multimedia, or who do not possess the basic understanding needed to operate computer systems.

Results of a survey of a low-strata neighborhood in 1980 showed, somewhat ironically, that "widely distributed information sources—neighborhood newspapers and participation in neighborhood organizations—contributed to knowledge levels of less educated residents, yet knowledge gaps were found between more and less educated groups in the neighborhood."[3] The results indicate that socioeconomic factors may lead to larger knowledge gaps, even though information sources are widely distributed.[4] Gaziano concluded:

Widely distributed information sources appeared to be vital to less educated groups' ability to learn about neighborhood issues. Neighborhood newspapers contributed to public affairs knowledge, but characteristics linked to social stratification were more influential in explaining knowledge disparities. Readership of neighborhood newspapers and group participation contributed to knowledge levels of all socioeconomic groups; however, these two widely distributed information sources did not compensate for lack of education because more information sources were available to better educated residents.[5]

Gaziano, therefore, notes that knowledge gaps are not merely information gaps deriving from communication effects. They are part of larger gaps "between well-bounded social strata and they reflect disparities in information as one among many resources which are less available to lower SES [socioeconomic study] groups"[6]

CRITICAL THINKING SKILLS

In the pre-television era, when the print media was the dominant vehicle for news, information, and entertainment, one set of critical thinking skills was needed and most of us assumed it was the only kind. It was a time when we could read the assertions of authors and—in nonfiction works—their sources, and we could take time to evaluate them for their veracity. The same was true in print advertising: Claims would be made largely based on logic, and we could sit and ponder as to how logical the assertions actually were or whether we were being manipulated. Telling the difference between truth and lies has never been an easy matter, but it did seem easier when we were reading claims instead of being subjected to fleeting images in 10- to 30-second commercial spots on television.

The point is that the nature of the informational medium exerts a strong influence on the type of education the country should be providing its students if part of the goal of the educational process is helping them to discern truth from lies in the hundreds of claims they encounter daily or weekly. Television analyst Neil Postman notes:

If, for example, we were living in a culture where all forms of important public discourse were a product of the printing press, and an oratory rooted in the printed word, then it would make sense to educate our students in logic, rhetoric, and semantics, and leave it at that.[7]

Postman adds that, while this type of education is still useful, it is inadequate to meet the needs that the electronic age of television has thrust on us. He quotes Leonard Goldenson, chairman of the board of the ABC television network in 1985 as saying:

We can no longer rely on our mastery of traditional skills. As communicators, as performers, as creators—and as citizens— the electronic revolution requires a new kind of literacy. It will be a visual literacy, an electronic literacy, and it will be as much of an advance over the literacy of the written word we know today as that was over the purely oral tradition of man's early history.[8]

In the case of television advertising, for example, it is obvious that drama, aesthetics, emotion, inference, and association have replaced logic and reason as the bases for the appeal of commercials. In the campaign used to launch the Infinity luxury car, for instance, viewers were not even shown the car for several months. Instead, they were treated to pastoral views of nature and calming sounds, over which a soft-spoken voice associated these pleasing images to the new Infinity. There were no real claims or assertions made about the car, and it would be impossible to prove whether these scenes from nature had any bearing on this new automobile on the basis of logic or reason. In the end, the viewer might or might not enjoy the commercial, but that same viewer would find it impossible to confirm or reject the subjective, dramatic associations made with the product.

In large measure, this is the same basis on which America is sold its political candidates seeking office at election time. There is obvious imagery, there are associations with pleasing ideas and attractive people, there is even the commentary and news stories about how Candidate A's media handlers are putting a new spin on his or her campaign; yet, many Americans make themselves vulnerable to manipulation by these campaigns because they lack the necessary skills to critically evaluate these new kinds of information. Commenting on just how scarce actual issues are in political campaigns, PBS journalist Bill Moyers said about the 1988 presidential campaign involving Ronald Reagan and Michael Dukakis that less than 10 percent of the entire campaign focused on issues. The rest was on personalities and images[9] There was the image of George Bush in an Ohio flag factory, of Michael Dukakis in an Army tank, of both candidates reciting the pledge of allegiance, of Dukakis sitting in jeans on an Iowa haystack, and of Bush throwing out a ball at a baseball game. They weren't saying anything about what they were doing in each of these situations; they were just doing it, and the viewers were supposed to draw the correct inferences. Is this subject to empricial research or traditional critical thinking? No.

The same problem exists, to a greater or lesser degree, with television newscasts and with the concept of real-time reporting, discussed in Chapter 9 and seen vividly in the television coverage of the Gulf War. In a typical TV newscast, there are the attractive anchors and field reporters, the musical soundtrack leading into and out of each segment of the show, an upbeat rhythm (especially in local television) provided by the anchor-desk personalities, 10-second "readers" on stories that have no dramatic video (and which therefore rate little news value), and a series of 90-second news packages told in narrative form and written to the available video. All of these items are put together with little thought for context or discussion of even the immediate past history of stories. To be fair, these nightly news shows have been augmented successfully by weekly programs such as "60 Minutes," "Prime Time Live," "20/20," "48 Hours," and even nightly by "ABC Nightline," which analyze in depth from one to three stories a week. Yet even 22 minutes of airtime is still inadequate, especially when the subject seems to be polarizing a controversial subject by having two or more people offer their conflicting views. In the end, there is usually no resolution to the issue, and viewers are— in a sense—invited to choose sides and follow the guest who came across best on television. Another problem with these in-depth programs is that, after watching from 10 to 22 minutes on anything, it is not uncommon to think one has seen and heard everything there is to know on the subject, when, in fact, the surface has barely been scratched.

Assessing these problems, Postman makes the following suggestions:[10]

1. Realize that the traditional tools of logic, rhetoric, and semantics are still indispensable armaments with which to confront today's media-saturated society. In fact, educating students in the traditional subjects of history, literature, science, philosophy, and the arts can go a long way in girding individuals against the onslaught of trivia, emotional imagery, and manipulation.

2. Introduce a new subject area into the traditional curriculum: a course in the nature and impact of the media—what Postman calls "media ecology." It would focus on how the media control the form, distribution, and direction of information, and how such control affects cognitive and behavioral patterns.

3. Begin a program of media awareness as early as the elementary grades, focusing on the amount of time students watch television versus reading or listening to recorded music. Students can also discuss how what they see on television or in the news seems to effect life in their own households. They can discuss what Mom and Dad have to say at the dinner table and what instructions they give the children on evaluating television programs.

4. In high school, students should be exposed to a course or courses in how information differs in various symbolic forms. For instance, how are written communications different from visual messages and what are their different appeals? Which media seem to promote sequential, logical thought and which do not.

In addition to these suggestions, it is important to study the history of the media and mass communications. As McLuhan and others point out, the passage we are facing from a print to an electronic culture is very similar—if not identical—in its effects to the passage from the ancient oral traditions to written traditions and from the first eras of writing to the introduction of the printing press. By understanding how culture has changed in the past, students can better understand how culture is changing now, what the signposts are, and how they can critically evaluate mass communications today.

Also helping them is this understanding would be coursework in international and intercultural communications in which students can witness how other cultures—both Third World as well as advanced—have been affected by the state of their mass media industry, if one exists at all. Such an understanding shows students that their culture is not universal and that they can broaden their view of the type of culture they would like to be a part of—maybe even help create—by looking around at how other nations and people are living in relation to their communications system and mores.

Finally, educators must realize that simply because they were raised in one culture, it does not follow that their students will be living in the same one. Therefore, it is necessary for educators to look around and see what is happening now, as well as what is likely to happen, to the media. Only then can they fit their program of teaching critical thinking to the world that present students will face after graduation.

EFFECTS ON BUSINESS

It is difficult to overstate how much businesses are being—and will be—affected by the new information age. Already innovations such as teleconferencing, the revolution in desk and portable fax machines, and electronic and voice mail have resulted in major changes in the way America does business. Some of these changes in technology and their effects have been discussed in earlier chapters. Looking at one of these changes—videoconferencing—we can see the following.

Business has come to embrace videoconferencing because of the interruptions to work schedules and the growing expenses caused by so much business travel. Meanwhile, the costs associated with videoconferencing has fallen in recent years by a factor of 10, and videoconference systems are practically paying for themselves.[11] In addition, long-distance meetings via video seem to allow participants to reach decisions quicker. As a result, *Fortune* magazine notes, "The lure of such improvements could help make video communication the next big leap in the digital revolution. Analysts believe that by 1997 annual worldwide sales (of the equipment) might be as much as $8 billion."[12]

In a typical videoconference today, an array of equipment is rolled into a room for costs less than $40,000. Transmissions can be achieved for as little as $25 per hour, if the public telephone network is used. A video system might have one or two television monitors and an unobtrusively mounted camera, possibly behind a black glass window. A control panel allows participants to move the camera in the adjacent room to right or left, zoom in or out, and use an electronic stylus and a grid on the control panel to annotate a drawing on the screen, just as football analysts do on television during games. *Fortune* explains the technology this way:

At the heart of the system is a device called a codec (short for coder-decoder), which translates camera and microphone signals into the ones and zeros of computer language. At the receiving end, another codec turns the bits back into pictures and sound. Each video image comprises no fewer than 90 million bits of information per second, far too many to squeeze through a phone line. So the codec automatically discards unnecessary data, such as the parts of the picture that haven't changed since the last frame. Even so, most systems use fewer frames per second than regular TV, so the motion onscreen is less fluid.[13]

Dominating equipment sales of videoconferencing equipment are three American companies and one British firm. First on the scene was Compression Labs, Inc., or CLI, of San Jose, California. CLI was the first to transmit a compressed video signal over a standard telephone line. PictureTel of Danvers, Massachusetts, builds mobile systems. GPT of Britain makes mid-priced systems and is the leader in Europe. VideoTelecom of Austin, Texas, specializes in mediaconferencing, which is a system aimed at users who need to share information and graphics stored in PCs during videoconferences.

One of the challenges to the growth of videoconferencing is the same problem slowing the growth of HDTV: a uniform set of transmission and receiving standards. Standardizing these signals could cause the market to move into high gear as prices drop and the way becomes open for inexpensive desktop systems to enter the market.

Another form of videoconferencing is provided by the Public Broadcasting Service's Adult Learning Satellite Service (ALSS), discussed in detail later in this chapter. ALSS videoconferences are designed to meet the informational, educational, and training needs of geographically dispersed audiences. The subject of a videoconference if often quite specific. The *Opening All Doors* series, for example, offered architects the chance to become familiar with the new Americans with Disabilities Act. All ALSS videoconferences feature well-known national experts on a panel that is available for call-in questions from the ALSS audience. In most cases, host sites can make a videotape of the conference program and use it for the life of the tape. An indication of the kinds of videoconferencing programs that ALSS members developed and participated in can be seen in a partial listing of 1993 videoconferences:

- *Continuous Quality Improvement in Health Care.*
- *Creating the Live Event.* This particular program shows ALSS members how to develop and market videoconference programs via the service.
- *Successfully Employing People with Disabilities: What Managers Need to Know.*
- *Adults as Students: Their Status and Role in Higher Education.*
- *Getting to the Bottom Line with Corporations.*

Other changes in the information age are also in place, and still more are coming. Most will mean business executives will have to rethink the way they carry out their assignments. For instance, Ray Steele, director of the Center for Communication Science (CICS) at Ball State University, has formulated a list of four premises that he believes all information and communication professionals will need to understand when applying the new technologies to business:

1. Information-age solutions cross lines of interest and authority. This is discomforting to any management group.
2. Opportunity in the information age rarely resides in the traditional practice of simplifying, separating, and operating exclusive entities. That is a threatening prospect to any existing unit head.
3. Complexity, not simplicity, holds human and economic promise in an electronic information environment. That disrupts existing relationships.
4. Information and communication problems today require solutions that are integration oriented—first for people, and then for technologies.

Steele concludes, "In short, the answers to information age problems may come from several directions at once and involve people in what were once separate disciplines. Information specialists may find themselves working with computer people, human resources people, telecommunications people, on solutions that may not have clear-cut lines of authority."[14]

Daniel Yankelovich, one of the world's leading forecasters and public-opinion analysts, echoes this growing complexity in business relations. He predicts that by the year 2000 the relationships between a company and its customers, stockholders, suppliers, and competitors will become a more complicated arena that it is today.[15] For instance, in most larger firms today, a trio of executives share external-affairs duties and responsibilities for a company: the CEO usually represents the firm within the industry and at the higher levels of state and national government. A vice-president for public affairs and a vice-president for public relations, both reporting to the CEO, are the second and third members of the team. But, in the future, Yankelovich predicts:

Globalization will blur the boundaries between what is considered internal affairs and what is considered external affairs for corporations. As joint ventures spread, as more manufacturing is done "offshore," as R&D centers are distributed around the world, and as more work is contracted to people in remote locations, it will grow ever more difficult to draw a sharp line between "the company" and its suppliers and customers. The difficulties of dealing with "the government" will also increase as businesses face regulations from an array of governments around the world.[16]

Because of these changes, managing external affairs for a company will become even more important and challenging. Yankelovich argues for not divorcing communication from content. "How one addresses a sensitive issue will become as important as what action one proposes," he says.[17] This is the essence of business diplomacy, and it will become even more important than it is today.

Two other ways in which the new technologies will affect business are found in the concepts of "transnationality" and "banana dollars." *Transnationality* refers to what happens when information transcends national borders around the world. Just as this transfer of data will accelerate the pace of political change (students protesting in China during the Tianemen Square demonstration used fax machines to get their message out to the attention of the international media), such transfer of information will also affect corporate institutions as well. There are few geographic loyalties with corporations such as IBM when these companies produce and sell goods in several countries and when people all over the world own stock in such corporations.[18] Multinational companies are becoming more the norm than the exception, and they can take advantage of this new, fast international exchange of information and of the lowering of political barriers to international trade. In thinking of this concept the image of Arthur Jensen in the movie *Network* comes to mind. As head of the mythical Communication Corporation of America, Jensen made a dynamic plea to disturbed news anchor Howard Beale for understanding that there are no real national boundaries or national politics when it comes to international business. The world, he said, is one huge, international, interdependent corporation; there is no East, there is no West. There is only Exxon, IBM, and other multinational companies. As depressing as the message was—that the world is being run by and for large corporations and the profits they can generate for countries—there is also more than a modicum of truth to it.

Banana dollars refers to the electronic transfer of huge sums of cash all over the globe. International electronic funds transfers amounted to

$114 trillion in 1990, up from $72 trillion in 1985. As Peter Schwartz, president of Global Business Network, says, "Finance is not one of the biggest customers of communication services; it is by far the biggest customer."[19] Analysts Scott Cunningham and Alan L. Porter explain that these electronic funds, nicknamed bananas, resemble imaginary dollars charged for time on many computer systems. "Like bananas, electronic funds transactions are based less on tangible values than on fluctuations in demand on international markets. The massive flows of such banana dollars can rapidly destabilize all but the largest national economies."[20]

Yet another impact on business is that so many businesses are being advised that if they are in any way connected with manufacturing communication-related products or services they had better get involved now. The technology scene is changing so rapidly, with so many entrepreneurial businesses already exploring every conceivable niche in the industry, that the field is getting quickly crowded with competitors. *Newsweek* noted in 1993:

Some companies are way ahead. The regional phone companies . . . are racing the cable companies to lay the fiber-optic network that will make up—and control—the superhighway infrastructure. Microsoft, Intel, and General Instrument are reportedly near an agreement on joint technology, employing Microsoft's popular Windows program for an interactive TV-set-top system. Bill Gates' new company, Continuum, has been buying up the rights to computer storage for whole museums worth of paintings. Alongside—or in joint venture with—the giants, other companies are maneuvering for a piece of the action, whether it is to build the necessary black boxes, "smart TVs" and remotes that will manipulate some 500 channels, or the software and programming to run on them.[21]

Still another side effect for business is the flattening of organizational hierarchies and the decentralization of power in the giant corporations. Although international competition helped this trend along, so did technology. The reason? Middle management's role in a corporation historically has been that of an information conduit, sending data down the line from top executives and up the line from employees. This information, once stored in headquarter-centered mainframe computers, has been dispersed to a network of cheap desktop machines. Therefore, fewer middle managers are required to send this data back and forth. As business writers David C. Churbuck and Jeffrey S. Young note:

As companies decentralize and reform themselves around their information networks—tying branch offices, telecommuting employees and customers together with private networks, satellites, laptop computers and fax machines—the result is sometimes the end of entire middle layers of management.[22]

The disadvantage of this corporate downsizing is the tremendous loss of jobs formerly held by middle managers at the corporate level as corporate staffs are laid off. The advantage is often the energy and creativity felt by managers of operating units in the field who now have the power and flexibility to develop new products and services faster.

Analyst Stratford Sherman noted in 1993 that "more than any other agent of change, information technology is transforming the way business works. It is helping companies get leaner, smarter, closer to the customer."[23] New personal computer technology, spreadsheet programs, Microsoft's relatively user-friendly Windows software, E-mail, and local area networks linking groups of desktop computers bring ever more information out to where businesspeople need it. This also enables companies to flatten out their organizational structure; link teams across former barriers of specialty, rank, and geography; and create closer strategic and tactical relationships with customers as well as suppliers.[24] Sherman notes further that winning companies such as General Electric and Wal-Mart want to create structures that increase closeness among managers and between customers and suppliers. In the early 1990s, it was seen that neither the centralized mainframe computer nor the radically decentralized personal computer would provide the model business will use in the near future. Instead, businesses will be connected into increasingly coherent networks that connect all varieties of computers, from mainframe to laptop to the new wireless pocket devices. "The buzzword is client server," Sherman states. "The servers—whether PCs or mainframes—will act as efficient central repositories of data, holding anything from corporate files to videos and voice-mail messages."[25] The various computers will tap into these databases, obtain the information needed, and then managers will use that information to make quicker decisions, and hopefully better ones. Obviously, the companies that are more computer literate will be in the best position to take advantage of these coming networks of information.

In short, business is realizing that the idea of the information age applies not only to consumers but to business as well, as the country moves deeper and deeper into a post-industrial economy and more into a broadbased and extremely diverse communications products and services economy.

THE DECLINE OF INDIVIDUAL PERSONALITY

Psychologist Kenneth J. Gergen addresses the concept of *postmodern consciousness*, which he uses to describe the syndrome of Americans who are so bombarded with a multitude of media images, personalities, and relationships, that they have trouble hanging on to their own personal identity and recognizing the authenticity of traditional reason and emotions. Gergen believes the driving force behind postmodernism is technology—most notably communications technologies "that shower us with social relationships both direct and vicarious." Included in these technologies are the telephone, radio, television, motion pictures, mass publication, the photocopier, cassette recordings, CDs, satellite transmission, the VCR, computer, fax, and mobile telephone. All have become "standard equipment for a normal life." He continues:

No longer is our social existence tied to a small town, a suburban community, or an urban neighborhood. Rather, as we wake to "Good Morning America," read the papers, listen to radio talk shows . . . answer faxes and electronic mail . . . take an evening graze through cable-TV channels, we consume and are consumed by a social world of unbounded proportion. We are exposed to more opinions, values, personalities, and ways of life than was any previous generation in history. . . . There is, in short, an explosion in social connection.[26]

So what does all this have to do with the decline of human personality and to our sense of personal identity? Gergen lists the following:[27]

1. *A populating of the self, or an absorption of others into ourselves.* We come to see a myriad of possibilities for being—along with their opposites.

2. *The collapse of a centered self under the demands of multiple audiences.* The socializing technologies are erecting a huge mansion of conflicting demands for each of us. Gergen alludes to a man in today's environment who must simultaneously demonstrate professional responsibility, soft and romantic sensitivity, macho toughness, and family dedication; he must have expertise in sports, politics, software, the stock market, mechanics, food, and wine; he must have a circle of friends, a fitness program, the right CDs, interesting vacation plans, and an impressive car.

3. *An undermining of self-confidence through the repetition of images.* The countless reproductions of our ways of life slowly sap them of authenticity. Citing the case of romance, Gergen notes that by traditional standards expressions of love, passion, and desire should be spontaneous eruptions of one's basic self. However, through the constant bombardment of such expressions through television and the other media, "authenticity begins to wear thin. Substance slowly becomes style. One loses trust in romantic expressions; the words are stifled in the threat. Where am I? Hollywood?"[28]

Having laid out the dangers, Gergen provides a note of optimism by saying that in these expanding technologies there is a large possibility for positive human development. "Each new relationship is simultaneously an opportunity, an open door to growth of expression, appreciation, and skill."[29] This is especially true in the lives of young women, where a half-century ago, there was only one strong model against which women could measure their state: the devoted wife and mother. Today, however, there are innumerable models through media images—some true and some false. There are a lot of possibilities now to choose from when women want someone to emulate. Gergen concludes:

If the socializing technologies can break down the sense of independent selves, can we look forward to a time when the same can occur at the national and international level? As the technologies increase our contact with those from other walks of life, other value systems, and other cultures, we may continue to expand our range of understanding and appreciation. As we form relationships in business, government, education, the arts, and so on, we may further our sense of interdependence.[30]

THE IMPACT ON EDUCATION

Walk down the hallway of almost any school in America, look in an open classroom door, and one will probably see a television monitor mounted on a cart with a VCR located just beneath it. Such is the ubiquitousness of television in schools in the late twentieth century. In some schools, and in some grade levels, education via television is more a prominent part of the school day than in others. But all schools employ television in much greater degree than at any time in the past. Teachers at all grade levels through graduate school routinely augment their lectures with excerpts of videotaped programs. Some instructors even require outside viewing of particular instructional programs, as well as commercial films that are relevant to the subjects in the classrooms. Some of these programs are aired with permission of their owners; many are aired without such permission.

Adding to the interest—as well as controversy—that television education has created is one school-TV idea called Channel One, created and produced by Whittle Communications, Inc. Channel One is a daily news program—complete with commercials—aimed at children and teens that is in use in about 11,000 schools around the United States. Whittle provides the schools with a satellite dish, two VCRs, a television set in each classroom, and the cable to hook everything up; schools agree to show Channel One's 12 minutes of feature stories and news and two minutes of commercials to most students on at least 90 percent of the days school is in session.[31] It is mainly the commercial content of Channel One that is causing parents and children's advocate groups some concern, and some states and school districts are fighting the Channel One concept in their jurisdictions. There is also disagreement over the suitability of news and information content for children and, in both areas of news and advertising, children's advocate groups are worried about the possibility of manipulating the value structure of young minds. Also, teachers complain about the interruption to their scheduled lectures and labs created by the required daily viewing of Channel One. It seems to be most popular with social studies and civics teachers because the focus of the stories is most often on contemporary life and institutions. Science teachers, on the other hand, are among the most vociferous critics. In Woodhaven, Michigan, four Woodhaven High School science teachers decided to pull the plug on Channel One and instead let their students do necessary lab work. The teachers were presented with an ultimatum by school officials, however: resume the TV programming or face the possible loss of their jobs. The reason? If a school does not show the required 14 minutes of daily programming, or if the student population drops by more than 25 percent during the three years of the contract period, Whittle can cancel the contract and take back its hardware.[32]

Channel One is not, by any means, the only way in which television is reaching into the classroom. A study done in 1989 by the Office of Technology Assessment found "distance-learning" projects—mostly for-credit video courses with a two-way hook-up between teacher and students—operating or planned in all 50 states, up from about 10 two years earlier.[33] For years, cable networks such as C-Span have been pushing efforts such as "C-Span in the Classroom," and even the Public Broadcasting Service is competing. That should not be surprising, since PBS began as an educational television network three decades ago. But today PBS reports that use of its instructional TV programs, such as "Cathedral" and "3-2-1 Contact," has jumped enormously since 1985. In Oregon, for instance, half of all teachers used instructional programs in class in 1990, up from 23 percent in 1984.[34]

How effective is television as an educational medium? The *Wall Street Journal* reports the research is "inconclusive," adding, "One clear advantage, though, is that television makes possible instruction in subjects where qualified teachers are lacking."[35] Thus, languages such as Japanese or Korean (which nearly always give way to French, Spanish, and German) can be taught alongside these other languages in which teachers are more plentiful.

One service made available to schools around the country is the Midlands Consortium, which is a satellite network based in studios at Oklahoma State University in Stillwater, Oklahoma. The Midlands Consortium is one of at least four large satellite networks that have started operation since 1984 and that look to schools as their customers. The federal government even supports some of these groups via grants. As the 1990s began, the Midlands Consortium reached 60,000 students from kindergarten to twelfth grade in 29 states. Professors from Oklahoma State University and Kansas State teach subjects such as Russian and German, advanced placement math and science, as well as a course that prepares students for college entrance exams.[36]

Schools are also receiving more programming from cable networks and stations. In 1989, cable operators and networks formed a group called the Cable Alliance for Education, whose members promised free cable hook-ups to schools that did not already have such connections in place. In addition, many schools are broadcasting CNN News because owner Ted Turner waived virtually all copyrights on it, giving schools unrestricted use.[37]

As the available instructional programming increases, television's use in the classroom will only continue to grow, despite some opposition. Among the critics have been members of the National Educational Association who fear that television may be stifling the perceived need for adding more live teachers in schools that may now rely too heavily on televised instruction. They also oppose distance learning via television if a certified teacher is not present on the receiving end, underlining and clarifying points made in the video and answering students' questions about the material they see. Still television continues to be a growing force in education in the primary, secondary, and higher education levels.

One educational television service that has become an important part of university teaching, as well as continuing education programs is PBS's Adult Learning Satellite Service (ALSS). This programming service is based on the predictions of such observers as management specialist and author Peter Drucker.

In the next 50 years, schools and universities will change more and more drastically than they have since they assumed their present form more than 300 years ago when they reorganized themselves around the printed book. What will force these changes is, in part, new technology, such as computers, video, and telecasts via satellite; in part the demands of a knowledge-based society in which organized learning must become a lifelong process for knowledge workers; and in part new theory about how human beings learn.[38]

ALSS was established in 1988 to provide colleges, universities, businesses, hospitals, and other organizations with a broad range of educational programming via direct satellite. ALSS is part of the Adult Learning Service, a department of the PBS Educational Division. ALSS extends the educational mission of PBS by providing quality programs to schools and other institutions. It returns a percentage of its annual income to the educational outreach departments of local public television stations.[39] ALSS provides organizations with a method of acquiring educational video programs over their television. Organizations with satellite-receiving equipment can tape the programs when they are fed via satellite.

The business programming arm of ALSS, The Business Channel (TBC), offers programs specifically selected for their timeliness and content. Through TBC, many programs that were originally available to corporations only on videocassette are now available to both colleges and businesses via satellite, often at a fraction of the cost.

ALSS programs include the following:[40]

1. *Telecourses,* which can be offered as comprehensive college- credit courses for distance learners.

2. *Audiovisual resource programs,* including some of PBS's best prime-time programs, which can be used as supplementary learning resources for classes and libraries.

3. *Live, interactive videoconferences* that give organizations the opportunity to host local conferences featuring national experts on the most pressing issues facing education, business, health, and other fields. In most cases, the live program can also be taped and used later as an audiovisual resource.

Users of ALSS are given the opportunity to obtain a license for accessing the programs and are also charged a fee for the programs.

Integrating communications technology into teaching is an idea that has been adopted at varying degrees at almost every instructional campus in the United States. A wide range of approaches exist to the instructional use of computers and interactive video, ranging from enhancing traditional teaching techniques to supporting entirely new modes of learning. The approaches can be grouped into four different levels of technology use:

1. *Enhancing existing materials and approaches.* At the most basic level, a computer can help instructors do what they've always done—only better. For example, word-processing software makes it easy to revise course materials and lecture notes to bring in new information and insights. Computers can also be used to generate professional-quality lecture materials, such as overhead transparencies and even 35mm slides. In addition, a computer connected to a projector can serve as a dynamic blackboard.

2. *Using existing software.* No longer are computer programming skills a necessary prerequisite to instructional computer use. A wide variety of software is commercially available—applicable to an even wider variety of academic disciplines. This second level of technology use involves commercially available software. A recent trend has been for textbook publishers to bundle supplementary software with textbooks and create more interactive learning experiences for students.

3. *Adapting existing software and videodisks.* This can be as simple as creating spreadsheet-based templates that deal with discipline-specific problems or as complex as developing software that provides a discipline-specific context using an existing videodisk.

4. *Creating original coursework.* Developing a software package used to require years of programming training. But today, because of the ease of use of some authoring programs, it's a short step from adapting existing materials to cre-

ating your own. Scores of instructors have tapped their subject-matter expertise to create their own instructional software, and much of it is interactive.

One classic example of how a supertech classroom might look is found at DeBartolo Hall at the University of Notre Dame. There, representatives of hundreds of other educational institutions can see what the classroom of the future might look like. The building is being used for several different kinds of courses ranging from math and computer science to religion and literature. Each of the building's eighty-four classrooms is equipped with an innovative system for delivering instruction. Described as "Media-On-Call," it allows efficient use of all forms of multimedia from audio recordings to videotapes, from films to television, from satellite programming to multimedia software. A centralized command center is located in the basement of DeBartolo where the computers and AV devices are located. They are networked to buttons on consoles in the various classrooms, so the system's capabilities can be activated by each professor from the classroom itself. As many as six audio or video sources can be activated during any class period if the professor simply consults with educational media staff members in the command center to line up the day's resources. The system was designed by Dynacom Corp. of Mishiwaka, Indiana.

In a sampling done of other colleges and universities by the December 8, 1993 edition of *The Chronicle of Higher Education*, the following communications systems were in the development or initiation stages at that time:

• Marist College planned to experiment with a computerized telephone system that could respond to voice commands and even read sentences aloud from computer files.

• A University of Mississippi professor developed software to expedite communication among speakers of different languages. The program was designed to help participants talk to each other in business meetings and it lets those who use IBM-compatible computers communicate in any of a dozen languages and immediately translates comments between English and French, German, or Spanish.

• Christopher Newport University plans to make it possible for students to get degrees even if they never go to campus for classes. At present, more than a dozen of the school's courses are taught in part via an electronic bulletin-board system. Students with a computer and modem can connect over the telephone to read lectures and other course materials, ask professors questions, use simulations, and take tests. More classes are slated to be moved from the classroom to the bulletin board system in coming months and, by 1995, the university hopes to offer all of its courses this way.

THE VIRTUAL WORKPLACE

Adding to societal changes caused by the new communications technologies is what is coming to be known as the *virtual workplace*. According to this concept, a person's office is no longer defined by one specific location. The integration of computers, telephone modems, fax machines (fixed and portable), mobile phones, conference phone calls, and videoconferencing makes it possible for a person to take his or her office with them where ever they go. The result is that many professionals are choosing to work out of their homes and—for part of their day—out of their automobiles. In the writing profession, newspaper and magazine reporters are no longer confined to the newsroom but can go with greater ease to where the story is, no matter how remote the locations. When the reporters are ready to write their stories, they simply pull out their laptop computer, attach a phone modem, and transmit the written copy to a fax machine anywhere in the world.

This creation of a workplace virtually anywhere workers find themselves is becoming at least a partial solution to other problems, such as the worrisome and costly situation of providing day care for children. The parent or parents can work out of their homes, while their children play in the next room.

It also means companies no longer must locate in the population centers of the country such as New York, Los Angeles, and Chicago. As long as computers can be connected to phone lines through a modem, headquarters can be located anywhere. Thus, clothing manufacturer Patagonia locates its customer service staff in Montana, and Citicorp has located its credit card operations in South Dakota. Even Utah has turned into a software development center. One of the largest mutual fund investment companies, Fidelity, connects its Boston office with a branch in Covington, Kentucky, at a cost of less than one penny per minute over a voice-grade fax line. That is less than Fidelity spends for connections within Boston.[41] The advantage for Fidelity employees is that they do not have to pay the high housing costs and taxes that they would pay in Boston. They can live in Kentucky and still stay in constant touch with the home office.

Forbes Magazine noted in 1992 that this telecommuting will reach high gear when the country is fully wired with fiber optic lines, which will make even more data transmission and reception possible over computers.[42] The Integrated Services Digital Network long promised by the telephone industry is here at last, making video-phone connections affordable for corporate face-to-face meetings. In the mid-1980s, business videoconferencing equipment cost $250,000 at each end and ran up $1,000 an hour in connection charges. Now, cheaper chips and compression algorithms have cut these costs to $40,000 and $15 per hour.[43]

That's still steep, but much less so—and the price will come down even further.

About this telecommuting phenomenon, *Forbes* notes:

All manner of service-sector companies are becoming virtual employers with no one centralized home. Where is Journal Graphics? This vendor of transcripts of television shows has Grant Street, Denver, as its mailing address. But the company's guts are elsewhere, in employees' homes. Shows are taped on personal VCRs, transcripts are made there, and the material is directly uploaded to satellite channels, digital FM sideband networks and online databanks for access by subscribers within hours of a show's original transmission.[44]

Thus, communication technologies is replacing the more time-consuming and expensive physical commuting that has been in place for generations. No longer is it necessary to transport the worker to work, as long as you can transport the actual work they do to the office. Employees are beginning to negotiate their working sites, and many of them are choosing to work from home. The disadvantage of telecommuting, however, is the loss of social contact with friends and associates in the workplace. It is one thing to work with other people in an office setting. It is another to distance yourself from these people and be able to contact them only over the phone or fax. Telecommuting could, then, have a negative effect on a person's social development and contribute to a growing sense of isolation and loneliness.

CHANGING PATTERNS IN SHOPPING

The effects of the new technologies on advertising patterns is in chapter 7, but mention should be made here of how these changes are already starting to affect consumer shopping patterns. Certainly the past few years have shown the viability of two new kinds of shopping that have lessened the foot traffic at the area shopping malls. These are (1) direct mail shopping and (2) video shopping.

When considering video shopping, one has only to look at the popularity of the Home Shopping Network or the QVC programming to understand just how viable interactive television will be as a shopping medium. Television affords us the chance to get as close as we can to a product, without actually picking it up and holding it, to inspect it before making the purchase. There is also the feeling that, even though you are sitting alone in your living room, you are somehow linked to others doing the same kind of shopping. In fact, one network does call itself the Home Shopping Club. In the studio from which this video shopping originates, producers and directors work hard to get across the feeling that viewers truly are members of a club. There are usually bright personalities doing the selling and explanation of the products offered, and phones are often heard ringing in the background, giving the sense of connection. In the case of QVC programming, products are sold for only a limited time, and prices are often cut as the time progresses. An on-screen counter shows how many hundreds or thousands of shoppers have made the purchase while listening to an extended commercial for the product, which goes into great detail about its use and value. There are also phone interviews with individuals who have just made the purchase, asking them what features sold them on the product and praising them for their savvy shopping discernment. An evening's programming on QVC is grouped around classifications of merchandise, so there may be an hour-long show on fine furs, another on high-tech gadgetry, and so on. In effect, the television shopping networks are akin to the free-distribution weekly newspapers—also known as shoppers—which have little if any news or editorial content and are sold purely on the basis of the advertisements they contain.

Direct mail catalog shopping is also booming. Some catalog shopping firms are working on deals with cable channels and networks to transmit their products electronically in a kind of video catalog, just as the Yellow Pages are being aired over television in some markets. The concept is similar to the home shopping club of the HSN and QVC networks. In all cases, viewers realize that, with the blossoming of package express services, they will be able to receive their purchases within 24 hours and, in some cases, in even less time than that. Gone are the days of waiting four to six weeks for purchases made through the mail.

The changes in consumer shopping patterns may well be one of the most visible and most imminent changes in all areas discussed in this chapter. It will also mean that retailers will need to drastically rethink the ways in which they do business and—quite possibly—consider ways of tapping into this new form of electronic shopping or at least offering greater incentives for getting consumers out of their homes and into the shopping malls.

A GLOBAL VILLAGE OR TOWER OF BABEL?

McLuhan and Innis envisioned a kind of global village resulting from the growth and spread of television. In part, it was a world in which ideas and values would become more uniform as Western programming invaded alien cultures and, over time, brought them into Western thinking and behavior patterns because of the appeal of the entertainment programming. It would be a world shrunk down to size by a ubiquitous medium that delivered a more and more uniform type of cultural language and set of values through popular programming. To be sure, some of this vision has become a reality—often with tragic consequences. To some degree, the story of Third World countries, where hopes and dreams have been raised beyond the ability to be fulfilled, is the story of television's cultural imperialism. Indonesian President Achmed Sukarno, at one time during the 1960s, complained bitterly about the extravagant expectations that Western television sitcoms, showing large homes and two cars in every driveway, were creating among the economically deprived people of Jakarta. Journalist Richard Critchfield, who practices a kind of anthropology-based journalism in reporting from Third World villages, writes that the struggle of so many of these societies is basically the struggle they face in trying to adjust and adapt to Western societies and technologies that are presented to them via the media.[45] He notes that this adaptation often blurs a country's idea of its own identity, sometimes resulting in an outright loss of that identity as it becomes subsumed in the West's values and traditions. The tragedy of Iran under its last Shah is testimony to what can happen when an ancient country with ancient traditions is asked to adapt too quickly to Western ideas. In the case of Iran, the society was sent reeling back to the past as conservatives snuffed out the threat they perceived, exiled the Shah, and set up rule under the Ayatolah Khomeni.

Adding to this perplexing problem of cultural imperialism is that so much of the Third World is now receiving Western programming via crude—but effective—underground video clubs, where villagers in small and large groups might go together to buy a single television and VCR and then cluster around this system to view Western videos that are often pirated via a small satellite dish and that are often illegally viewed under the country's repressive regime. Others look at this situation, however, and see the possibility of new ideas, hopes, and expectations in countries that desperately need them. They see in this situation the opportunity to plant the seeds of democratic values and hope those seeds will grow into revolution.

Opposing this view of a global village is another view of what the new communications technologies might portend: a kind of Tower of Babel scenario in which everyone, instead of speaking the same language, is speaking radically different languages and pursuing radically different interests. This scenario began surfacing in the minds of some media analysts when the world of magazines turned from the production of general-interest, mass-circulation magazines to narrow-interest, small-circulation magazines. This specialization in magazines, which began in earnest in the 1970s, led to a plethora of magazines targeted at thousands of special interests, most of which are narrowly defined. The hobby and sports category of books was broken into hundreds of subcategories; so were women's magazines and almost every other category of magazine in existence. Some observers perceived a scenario in which the typical American family would come together around the dinner table, fresh from perusing a different magazine. In this scenario, Dad might have been reading *Scuba Diving*, Mom might have been reading *Martha Stewart Living*, while each of the children have been reading *Tiger Beat*, *Model Airplane*, and *Popular Photography*. In so doing, some would ask, what is the common thread of conversation or of interests? Unless members of a family are able to adapt to the different interests of each other, there might be little talk at all around the table, and even if there is it might be little understood by individual family members who have just come out of a different culture of reading content and jargon.

If such a scenario exists because of special-interest magazines—which often hold only a portion of the reader's attention—how much more realizable might this scenario be in the age of cable and interative TV? It has been seen elsewhere in this book that experiments are underway in several cities around America to beam hundreds of different cable channels into homes. Each of these channels and networks is somewhat different—in some cases vastly different as is the case with ESPN and A&E networks. Add to this the average American family with its two to four television sets, and the possibilities for a familial Tower of Babel seem strong indeed. If such a scenario were to occur, then individuals within the family who choose to spend hours each day watching or interacting with their television sets might find themselves cut off not only from friends outside the home, but from other family members within the home as well.

SUMMARY

Predicting the future is a risky business. So it is with predicting the kinds of changes that might result from the new communications technologies and the intensity of those changes. Nevertheless, the suggested changes discussed in this chapter seem likely by-products of the new technology. In fact, many of the changes such as telecommuting, the use of television in education, and television shopping are already with us.

One question that always lurks around new developments on the horizon is how quickly they might actually arrive and be pressed into service. For many of the technologies discussed in this book, the answer is that the time is at hand; change is imminent. For other changes, such as the rewiring of the country with fiber optic lines, the implementation of changes and their resulting effects could take another decade. No one should take the changes in communications technology lightly, however. We are all on the threshold of great societal changes brought about by the ability to compress a great amount of information through digitalization, and the sending of that information across hair-thin glass lines known as fiber optic lines. The societal changes resulting from these twin technologies will be as great—or greater—than any technological developments since movable type and the printing press.

NOTES

1. Cecile Gaziano, "The Knowledge Gap and Class Communication," *Mass Comm Review*, Fall 1989, 29.
2. Werner J. Severin and James W. Tankard, Jr., *Communication Theories: Origins, Methods, and Uses in the Mass Media*, 3rd ed. (New York: Longman, 1992), 236–237.
3. Gaziano "The Knowledge Gap," 33–35.
4. Ibid.
5. Ibid., 35.
6. Ibid.
7. Neil Postman, "Critical Thinking in the Electronic Era," *Phi Kappa Phi Journal*, Winter 1985, 4.
8. Ibid., 5.
9. Comments from Bill Moyers in the PBS program, *The Public Mind: Illusions of News*, November 1989.
10. Postman, "Critical Thinking," 8–9.
11. Andrew Kupfer, "Prime Time for Videoconferences," *Fortune*, December 28, 1992, 90.
12. Ibid.
13. Ibid., 91.
14. M. William Lutholtz, "Technology May Complicate Our Jobs," *IABC Communication World*, September 1988, 16.
15. Daniel Yankelovich, "Tomorrow's Global Businesses," *The Futurist*, July-August 1991, 60.
16. Ibid.
17. Ibid.
18. Scott Cunningham and Alan L. Porter, "Communication Networks: A Dozen Ways They'll Change Our Lives," *The Futurist*, January-February 1992, 21.
19. Ibid.
20. Ibid.
21. John Swayne, "The New Communications Revolution," *Newsweek*, April 19, 1993, 21.
22. David C. Churbuck and Jeffrey S. Young, "The Virtual Workplace," *Forbes*, November 23, 1992, 186.
23. Stratford Sherman, "The New Computer Revolution," *Fortune*, June 14, 1993, 57.
24. Ibid.
25. Ibid.
26. Kenneth J. Gergen, "The Decline and Fall of Personality," *Psychology Today*, November/December 1992, 62.
27. Ibid., 63.
28. Ibid.
29. Ibid.

30. Ibid.

31. Dudley Barlow, "Channel One Update," *The Education Digest*, October 1992, 26.

32. Ibid.

33. Gary Putka, "Schools Giving TV Warmer Reception," *The Wall Street Journal*, December 26, 1989, B1.

34. Ibid.

35. Ibid.

36. Ibid.

37. Ibid.

38. Peter F. Drucker, "The New Society of Organizations," *Harvard Business Review*, September-October 1992, as quoted in: *ALSS Programming Line-Up Booklet*, Winter/Spring 1993, PBS Education Adult Learning Service, Alexandria, VA, 1.

39. *ALSS Programming Line-Up Booklet*, Winter/Spring 1993, PBS Education Adult Learning Service, Alexandria, VA.

40. Ibid.

41. Churbuck and Young, "Virtual Workplace," 184.

42. Ibid.

43. Ibid., 188.

44. Ibid.

45. Richard Critchfield, "The Village Voice of Richard Critchfield," *Washington Journalism Review*, October 1985, 27–28.

Glossary

Analog Technology: Conventional signal transmission that is an electrical representation of (analogous to) sound waves and that is continuously variable and varying, changing in agreement with the sound waves. Analog signals are incompatible with digital signals, although analog signals can be converted to digital signals through the use of a converter. Digital transmission is seen as superior to analog for a number of reasons, including the amount of data sent and the speed with which that data is transmitted.

Audiotex: A voice information service, usually accessed via special "900" numbers, in use by many newspapers around the United States and offering readers up-to-the-minute information on such topics as weather, sports, finance, and even soap operas. Newspapers and magazines are also offering voice classified advertising.

Bandwidth: The bandwidth on a particular communication channel is the capacity of that channel to dictate the range of frequencies and the amount of data the channel can carry in a short amount of time. A wider bandwidth allows for faster communication of more data.

Cable Communications Policy Act of 1984: A federal act weakening the power of local government to control cable subscription rates, although authorizing the same local governments to regulate cable systems to some degree. The act also set federal standards for cable franchises.

Cable Act of 1992: Congress approved this act on September 22, 1992, despite severe lobbying efforts by the cable television industry and a threatened veto by President George Bush. The act was a significant update, and in some ways a reversal, of the 1984 Cable Act, which had gone a long way toward deregulating cable and freeing it from government price controls. Among the provisions of the

1992 act are that (1) cable programming must be made available to competitors, (2) cable companies must negotiate with local broadcasters before carrying their signals but cannot refuse to carry those signals, and (3) the FCC must determine "reasonable" rates for basic cable service.

Cable Television: A distribution system for television programming that uses coaxial cables, which connect local cable companies to subscribers' homes. Cable has the capacity to carry more data than conventional copper telephone wires, but less than fiber optics. Nevertheless, by the 1990s, cable television was bringing in a total of $15.1 billion annually in revenue, the number of basic cable subscribers was over 50 million households, and cable is now positioned to be a major player in the multimedia age.

Cellular Transmission: Over-the-air transmission system using radio waves and a computer-controlled array of transmitting towers to ensure that the signal will be carried over a wide area, composed of a large number of "cells" that cover specific geographic regions round the United States. This is the transmission system used for cellular telephones, now widely used in the United States, and for new wireless communications products on the market.

Closed-Captioning: Subtitles delivered within a television receiver's vertical blanking distance (VBS) and appearing on the screen for hearing-impaired viewers.

Compact Disc: A nonerasable, prerecorded digital optical disc system that is used to store and playback music. Playback is accomplished when a CD player uses a light beam, produced by a laser, to "read" the information stored on the disc, producing a much higher quality sound than current audio tapes or radio broadcasts.

Compact Disc-Read-Only Memory (CD-ROM): A nonerasable, prerecorded digital optical disc system that is used to store and play back computer compatible data. A CD-ROM can hold textual data as well as computer graphics. Additional data cannot be stored on these discs. Suitable for distribution of a great volume of data.

Cyberpunk: The virtual reality cult. This term is used for combining the related cults of techno-bohemians—primarily computer hackers—and "phreaks" or practitioners of the art and science of cracking the telephone network.

Desktop Publishing: A concept that has grown in popularity in the 1980s and 1990s whereby an individual possessing a personal computer, low-cost software, and a laser printer can carry out many of the functions, such as typesetting and composition, once reserved for large publishing ventures.

Digital Audio Broadcasting (DAB): A recent technical development in digital technology that promises a higher-quality sound over radio than is available with current compact disc transmission. As the 1990s began, DAB was being touted as the greatest event in decades of radio broadcasting. The radio industry is working now to develop a universal DAB system that will cause a minimum amount of

economic upheaval to broadcasters, provide the most sensible technological solution, and generate the greatest enthusiasm and use by listeners.

Digital Technology: A system of transmission whereby letters, numbers,
sounds, and images are reduced to a sequence of zeros and ones. With computers, these bits are endlessly interchangeable. Digital transmission makes interactivity between provider and user possible and allows more data to be transmitted
across conventional phone lines or fiber optics than analog transmission.

Direct Broadcast Satellite (DBS) Transmission: Direct television broadcasting via satellite suspended 22,000 miles high in space was operational in the
United States in 1984. The signals are sent directly to consumers' homes, which
are equipped with small receiving dishes. Seen as a challenge to the cable industry
as well as fiber optic transmission, DBS ran into trouble when major companies
such as CBS pulled out of this form of technology. Transmission via fiber optics
is generally seen as a superior form of transmission, oblivious to atmospheric
conditions, and cheaper for the consumer to access.

Electronic Bulletin Board System (BBS): An interactive messaging component of a larger interactive service in which a user with a personal computer and
modem (if terminals are not directly connected via fiber optics) can trade information with other users belonging to the same BBS network or scan information
bulletins left by a PC communications center.

Electronic Database: A storage/retrieval system containing a huge amount of
data that the user may access via PC and telephone modem. Electronic databases
are available for professional, business, and home use. Professional databases include LEXIS/NEXIS and Dialog, while home services include Prodigy and
CompuServe. There are also databases, such as InfoTrac, which are used largely
in reference libraries.

Electronic Mail (E-mail): An electronic version of traditional mail whereby
users in the same system can send messages to each other via their PCs and have
those messages stored for retrieval at the user's convenience.

Federal Communications Commission (FCC): Federal government agency
that regulates broadcasting, cable, and other areas of telecommunication. The
FCC will play a significant role in regulation concerning the multimedia age.

Fiber Optics: A transmission vehicle composed of hair-thin glass cables through
which data such as text, voices, or images can be reduced to pulses of light and
transmitted with great speed and clarity. Fiber optic lines permit the transmission
of more data at a much faster speed than do conventional copper telephone lines
or even coaxial cable. Fiber optics lies at the heart of the concept of interactive
media.

Gateway: A universal switching point that allows a user to gain access to different external computer systems that are ordinarily incompatible and inaccessi-
ble. A videotex service, for instance, may have a number of gateways available to
subscribers that allow them to access different kinds of services and information
from different information providers.

High Definition Television (HDTV): A television receiver, currently operational in Japan, that offers a sharpness and clarity of image that is far beyond the range of conventional television. With HDTV, the number of lines on a television screen are doubled, from 525 to 1050, although debate is still underway as to which format should be used in North America. The FCC has declared, however, that the HDTV standard adopted will be digitally based. HDTV screens are also wider and change the current 4:3 "aspect ratio" of the screen to a 5:3 ratio.

Highly-Immersive Systems: A form of virtual reality technology in which users' senses are enveloped with virtual stimuli. Equipment consists of a head-mounted display, speech recognition system, spatial audio system, position tracker, data glove, treadmill, motion platform, and several other types of related accessories.

Infomercial: A hybrid television program that walks the line between a talk show and an extended commercial. The programs, running 30 minutes or longer, are aired on time purchased by the advertiser. Often celebrity hosts are used to talk with the developer of the product or service and to the "satisfied" customers.

Information Agent: An impartial information provider designed to benefit consumers by offering unbiased and informed commentary about products and services offered for sale. Deemed by some analysts to be a key part of the future of interactive television, these agents will act as a kind of video version of *Consumer's Digest* or *Consumer Reports*.

Information Highway: Also called the electronic superhighway, this concept is the technological buzzword of the 1990s. It is analogous to the interstate highway system for vehicular traffic, only this "highway" would transmit all forms of data from all forms of media. Hundreds of communications companies are juggling to own a piece of this highway, which will be made possible by technological advances such as digital compression of data, fiber optic wiring, and new switching techniques.

Information/Service Provider: A company or group that provides a certain kind of information or service to users via an interactive, videotex system. Several providers might be offered by the same videotex service, as was the case with Knight-Ridder's Viewtron service, which began with 50 information providers in the 1980s.

Intelligent Remote: Also called the universal remote, this is a handheld unit that the viewer will use to, among other things, automatically scan television channels like a radio scanner and to switch automatically to another channel when a commercial is encountered.

Interactive Media: Media with two-way capabilities between service or information provider and user. A number of different media formats are mixed together, and the user can access any or all of them, from text to graphics (moving or still), to audio formats. The media is a kind of buffet from which the user may choose with what he or she wants to see, hear, and/or interact.

Internet: A worldwide network established by the U.S. Department of Defense in 1969 for E-mail users. Over ten million people in the world have E-mail now, most of them in America.

ISDN: The Integrated Services Digital Network created by AT&T as it moved to become a major player in the age of interactive media. With the ISDN, voice and data can travel side by side over the same wires, which are being upgraded to fiber optic lines in many parts of the country. By the end of the 1980s, a large international effort was underway that would link every world telephone system with an ISDN network that could carry all kinds of signals. More than 100 countries were participating.

Laser Printer: An essential element of the desktop publishing system employing a small semiconductor laser in the print motor and offering 300 dots per inch (dpi) printing resolution that is suitable for most commercial needs.

Media Blur: In the age of multimedia, the traditional boundaries separating print and electronic media are falling as newspapers, magazines, books, television, the telephone, and the computer all begin to merge into one interactive multimedia system.

Multimedia: An all-embracing term reflecting the combination of media forms and presentations resulting when different forms of print and electronic media couple with the computer, CD-ROM technology, and the telephone system to offer the user one all-purpose, interactive media system.

Pay-Per-View (PPV): Cable programming for which subscribers pay individually for each program accessed. Also a feature of several videotex systems.

Postmodern Consciousness: The syndrome describing many Americans who are so bombarded with a multitude of media images, personalities, and relationships, that they have trouble hanging on to their own personal identity and recognizing the authenticity of traditional reason and emotions.

Print Television: Another way of describing electronic newspapers or magazines which are "published" in an electronic format and appear on home television or personal computer screens.

Psychotechnology: Any technical device which extends or emulates one human psychological feature or another, or a group of them. They can include live information-processing devices and networks, public and domestic, such as the telephone, radio, television, computers, or satellites.

Qube: An early American experiment in interactive TV that began in 1977 in Columbus, Ohio. The primary goal in designing Qube was to offer Columbus television viewers an opportunity to tailor their viewing to their own personal tastes. A cable-based system, Qube offered all the cable programming options available at the time and also offered a pay-per-view option. Its interactive feature allowed subscribers to register their comments and feelings about everything from presidential speeches to local city council meetings, via a remote-control keypad. Qube computers quickly analyzed and presented the results back over the television screen to subscribers. The Qube system was still operational in the early

1990s, but it was downgraded to offering traditional cable programming and PPV programs. The interactive features were suspended.

RBOCs: The seven regional bell operating companies that were given a independence and autonomy when the gigantic AT&T complex was broken up by federal ruling. The RBOCs were given further freedom when they were allowed, in the early 1990s, to enter the information-providing business. Some of the RBOCs, such as Southwestern Bell, have moved to acquire cable television companies and become a major player in the multimedia era.

Smart TV: A product which represents the merging of the home computer and television. Smart TV is similar to a personal computer with a high-resolution display screen. Inside the set are digital instructions that permit the set to receive any broadcast or cable network, or any other form of signal transmission that may someday be developed. Smart TV is actually a telecomputer that could be used in videotex transmission. The technology is available, and the system is waiting to be incorporated into regular use.

Teletext: A one-way transmission system whereby alphanumeric text and graphics are carried over the air on traditional broadcast or cable television channels for display on home television monitors. The signal is piggybacked on the television signal and uses the vertical blanking interval (VBI) found between video frames on the television screen. It is unscrambled by a special decoder in the set. With a teletext system, when the user accesses the appropriate channel, "pages" will scroll by quickly and the viewer can use a remote-control keypad to stop the desired page and read it. Generally, teletext systems are easier to use than videotex systems.

Turbonews: News and information at the speed of light, delivered in written, oral, and/or visual form over fiber optic lines with immediate access by users and capable of being continually updated.

Universal Remote: See Intelligent Remote.

User-Modeling: An approach to tailoring interactive media content to individual users by monitoring the user's viewing habits, combined with an established databank of the user's interests and preferences in news, information, and entertainment.

Videoconference or Teleconference: A kind of electronic meeting in which individuals or groups can interact visually and orally over an electronic hookup via fiber optics or—more prominent today—by uplink and downlink satellite technology. Videoconferences can be either one-way or two-way in design, depending on whether the purpose is to transmit information to a group or groups of individuals or to have the groups interact with the information provider and/or each other.

Videotex: A two-way system of transmission that electronically transmits text, graphics (moving or still), and sound via conventional telephone lines, coaxial cable, or fiber optics to a PC screen or dedicated terminal that is designed to decode the signal. A large number of information and service providers may make data and interactive services available for the subscriber to the videotex system. Use of videotex is somewhat more complicated than use of teletext systems, although it can offer more data and services.

Viewdata: Another term for videotex, originated in Great Britain at the then-British Post Office (now British Telecommunications) in the early 1970s. It describes interactive information products and services available over television sets and/or specially dedicated PCs.

Virtual Reality (VR): An experimental media form that allows the user a greater sense of presence or entry into worlds he or she cannot literally encounter. VR has been called the ultimate form of interaction between humans and machines. The necessary equipment used to "transport" users consists of a head-mounted display, speech recognition system, spatial audio system, position tracker, data glove, treadmill and motion platform. Other items may be added for greater believability.

Bibliography

BOOKS

Altheide, David L., and Snow, Robert P. *Media Worlds in the Postjournalism Era*. New York: Aldine de Gruyter, 1991.

Aumente, Jerome. *New Electronic Pathways*. Newbury Park, CA: Sage, 1987.

Berger, Arthur Asa, ed. *Media USA: Process and Effect*. New York: Longman, 1988.

Brand, Stewart. *The Media Lab: Inventing the Future at MIT*. New York: Viking, 1987.

Brody, E. W. *Communication Tomorrow: New Media*. Westport, CT: Praeger, 1990.

Conhaim, Wallys. *Videotex: Growing Public Awareness*. White Paper Report prepared for the Newspaper Association of America, Reston, VA, 1991.

Cook, Phillip S.; Gomery, Douglas, and Lighty, Lawrence W. *The Future of News: Television, Newspapers, Wire Services, Newsmagazines*. Baltimore, MD: The Johns Hopkins University Press, 1992.

Crowley, David and Paul Heyer. *Communication in History*. New York: Longman, 1991.

Dizard, Wilson P., Jr. *The Coming Information Age*, 3rd ed. New York: Longman, 1989.

Donou, Kenneth R., and De Sonne, Marcia L., eds. *HDTV: Preparing for Action*. Washington, DC: National Association of Broadcasters, 1988.

Hilliard, Robert L. *Television Station Operations and Management*. Boston: Focal Press, 1989.

Husted, Stewart W.; Varble, Dale L., and Lowry, James R. *Principles of Modern Marketing*. Boston: Allyn & Bacon, 1989.

Kantrow, Alan M. *The Constraints of Corporate Tradition*. New York: Harper & Rowe, 1988.

Keirstead, Phillip O., and Keirstead, Sonia K. *The World of Telecommunication:*

Introduction to Broadcasting, Cable, and New Technologies. Boston: Focal Press, 1990.

Manoil, Daniel. *Telecommunications Technology Handbook.* Boston: Artech House, 1991.

McLuhan, Marshall. *Understanding Media.* New York: Mentor, 1964.

———. *The Gutenberg Galaxy.* Toronto: University of Toronto Press, 1969.

Mirabito, Michael M., and Morgenstern, Barbara L. *The New Communications Technologies.* Boston: Focal Press, 1990.

Nmungwun, Aaron Foisi. *Video Recording Technology: It's Impact on Media and Home Entertainment.* Hillsdale, NJ: Lawrence Erlbaum Associates, 1989.

Noll, A. Michael. *Introduction to Telephones & Telephone Systems.* 2nd. ed. Boston: Artech House, 1991.

Parker, Edwin B., et al. *Rural America in the Information Age: Telecommunications Policy for Rural Development.* Lanham, MD: University Press of America, 1989.

Robinson, John P., and Levy, Mark R., with Davis, Dennis K. *The Main Source: Learning from Television News.* Beverly Hills, CA: Sage, 1986.

Sterling, Christopher H. *A Guide to Trends in Broadcasting and Newer Technologies 1920–1983.* New York: Praeger, 1984.

Sussman, Leonard R. *Power, the Press, and the Technology of Freedom: The Coming Age of ISDN.* New York: Freedom House, 1989.

The Veronis, Suhler & Associates Communications Industry Forecast, Industry Spending Preview, 1991–1995. 5th ed. New York: 1991.

Willis, Jim, and Willis, Diane B. *New Directions in Media Management.* Boston: Allyn & Bacon, 1992.

Wilson, Kevin G. *Technologies of Control: The New Interactive Media for the Home.* Madison, WI: University of Wisconsin Press, 1980.

Yoakam, Richard D., and Cremer, Charles F. *ENG: Television News and the New Technology.* 2nd ed. New York: Random House, 1989.

ARTICLES

Alexander, Suzanne. "Interactive TV Test Is Watched to See Who's More Than Remotely Interested," *The Wall Street Journal,* May 10, 1990.

Arnett, Nick. "Multimedia: Where Is the Industry Going?" *The World of MacIntosh Multimedia,* January 1991.

Aumente, Jerome. "Battling the Telcos," *Washington Journalism Review,* May 1990.

Biocca, Frank. "Virtual Reality Technology: A Tutorial," *Journal of Communication,* Autumn, 1992.

Bishop, Philip. "The World on a Silver Platter," *Home Office Computing,* June 1993.

Bogart, Leo. "Shaping a New Media Policy," *The Nation,* July 12, 1993.

Brody, Herb. "Sorry, Wrong Number," *High Technology Business,* September 1988.

Burgi, Michael. "No U Turn," *MediaWeek,* April 19, 1993.

———. "Ads on Pay-Per-View? Maybe," *MediaWeek,* April 21, 1993.

Callahan, Sean. "Eye Tech," *Forbes ASAP*, June 1993.

Charbuck, David C. and Young, Jeffrey S. "The Virtual Workplace," *Forbes*, November 23, 1992.

Chisholm, Patricia. "Getting the Picture," *MacLean's*, November 9, 1992.

Cobb, Nathan. "Cyberpunk: Terminal Chic," *The Boston Globe*, November 24, 1992.

Cole, Patrick E. "The Next Magic Box?" *Time*, January 18, 1993.

Conhaim, Wallys. "Videotex: Growing Public Awareness," *White Paper Report* prepared for the Newspaper Association of America, Reston, Va, 1991.

Conniff, Michael. "Enter the Personal Newspaper," *Editor & Publisher*, January 16, 1993.

Cook, William J. "A Clear Picture for TV," *U.S. News & World Report*, June 7, 1993.

Cox, James. "Regulation Bill Sets Off Lobbying Brawl," *USA Today*, September 17, 1992.

Cox, Meg. "NBC Will Mix Tech and Talk with Live Poll," *The Wall Street Journal*, August 28, 1989.

Coy, Peter. "Satellites Affect Face of Communications," *Albuquerque Journal*, July 12, 1987.

Cunningham, Scott and Porter, Alan A. "Communication Networks: A Dozen Ways They'll Change Our Lives," *The Futurist*, January/February 1992.

Dennis, Everett E. "New News Technology," *Television Quarterly*, Winter 1990.

Deutschman, Alan. "Bill Gates' Next Challenge," *Fortune*, December 28, 1992.

Donlon, Brian. "Cable Is Overflowing with New Options," *USA Today*, June 7, 1993.

Elmer-Dewitt, Philip. "Take a Trip into the Future on the Electronic Superhighway," *Time*, April 12, 1993.

Elmer-Dewitt, Philip. "Who's Reading Your Screen?" *Time*, January 18, 1993.

Fitzgerald, Mark. "What Do Callers Think?" *Editor & Publisher*, February 22, 1993.

Flanagan, Patrick. "Wireless Modems: CDPD Standard Gaining Acceptance," *Telecommunications*, February 1993.

Garneau, George. "The New Media Landscape," *Editor & Publisher*, May 8, 1993.

Gaziano, Cecile. "The Knowledge Gap and Class Communication," *Mass Comm Review*, Fall 1989.

Gilder, George. "Forget HDTV, It's Already Outmoded," *New York Times*, May 28, 1989.

Greenfield, Meg. "Misled by the Facts," *Newsweek*, June 26, 1989.

Hamilton, David P. "Japanese Push to Switch on Sales of HDTV," *New York Times*, April 1, 1993.

Hass, Nancy. "Telecommunications: A Global Report," *FW*, September 15, 1992.

Impoco, Jim. "Technology Titans Sound Off on the Digital Future," *U.S. News & World Report*, May 3, 1993.

Jahnke, Art. "Not Just Another Pretty Picture," *Boston Magazine*, March, 1990.

Kanter, Rosabeth. "Even Closer to the Customer," *Harvard Business Review*, January/February 1991.

Kaplan, Rachel. "Video on Demand," *American Demographics*, June 1992.

Karlgaard, Rich. "Fast Forward Forever," *Forbes ASAP*, June 7, 1993.

Karraker, Roger. "Highways of the Mind," *Whole Earth Review*, Spring 1991.

Katz, Jon. "New World of TV," *Washington Journalism Review*, February 1993.

Kripalani, Anil T. "A Seamless and Smart Network Is the Key to Great PCS," *Telephony*, March 8, 1993.

Krumenaker, Lawrence. "Get a Clue!" *Quill*, June 1992.

Kupfer, Andrew. "Prime Time for Videoconferences," *Fortune*, December 28, 1992.

Landler, Mark. "Time Warner's Techie at the Top," *Business Week*, May 10, 1993.

Levitt, Theodore. "Marketing Myopia," *Harvard Business Review*, September/October, 1975.

Lewyn, Mark. "This Isn't the Response TV Answer Expected," *Business Week*, June 29, 1992.

Liebman, Hanna. "The Microchip Is the Message," *MediaWeek*, November 2, 1992.

———. "2002: Interactive Adland?" *MediaWeek*, May 17, 1993.

Lippman, Andrew. "Feature Sets for Interactive Images," *Communications of the ACM*, April 1991.

Lutholtz, M. William. "Technology May Complicate Our Jobs," *IABC Communication World*, September 1988.

Lynch, Dennis. "New Online Service Has More for Less," *Chicago Tribune*, January 26, 1990.

Maney, Kevin. "Southwestern Bell Wires into Cable TV," *USA Today*, March 19, 1993.

McNamara, Donald. "At the Front: Clash of Cultures," *Media Studies Journal*, Spring 1992.

Nyhan, David. "MIT's Multimedia Marvels: Future Schlock?" *Washington Journalism Review*, April 1988.

Pearce, Kevin. "Pies in the Sky?" *Channels Field Guide*, 1991.

Petersen, Lisa Marie. "Cable: Targeted Audiences Help Break New Categories," *Media Outlook*, September 14, 1992.

Piirto, Rebecca. "Battle for the Black Box," *American Demographics*, November 1992.

Postman, Neil. "Critical Thinking in the Electronic Era," *Phi Kappa Phi Journal*, Winter 1985.

Putka, Gary. "Schools Giving TV Warmer Reception," *Wall Street Journal*, December 26, 1989.

Rosenblatt, Roger. "Journalism and the Larger Truth," *Time*, July 2, 1984.

Rosenthal, Steve. "Interactive TV: The Gold Rush Is On," *New Media*, December 1992.

———. "Interactive Network: Viewers Get Involved," *New Media*, December 1992.

Schneidawind, John. "US West Plugging in to TV," *USA Today*, May 18, 1993.

Shannon, L. R. "Visiting a Mall, by Phone," *New York Times*, September 5, 1989.

Sherman, Stratford. "The New Computer Revolution," *Fortune*, June 14, 1993.

Slutsker, Gary. "The Tortoise and the Hare," *Forbes*, February 1, 1993.

Snider, James H. "Shopping in the Information Age," *The Futurist*, November/December 1992.

Solomon, Jolie, et al. "A Risky Revolution," *Newsweek*, April 26, 1993.

Sternberg, Bill. "A Theory of Critical Mass," *MediaWeek*, May 10, 1993.

Susman, Andrew. "Switching the Channel," *Direct Marketing*, January 1993.

Swayne, John. "The New Communications Revolution," *Newsweek*, April 19, 1993.

Toor, Mat. "When TV Advertising Means Playing the Game," *Marketing*, April 30, 1992.

Underwood, Doug. "Reinventing the Media: The Newspapers' Identity Crisis," *Columbia Journalism Review*, March/April 1992.

Williams, Frederick. "Network Information Services as a New Public Medium," *Media Studies Journal*, Winter 1991.

Wilks, Stephen. "Science, Technology and the Large Corporation," *Government and Opposition*, Spring 1992.

Wrubel, Robert. "Strange Bedfellows," *FW*, September 15, 1992.

Yankelovich, Daniel. "Tomorrow's Global Businesses," *The Futurist*, July/August 1991.

Zachary, G. Pascal. "HP Is Building Gadget to Make TVs Interactive," *The Wall Street Journal*, February 27, 1992.

Index

ABOUT THE AUTHOR

JIM WILLIS is Associate Professor of Communication and Chairman of the Department of Communication at Boston College. He is the author of four books and numerous articles on journalism and the mass media. A veteran of twelve years in the news media, he served as a teaching editor at the University of Missouri School of Journalism, co-founded the graduate program in journalism at Northeastern University and served as its director for several years, and then directed the News-Editorial Sequence in the Department of Journalism at Ball State University.

1940